RY AND LE

a:

A Facilitator's Handbook for Working in Community

Applied Drama:
A Facilitator's Handbook for Working in Community

by Monica Prendergast and Juliana Saxton

intellect Bristol, UK / Chicago, USA

First published in the UK in 2013 by Intellect,
The Mill, Parnall Road, Fishponds, Bristol, BS16 3JG, UK

First published in the USA in 2013 by Intellect, The University of Chicago Press,
1427 E. 60th Street, Chicago, IL 60637, USA

A catalogue record for this book is available from the British Library.

Series: Theatre in Education
Series ISSN: 2049-3878
Cover design: Ellen Thomas
Copy-editor: Emma Rhys
Typesetting: John Teehan

ISBN 978-1-84150-740-8

Printed and bound by Hobbs, UK

Contents

ACKNOWLEDGEMENTS

The authors wish to thank the following for permission to use their work:

"The Man Who Finds His Son Has Become a Thief" is reprinted from *Collected Poems of Raymond Souster* by permission of Oberon Press.

We are grateful to Intellect for its support and attention, particularly our production manager Bethan Ball, marketing representative Amy Damutz, and copy-editor Emma Rhys.

Drama educators get their best ideas from each other. We are forever grateful to our colleagues worldwide who share their work with such generosity.

Experts tell us it takes 10,000 hours to gain expertise in anything. Any expertise we can claim is due to our (probably 10,000) students, past, present and future. Teaching drama is a conversation, but without the engagement of our students it would be very one-sided; their tact and responses have shaped our teaching.

We wish to dedicate this book to our first mentor in drama education, Brian Way. He was a wonderful teacher and a lovely man from whom we learned so much about the art form of drama and its power as aesthetic experience.

Start from that point–from where you yourself feel interested and confident. Keep reminding yourself that what you are concerned with is the development of every one of the manifold facets of human beings; the circle can start at any point on the circumference of that circle.

– Brian Way, 1967, pp. 8–9

December 2012
Victoria, British Columbia

How is applied drama different from applied theatre?

This handbook is intended to be a companion volume with a previously published collection of case studies dealing with applied theatre called *Applied Theatre: International Case Studies and Challenges for Practice* (Prendergast & Saxton, 2009). In that book, written as an introductory text for students new to the field, we focus on laying out the range of practices available to those who wish to engage communities through theatre. Our definition of applied theatre, as distinct from mainstream theatre practice, is theatre that happens "most often ... in spaces that are not usually defined as theatre buildings, with participants who may or may not be skilled in theatre arts and to audiences who have a vested interest in the issue taken up by the performance or are members of the community addressed by the performance" (p. 6). In applied theatre a *performance*, to and with an audience, is an essential characteristic.

> Applied theatre happens within a new *theatron* where not only viewing happens, but where a new pedagogy is being taught, a pedagogy which asserts that viewing is not enough… we need to act upon our viewing as means of transforming the kind of world we live in.
>
> – Philip Taylor, 2003, p. 38

One of the clearest ways to identify the difference between applied theatre and what we are focusing on in this text, *applied drama*, is to remember the difference in the root meanings of the words "theatre" and "drama." Theatre comes from the Greek word *theatron* defined as "seeing-place" which, over a long period, has come to be understood as a space or venue dedicated to theatrical performances. Drama, on the other hand, has its roots in the Greek verb *dran* which means "to do" or "to act." This text is about the *doing* of drama, which may or may not be connected to a theatre performance. Drama in this sense is akin to what we know as the rehearsal process of performance. In rehearsal, actors, directors and designers come together as an "interpretive community" (Fish, 1980, in title) for the purposes of illuminating a dramatic text for a paying audience. Rehearsal can be seen as a collaborative process of investigation, research, trial and error, negotiation and often improvisation that leads to a fixed version of a playtext prepared for the public. Rehearsals most often occur in private, in safe spaces where participants are encouraged and feel confident in testing out and sharing creative ideas. Dramatic process involves these same kinds of communal and cooperative engagements but in a different context, one that, most importantly, lacks the performance pressure that attends theatre-based rehearsal.

The contexts in which applied drama may occur include classrooms in schools, community groups of all kinds (including at-risk, disadvantaged, developing or otherwise marginalized groups), employment or training settings, healthcare education, and many other locations (See Appendix B, pp. 207–210). As with applied theatre, applied drama serves as an umbrella term under which many practices are located. An applied drama facilitator (or practitioner) is the name given to a theatre/drama artist who most often comes from outside the locations into which he or she enters to work, often in partnership with non-government organizations, businesses, social agencies or institutions. The participants in an applied drama project are generally not skilled as actors or other kinds of theatre artists, but are brought together by a common concern or interest to work with a highly-skilled facilitator. An applied drama facilitator knows and is capable of using theatre and drama strategies and techniques to serve the needs of these diverse communities. Those needs, often identified by the outside partner, may or may not be seen as valuable by the participants and will never be addressed usefully unless or until they are self-identified by the group. Helping an applied drama facilitator to develop and hone these varied and specialized skills is the intention of this text.

> The difference between theatre and ... drama is that in theatre everything is contrived so that the audience gets the kicks. In [drama] the participants get the kicks. However, the roots are the same: the elements of theatre craft.
>
> – B. J. Wagner, 1976, p. 147

As co-authors of this handbook, we are drawing upon our backgrounds as theatre and drama educators in elementary and secondary classrooms, in postsecondary theatre departments and in teacher education. Our careers began in the professional theatre as actors and over time followed distinct yet parallel lines that led us, due to growing interest in working with young people, into the field of drama/theatre education. Over the past decade, this field has developed a focus on working through drama and theatre in settings outside of schools. Our first collaborative text on applied theatre came out of a real necessity when we began teaching an introductory applied theatre course and realized there was no survey text available at that time. There are a number of excellent practical handbooks on specific areas of applied drama/theatre, and there are theatre and drama education texts; we will refer to many throughout. Yet, within the relatively new field of applied drama we feel the need for an introductory handbook to support facilitators and teaching artists working in community settings through dramatic process. Our inten-

Entertainment is crucial to the ability of the arts to offer perception and hope… it is the way in which performance offers a venue for exploring difficult issues without crippling anxiety.

– Martha Nussbaum, 2010, p. 110

tion here is to offer a set of practical opportunities within which our readers may find the freedom to play.

In our view, effective facilitation in applied drama is closely connected to effective pedagogy in drama/theatre education. Therefore, our focus in this text is to draw on best practices that we see as transferable into the diverse settings within which applied drama projects occur. Drama education is a practice that grows from a culture of sharing and as "friendly thieves" we cannot claim any of what you will read here as entirely our own. Like crows, we pick out the shiny bits of the practices of others. Indeed, in your own practice we hope you will take these ideas and adapt them according to the needs of your participants and the settings that you are in.

How to read this book?

One of the most effective ways in which to help participants make meaning is to contextualize each session. Context is the frame or setting within which everything else is contained. Caine et al. (2008) tell us that the brain is able to look at parts and wholes at the same time and it is the imagined contexts that transform learning into meaningful and relevant activity. For that reason, the workshops in this text are built around

It is the context that provides us with the feeling of what is real and important and this has significant implications for learning in terms of "ownership, motivation, [and] engagement."

– John Norman, 1999, p. 11

concepts or stories that serve not only as holders of meaning but also as a kind of shorthand—collective containers of memory to which the whole group can make reference easily and quickly as they progress. The work is recursive in nature, reflecting back on itself as it moves forward.

Our two opening chapters offer a survey of applied drama practice and key concepts that underpin the work. The book is then divided into three sections. Sections 1 and 2 focus on building dramatic skills, confidence and group dynamics in a developmental way. We introduce drama strategies and techniques such as working through role, creative movement, and improvisation in a safe and low-risk approach intended for people who may be very new to this kind of activity. The focus here is the process. Section 3 moves the work, for groups that wish to do so, toward some form of shared presentation. Here we offer strategies for devising (also called playbuilding), creating monologues and scenes, and giving suggestions on how to piece these elements together into an artistically satisfying form. We conclude with a chapter that addresses how to reflect meaningfully on an applied drama project, along with the facilitator's responsibilities for reporting on and exiting from a participant community and its process.

Our writing collaboration is a process in which we share ideas, accepting some and setting many others aside along the way. This work is difficult but also great fun, at times surprising, and like all processes is a continuing spiral of learning and change. As you engage with your communities through dramatic process, we wish the same for you.

Monica Prendergast
Juliana Saxton
June 2012

1.1 What is applied drama?

Applied drama is a field of dramatic arts practice that is process-based, one in which spectatorship and performance happen within communities in ways that are private or semi-private, for a variety of purposes that would be inhibited by the presence of an audience. By this, King (1981; see Appendix A, p. 205) means dramatic work that is done for the benefit of the group and those individuals within the group. Applied drama is not concerned with making meaning for someone who is outside this process (as in a public audience). This definition serves as a starting-point only.

> The application of drama to different institutional or community settings illuminates fundamental questions about the role and significance of *all* theatre practice to society, and about how theatre-making articulates and challenges contemporary concerns.
>
> – Helen Nicholson, 2005a, p. 5

A glance at the range of topics addressed in applied drama projects shows the diversity of its applications. "Appendix B: Selected peer reviewed publications on applied drama, 1996–2012" (pp. 207–210) illustrates clearly the broad range of locations and intentions of applied drama projects. Areas such as crisis management and conflict resolution, professional training, healthcare, museum programs, learning about ethical practice, second-language learning and many more topics and issues may be seen on this survey list. Even amongst such a broad range of applications, there are common qualities:

Applied drama
- Is a process-oriented means of exploring issues of concern to participants without the pressure of performance.
- Is a facilitated process in which the value of the work lies in what it does for participants rather than for an audience.

- Uses many of the same strategies as in the rehearsal stage of a devising project where the focus is on generating material from the group or ensemble.
- Involves looking at ourselves looking at ourselves through *self-spectatorship* and continual reflection (Bolton, 1998, p. 266).
- Works with and through the artistic skills of theatre; these will lie in the domain of the facilitator rather than be expected of participants.
- Engages facilitators and participants in the Five Cs: Communication, Cooperation/collaboration, Concentration, Commitment and Caring.
- Is a social laboratory for developing critical consciousness; that is, a heightened awareness that moves toward action.
- Is an artistic and aesthetic process that is concerned with the making of things perceptible by and through the senses (primarily seeing, hearing and feeling) as developed through the actions of dramatic play.

> [Devising] is determined and defined by a group of people who set up an initial framework or structure to explore and experiment with ideas, images, concepts, themes or specific stimuli.
>
> – Alison Oddey, 1996, p. 1

Apart from the absence of a performance outcome, the length of time for applied drama work is much more flexible than in applied theatre. Often a single half-day workshop may be sufficient to accomplish the stated needs of the group.

1.2 Who does applied drama and what are the benefits?

Referring again to Appendix B (pp. 207–210) we can determine the kinds of groups that have participated in various applied drama projects. Here we can see students in schools, pre-service and in-service teachers, postsecondary business students, university students in a variety of disciplines, workers in healthcare and crisis management/conflict resolution/anger management, electronic game designers, occupational therapists, peace activists, patients with physical or mental challenges, and those in medical, police or military training. In fact, any group of people who need or are required to work together in any educational, socio-political, employment, cultural or community context may be interested in engaging in an applied drama experience. However, it is equally possible that an applied drama process may be imposed on a group from the outside; that is, medical students may be required to participate in role played patient interactions as a

> There are at least three levels of spectatorship involved… an awareness of what is happening… an awareness of what is being "made"… and an awareness of what could happen or needs to happen to further the drama.
>
> – Gavin Bolton, 1998, p. 199

component of their training. In these cases, an insider co-facilitator(s) from the organization should be part of the project. But, whether the impulse comes from inside or outside the group, the overall intention is that it will be of benefit to the participants.

One way in which applied drama may benefit group members is that it builds the Five Cs as outlined above. In a business setting, for example, improving communication skills may be all that is required for a team to begin to work well together. *Communication* is bound by social, cultural and hierarchical structures. In building a group through dramatic process, communication happens in many ways—both verbal and non-verbal. Working through fictional situations can make the challenges of communication more apparent by neutralizing the constraints felt in the "real world." Dramatic process is the most social of arts-based ways of working, and building fictional situations *cooperatively* offers people with a variety of skills and interests the chance to work together in an inherently *collaborative* social process. *Concentration* calls for participants to stay focused within a process and to pay attention to emotional, bodily and sensory responses that arise moment to moment within a group. *Commitment* requires that participants see the work as mattering as they enter into "acceptance, engagement and responsibility to the work and to the group: it is the initial action of empathy" (Morgan & Saxton, 1987, p. 24). *Caring* extends from commitment into shared responsibility—put into and held in place by the facilitator throughout—so that every member of the group feels a sense of safety and respect that, in turn, allows them the freedom to explore and express themselves without fear of negative critical judgment.

In theatre, part of an actor's training is to discover a "neutral self" upon which they can build other characters. What drama does, on the other hand, is to enable participants to explore who they are in relation to whatever is under investigation. Margaret Lepp (O'Toole & Lepp, 2000), for example, works with nurses through drama to help them reflect on their attitudes toward illness and patient care. It is through a conscious examination of attitudes and the cultural ethos that have shaped us that we can come to understand more clearly our reactions to events in our professional or personal lives. Safety is at the core of applied drama practice; paradoxically it is working in safe spaces and in safe ways that helps us to look at the risky issues that can arise in our lives. Dramatic process offers multiplicities of ways of thinking; participants are challenged to become more critical thinkers, to accept ambiguity (a tolerance for open-endedness), to be aware that there is rarely one "right" answer, and to think collaboratively in more creative, non-linear ways. Drama, as all art forms, works through the language of metaphor that allows participants the necessary "aesthetic distance" to deal with issues that may otherwise feel too close. This is known as the "protection of the role":

> [Working] flexibly and creatively… can enable participants to think and perceive dramatically, to use the aesthetic distance of theatrical metaphor, to confront difficult issues and to find new forms of identification with others.
>
> – Helen Nicholson, 2005a, p. 54

> With drama, participants feel more protected and work with more convic-
> tion if they are framed at some distance from the moment of real-time
> enactment. If too much is at stake, the role distance is often too close for an
> exploration of the situation, and the performance frame becomes blurred
> while the belief in the convention and protection of the role is lost. (Carroll
> & Cameron, 2005, p. 7)

Applied drama always takes place within a *community of practice*; with children or the elderly, with prisoners or museum visitors, with disadvantaged or otherwise chal- lenged community groups, with doctors or police officers-in-training. The focus in each of these sites is the understanding that, as human beings, we can learn from each other in meaningful ways. This can be seen as akin to the apprenticeship model still used in some professional training (or as a coach of a sports team), where a "master" works alongside and in tandem with a trainee/apprentice and mentors the learner into mas- tery of the form, whether it be a sport, woodworking, cake baking or dramatic process- ing.

1.3 How is applied drama done?

The facilitator, sometimes called the practitioner (or in schools, the teacher), is some- one who has the necessary education, background and artistic skills to lead a group that is often relatively unskilled in dramatic process. Applied drama facilitation is es- sentially grounded in drama education strategies and techniques, delivered by someone who knows about theatre and who possesses pedagogical skills honed by training and experience:

> That is to say, a facilitator knows how to do something, and knows why it
> is appropriate, when it needs to be used and how to do it in the most ef-
> fective way. … In addition, participants benefit from a facilitator who is
> a communicator and a listener who possesses both social and empathic
> intelligence… in order to work with people in groups and help them ar-
> rive at decisions. It requires skills of diplomacy because this kind of work
> is fraught with difficulties around what is left in and what is taken out and
> how an aesthetic product is shaped out of dramatic process. Also key to…
> facilitation is the recognition that the community participants… hold the
> knowledge of the subject under investigation, whereas the facilitator will
> hold the aesthetic knowledge of the theatre form. (Prendergast & Saxton,
> 2009, p. 18)

This quotation identifies a formidable list of necessary attributes! However, over time, facilitators will grow the skills needed to develop their applied drama practice, much as new teachers move from apprenticeship to mastery.

Another characteristic of facilitation is the ability to work in partnerships with others who have knowledge and skills in other areas. For example, a facilitator who is training actors to improvise in role as patients in a medical education program must partner with clinicians and instructors who have the medical knowledge necessary for preparation.

In summary, an applied drama facilitator should be the kind of person who enjoys people, is comfortable in new situations, can tolerate lots of change, can improvise in the moment as a response to change, is a deep listener, a curious questioner and is able to "de-centre"; in other words, to see the work as about and coming from the participants rather than from him/herself. Where does one go to gain such training? Working as an apprentice/trainee in a theatre company with a mandate to address social issues is one avenue. For example, Vancouver, Canada's Headlines Theatre—based on the work of Augusto Boal—holds regular workshop programs. Sojourn Theatre in Portland, Oregon and Geese Theatre in Birmingham, England are two other companies that offer ongoing training for those who are interested in working in sociopolitical contexts (Sojourn) or with offenders and/or youth at-risk (Geese Theatre) (see Further Reading for websites). A second avenue for applied drama training is through a university degree program, although these programs are most often framed as applied theatre. In researching these programs, it is useful to keep these questions in mind: Does the program offer both undergraduate and graduate training? Are there opportunities for community placements? Another aspect is to look over the courses offered in any program to consider their breadth, variety and cross-disciplinary offerings. Guiding questions in making your choice are: How well might the skills listed above be developed in the program you are considering? How well does the program you are considering mesh with your own skills and interests?

1.4 What is the nature of applied drama?

Applied drama involves the physical/biological body working in harmony with the phenomenal/experiential body (Bresler, 2004, p. 7). This means that our minds and memories, thoughts and feelings are a part of how our bodies operate in many settings, including dramatic ones; this is called *embodied learning*. Our bodies and our minds work together, in concert, to explore issues, themes, ideas and situations through improvised role play and other process-based activities. Of course, we know that our bodies and our minds are not separate, yet in many ways we have set up social functions—such as education—that tend to privilege the mind over the body and lead to *dis*embodied learning. When our minds and our bodies are seen as one and the same, rather than as separate entities, embodied learning can be powerful, memorable, aesthetic and dramatic. As Davidson (2004) says, embodied knowledge involves "a recognition of the embeddedness of thought *in* experience *as it emerges* in our interactions with the natural and technical world" (p. 198, emphasis added). This notion of "thought in experience as it emerges" is how improvisation works, and is a key way of working in educational and community settings in applied drama.

> Process Drama can be seen as a framed activity where role taking allows the participants to behave "as if" they are in a different context and to respond "as if" they are involved in a different set of interpersonal relationships. ... [R]ole performance is seen as a mental attitude, a way of holding two worlds in mind, the world of real life (RL) and the world of the dramatic fiction simultaneously. The meaning and value of the drama lies in the interplay between these two worlds.
>
> – John Carroll & David Cameron (2003, n.p.)

The other side of this coin is our basic human social ability to "read" the "dynamics of concealment and revelation, identity and disguise in human behaviour. The pleasure of exercising this skill and the [reading] of bodies and their actions are among the important pleasure of theatre spectatorship," Conroy (2010, p. 75) points out. In applied drama, the significance of the work is for its producers rather than, as in applied theatre, for participants and consumers (audiences). It is as if we are in a sort of continual rehearsal in which what we are doing becomes the "basis… in which all possible decisions and their consequences can be explored" (Rideout, 2009, p. 48).

A big part of the pleasure we can experience through dramatic activity is the shared sense of both making and perceiving that happens at one and the same time. This "fun" payoff is a really important component of effective applied drama practice; the kind of "serious fun" that involves complex and challenging skills that must be developed and practised by both teacher/facilitators and participants in situations that engage in multifarious ways.

Situated learning, also known as situated cognition, involves a broader awareness of the contexts within which an experience happens. Unlike much of the learning that we know of and have experienced ourselves, that is, subject-specific and delivered in "organized chunks" (Doll, 2008, p. 6), situated learning evolves out of particular settings and "takes place in certain sorts of communities of practice typically outside of school" (Wolfson & Willinsky, 1998, p. 22). For an applied drama facilitator, situated learning means paying close attention to the spaces and places where the work is happening. There will be a difference between working in a school gymnasium to working in a lounge in a senior citizens' home to working in a dedicated theatre studio. The latter option (which

> [T]he arts, by generating pleasure in connection with acts of subversion and cultural reflection, produce an enduring and even attractive dialogue with the prejudices of the past, rather than one fraught with fear and defensiveness.
>
> – Martha Nussbaum, 2010, p. 109

is also the most rare) is the most ideal, of course, as it brings with it its own authority. Working in the lobby of a theatre company brings with it a wholly different sense than working in a rehearsal hall, a sense of which will greatly affect the quality of the work carried out. How a chosen space is set up also has a big impact on the situated learning possibilities available; an applied drama facilitator needs to be well-organized in taking the time necessary to set up a space before participants arrive. Arriving in a space where chairs are arranged in a circle, music is playing, and chart paper with notes from previous sessions is up on the walls for review is far preferable to arriving in a space to meet a facilitator who is flustered and a space that is in chaos.

The most powerful aspect of situated learning, however, is the metaphor and story that is being addressed by the group. If participants feel a strong sense of connection to the work that is occurring, that it has meaning and value, then an applied drama facilitator has done her job. Applied drama is less about building drama skills (as in actor training) and more about the investigation at-hand.

An applied drama facilitator who is attending to situated learning/cognition within a group will be consistently responsive to all of the contextual factors at play in each session: Who are these people? What do they bring with them? How are they different today from yesterday? How does this space shape what we do? What is the social health of the group?

> Learning awakens a variety of internal developmental processes that are able to operate only when the child is interacting with people in his environments and in cooperation with his peers.
>
> – Lev Vygotsky, 1978, p. 90

Good facilitation is always centred around the kinds of reflective questions given above. A facilitator becomes more effective as s/he asks these kinds of questions regularly throughout a dramatic process and is able to make use of responses as an integral part of the work. The work that a facilitator does outside of the process involves thinking deeply and contemplatively about what is happening and where a process is going. Being able to see clearly is key and the workshops we offer in the chapters that follow are designed to allow for reflection both inside and outside a particular dramatic process.

Reflection is interwoven throughout any applied drama project. Reflection is about looking inward, both individually and collectively, to explore the emotional and intellectual impact of a dramatic process. There may be times when the reflection is actually richer than the process itself; reflection can enrich perception in very meaningful ways. *Reflection-in-action* and *reflection-on-action* are not only the responsibility of a facilitator in terms of thinking through what is happening within a group; the group members themselves must also have plenty of time and opportunity to reflect. Reflection-in-action can be done through a number of drama activities: writing-in role, hot-seating, pair-share and reportage are all reflection strategies (as will be seen throughout this book), and happen inside a drama structure. Reflection-in-action for a facilitator is about being deeply aware of what is happening at any moment and therefore able to sense when and how the work may need to be re-directed to better meet the needs of the group. Reflection-on-action usually occurs at the conclusion of an activity or a session as well as at the end of a workshop series.

[In reflection-in-action] [t]here is some puzzling, or troubling, or interesting phenomenon with which the individual is trying to deal. As he [sic] tries to make sense of it, he also reflects on the understandings which have been implicit in his action, understandings which he surfaces, criticizes, restructures, and embodies in further actions. It is this entire process of reflection-in-action which is central to the "art" by which practitioners sometimes deal well with situations of uncertainty, instability, uniqueness, and value conflict.

– Donald Schön, 1983, p. 50

Reflection-on-action involves guiding a group into a richer understanding of the meaning of the work through questions and discussion.

Through reflection, a skilled facilitator will draw participants' attention to key moments when something significant happened, an "ah-ha" moment when a shift or change occurred in the work, when a palpable risk was taken, when a metaphor took hold. Making connections between what happened in the fictional world of the drama with what has happened (or may happen) in participants' real lives is central to good practice in applied drama. Apart from the knowledge building that reflection generates, it is also a means of building trust, communication skills, safety and, paradoxically, risk-taking. Reflection may take place within the whole class, small groups, pairs, or simply thinking individually about something done and then shared with a partner.

Reflection conceived in these ways can be seen as a type of artistry in itself, as Donald Schön makes clear (see textbox). Effective questioning is at the heart of reflection; good questions allow a facilitator "to competently, responsively, responsibly intervene in talk, so that it moves from routine and predictable to surprising, innovative, even transgressive [and] makes… the facilitator a true artistic collaborator, with [participants], in a creative act" (Goodwin, 2004, p. 332). Questions can be categorized ranging from relatively superficial elicitations of what has happened to questions that help participants shape their understanding, to the deepest questions that press for reflection, that "press participants into deeper thought, into the kind of learning that considers any information as conditional upon its context, the possibility of a variety of perspectives, and the questions that lie therein" (Morgan & Saxton, 1994/2006, p. 52). It is also important to encourage participants, especially those who have been disempowered in some way, to ask as well as answer questions throughout a reflective process. A facilitator both asks questions and models how to ask questions; very often participants will know what they want to know but will lack the language needed to phrase the question. Helping participants find ways of asking questions that

First there is the doing (process); then, the thinking on the doing (reflection). Finally, there is a redoing (process informed by reflection) that restarts these interactions again.

– Jessica Hoffmann Davis, 2005, p. 13

move to the heart of what really interests them is a large part of applied drama—and democracy—in practice.

1.5 Questions for Reflection, Suggested Activity and Further Reading

Questions for Reflection

1. Identify an area of study in your institution, or work setting, where you see possibilities for the use of applied drama. What are those possibilities? For example, if you identified law, one of the applications for drama might be practising for client interviews. How do you see the Five Cs of applied drama being evidenced in a process such as this?
2. There are many skills required of an applied drama facilitator, some inborn (good communicator) and others acquired (guitarist/juggler). What are the skills you already possess that will serve you well in applied drama facilitation? What skills do you feel you will need to develop? Create a Skills Inventory for yourself and maintain and update it as you begin to work in applied drama settings (see Weigler, 2001, "Chapter One: Developing an Ensemble and Building Skills").
3. What training possibilities are available to you that will build your Skills Inventory? What can you find through research and the Internet to access training opportunities in your community or beyond?

Suggested Activity

This activity practises the process of asking open-ended questions that may do any one or all of the following: (1) help to open things up in a group setting, (2) be useful for developing interview skills, and (3) looks at questioning as an integral part of a planning process.

> You wonder why life seems to go on for everyone else. Why are their lives so good and ours so terrible? You are angry. You can't stand to be around people yet you can't stand being alone. You can't bear to hear people laugh and talk, but you leave the television on all the time for the noise. (Letter to Ann Landers)

Read the quote above and write a list of open-ended questions—that is, questions that cannot be answered with a simple Yes or No response—that explores who this writer may be and what he or she has experienced. Consider not just what happened (plot), but how it might have happened, how it affected those involved, and what may occur in the future.

Further Reading

Select two or three articles from Appendix B (pp. 207–210) to read as other lenses to expand on this introductory chapter to understanding the field of applied drama.

The websites below offer views of theatre companies in Canada, the United States and the United Kingdom dedicated to working in communities through dramatic process.

Headlines Theatre: www.headlinestheatre.com
Sojourn Theatre: www.sojourntheatre.org
Geese Theatre: www.geese.co.uk

In this chapter we introduce three key concepts and their functions in applied drama. These concepts—*process, role and improvisation*—have been and continue to be key aspects of theatre-making in the traditional sense of rehearsing a scripted play. They may be seen as placed on a continuum where process moves toward "product" (a play in performance), a role becomes a refined character, and an improvisation is used as preparation for presenting a scripted scene.

Applied drama, by contrast, uses process, role play and improvisation as means and ends in themselves. These ways of working have both aesthetic and social value without having to be focused on producing a piece of publicly performed theatre. In taking up this position some may see it as opening up old debates, specifically in the field of drama education, over the "false dichotomies" (Ackroyd, 2004, p. xiv) between drama and theatre. We do so here because we believe theatre-making processes should be available to everybody. Everyone should be able to access the tools needed to create meaningful dramatic experiences without having to have the rarer qualities of gifts and talents held by those who make theatre their chosen profession. In the work of applied drama, the focus is not on the making of a performance but on the dramatic investigation of content that is of interest to a particular group and for particular reasons.

2.1 What is the nature of dramatic process?

What is *process*? Process is a word that everyone uses and, in drama and theatre, one that generally refers to work, or things that are happening, before they are "fixed" as a product or outcome. There is the sense, with process, that something is still in action, still being considered, played with, not yet finished. Process is part of an implied hierarchy of which everybody is aware: that something finished is "better" than

Process is well-illustrated in Marcel Duchamps (1913) painting, "Nude descending a staircase," in which a series of nested bodies give the observer a "stop motion" view of a body in movement—paralleling early camera animation techniques.

For those who work in the area of process studies, process is relational and crosses disciplines: Aesthetics, Biology, Cosmology, Economics, Education Theory, Ethics and so on are all academic fields interested in process.

– "Process Philosophy," 2012

something that is not yet completed. The sense of pleasure that comes with being "done" and the need to be "done" is deep in our DNA (certainly in our parents and teachers!); it gives us a great sense of fulfillment to complete, tidy and put away in order that we can move on to something new. It is as if we have metaphorically "filled in" a bit of the pattern of our lives by working something through or, to put it another way, by making meaning. But is it really possible to be truly finished with anything or is it, in fact, only another step in a process?

The Greek philosopher Heraclitus (535–475 BCE) is considered to be the founder of "process philosophy." One of his most famous quotes was, "Everything changes and nothing remains still" (Wikipedia entry on Process philosophy) which is another way of saying that the universe is made up of constant processes of being and becoming that are neverending. Alfred North Whitehead, credited as the founder of the modern school of process philosophy, saw "individual entities as series of moments of experience instead of as masses of static substance. Within each moment, an entity is influenced by others, creates its own identity and propels itself into further experiences" (Pawar, 2012, n.p.). What is important in applied drama contexts is that although being inside a process (such as working in a group) may seem to be rather messy and unfocused, it has an inherent organization that involves distinct stages that happen over time and within certain shapes or forms. It is often only in reflection that we can see the distinct stages and forms of a dramatic process.

Our second question "What is *dramatic* process?" takes these general ideas about process and places them into dramatic contexts. Drama theorist Richard Courtney (1980) describes dramatic process as thoughts emerging from what is seen or imagined and then acted upon (p. 24). A simple dramatic process based on Courtney's definition could involve viewing Goya's *The Executions of the Third of May, 1808*, creating a group tableau that responds to this great painting and then animating this image to hear the voices, thoughts and feelings that emerge. Drama educator and theorist John O'Toole (1992) goes further. He describes dramatic process as involving multiple processes having an "evanescent and slippery quality" (p. 231) that include:

- Varied levels of *context* (fictional and real), which in the example of Goya's work entails seeing both the "fictionalized" painting and knowing, experientially or vicariously, the real events that happen in war.
- *Engagement* (from shallow to deep), in our example, begins with a simple viewing of a reproduction of a painting and moves to placing participants imaginatively "inside" this setting through image-making, role play and improvisation.
- *Meaning-making* (inside and outside of the drama), that asks participants to consider their work both in and out of the dramatic world they have created.

So there are processes within processes, wheels within wheels. Processes of seeing (perception), of engaging with metaphor (images and imagining) and of acting (doing) are all stages of any applied drama workshop or project.

O'Toole also offers a model of what he calls the "dynamic processes" (1992, p. 6) of drama:

- It normally exists in physical action, in three dimensions, and in time—both in the moment, and in the passage of time.
- Drama is a group art, involving a number of people directly and indirectly in the action, with a number of different functions, taking part simultaneously as individuals, as sub-groups clearly identified by functions, and as a whole group within the dramatic event.
- [T]he relationship between [members of a group] is almost infinitely negotiable, and the meanings emergent between them are inevitably dynamic and shifting.
- The contexts in which drama presents itself are invariably complex and never exactly reproducible (O'Toole, 1992, pp. 6–7).

> We need to let go of our engrained ways of seeking goals and objectives, letting the process be the essence of being, not doing.
>
> – Daniel J. Siegel, 2007, p. 243

We add to Courtney's and O'Toole's descriptions of dramatic process another element that is particularly relevant to applied drama: that of reflection. Applied drama seeks to bring about awareness and/or shifts in understanding. Through the process of reflection, we consciously can see or be enabled to see the meanings of what has been done. Dramatic process can, therefore, be experienced as a series of "tiny products" from which we are able to step back in order to see what we have made to know better where we might go next.

For many of the participants with whom we work, the practice of dramatic process can be difficult for a number of reasons. There is not too much opportunity in our lives to attend to process, and both process and the attending to it is often seen as uncomfortable and messy. Group work, if it is not understood as a process, is often regarded as repetitive and boring—going round and round with little to show for it; there is always the temptation to "leave it to someone else" to make decisions or come up with ideas. Although group members will sometimes let that happen, they may also be resentful when they see themselves as being taken over by a "self-appointed" leader. Effective practice in dramatic process demands a great many strategies and techniques to keep individuals and groups moving forward, and these will be built in to the work that follows.

> The doing; process is goal, and goal is endless process; there can be no final statement on a character, relationship, scene, system of work.
>
> – Viola Spolin, 1963/1983, p. 389

2.2 How does the key component of role function in applied drama?

An applied drama process is not the same as an acting workshop. Working in role is a key part of dramatic process, but role is distinct from acting and this distinction should be made clear in any applied drama setting. The focus of an acting workshop is to build specific skills that enable a participant to shift into a character and perform that character effectively on the stage for an audience. In applied drama, however, our shared intention is not to produce "good" actors, or even actors of any kind; rather, the goal is to allow participants to take on self- and/or collectively-created social roles for the purposes of shared investigation. This difference can be further understood as the difference between the aesthetic role of "acting a part" (which is most often pre-determined in scripted form) and the social role of taking on a particular set of attitudes and points of view (which is created by and for a group).

For applied drama practice, role theory drawn from sociology provides a strong starting-point for understanding role in dramatic process:

> At the heart of all drama and theatre is the opportunity for role-taking—to imagine oneself as the other. To try and find oneself in the other and in so doing to recognize the other in oneself. This is the crucial and irreducible bridge between all forms of drama and theatre work.
>
> – Jonothan Neelands, cited in O'Connor, 2010, p. 122

> Role theory is designed to explain how individuals who occupy particular social positions are expected to behave and how they expect others to behave. Role theory is based on the observation that people behave predictably and that an individual's behavior is context-specific, based on their social position and situation. (Hindin, 2007, p. 3959)

Any given role in a fictional setting begins with a need to know who this person is and how they might be expected to behave in relation to a given situation. Of course, the power of drama is often seen in the conscious subversion of these expected social roles, so that a child may berate a parent for staying out too late at night, or a police officer may break into tears while making an arrest (Booth & Lundy, 1985, p. 53). The predictability of a role may be necessary for sociologists, but is less desirable in the making of imaginative and effective drama. However, effective applied drama role play must be believable enough that participants may benefit from the meaning-making that emerges. Bringing together all of these characteristics within a role is a very real challenge faced by an applied drama facilitator. Good facilitation will create spaces for participants to play with social roles and behaviours for the purposes of dramatic investigation, creative storytelling and significant opportunities for shared experience.

One exception to these qualities lies in role play for the purposes of professional training or development. When learning how to be a doctor or a counsellor or a salesperson

In role-play it is not what our finger can successfully point to that we are interested in opening up. It is the emergent meaning that requires our attention. [Meaning lies] in whatever the whole context is of which that role-player... is but a part.

– Gavin Bolton & Dorothy Heathcote, 1999, pp. viii–ix

through drama, it may not be necessary to move beyond the mostly predictable social codes of behaviour. In fact, a kind of consistency in professional behaviours may be viewed as highly desirable in these kinds of applied drama programs. A facilitator whose intent is to help participants learn, may find the possibility of playfulness in employee training lies in the creation of roles that will surprise by disrupting the expectations of the professional trainee. For example, in a recent applied drama project carried out in Vietnam, women who were training to deliver HIV prevention programs were struggling to address a topic which, in that particular culture, is not considered appropriate (Cahill, 2010). Researcher Helen Cahill writes about how the atmosphere shifted when she asked the women to role play as lifesized humanoid condoms in a talk show format. The playfulness and humor of the genre allowed participants to discuss openly and frankly what had previously been hidden.

It is important to understand that there are two main types of role play. Role play as developed in sociology and seen in management and other forms of training is most often short-term with fixed goals and directed toward solving specific problems. For example, human resource staff may benefit from a role play workshop that helps them to fire employees in ways that are more humane and considerate (see the movie *Up in the Air* [Reitman, 2009]). Role play as used in dramatic process most often involves a longer-term engagement in which the goal and the issues arise from the investigation itself. Participants may take on a number of roles in the building of a dramatic context, even the creation of a whole dramatic world. The purposes of this second kind of role play, in educational and/or community settings is to "call on one's humanness" (Bolton & Heathcote, 1999, p. 58) in order to explore more richly an issue, topic or theme of significance to participants.

Another key distinction between these two types of role play is that professional training uses role in mostly nonfictional ways in which the role played sits very close to the actual role of the trainee and occurs in places and situations that are recognizable to all involved. On the other hand, in more open-ended dramatic role play processes, a group may enter into highly fictional roles and worlds that involve a broad range of possible genres such as fable, science fiction, silent movie, ritual, historic events or clowning. Roles taken on by participants in this kind of applied drama work may be very "other" than real life, but the overall purpose of human investigation remains central.

All effective performances share [a] "not—not not" quality: Olivier is not Hamlet, but also he is not not Hamlet: his performance is between a denial of being another (= I am me) and a denial of not being another (= I am Hamlet).

– Richard Schechner, 1981, p. 88

The process of human investigation through role play leads us to a theory that resonates with our discussion of role in applied drama: aesthetic distance. Aesthetic distance allows applied drama participants to address and work with their own lived experiences and concerns in a safe way, through the distancing provided by translating reality into fiction. This complex idea has been discussed by philosophers and theorists over many centuries and has been usefully synthesized by Daphna Ben Chaim (1984) as involving three elements: "An awareness of fiction is the most basic principle of distance in which there appears to be three distinguishable but interrelated components: (1) tacit knowing; (2) volition; and (3) perception *as* unreal" (p. 73).

People often think that a fiction is something untrue, but this is wrong. The word derives from the Latin *fingere*, to make. As something made, fiction is different from something discovered, as in physics, or from something that happened, as in the news. But this does not mean it is false. Fiction is about possible selves in possible worlds.

– Keith Oatley, 2009, p. 1

Tacit knowing, according to philosopher Michael Polanyi (1967) means that "we know more than we can tell" (p. 4). If we try to describe how we acquired the ability to talk, or to ride a bike, or to sense if someone is lying to us, we have difficulty finding the words. We are left only with a sense of trusting our lived experiences, our hunches, guesses, trials and errors and imaginations. In dramatic process we build roles on a foundation of tacit knowledge and it is this foundation upon which much of our actions and responses are drawn. *Volition* involves free will: we are engaged in a process by choice and therefore can remove ourselves from it whenever we want. This is a very important point in role play. Participants must always be given the option to exit a role, to feel a sense of safety at all times that allows any one person to say, "Stop." If we think about how young children enter into and exit their own dramatic play, we can see how stopping and starting does not necessarily inhibit the drama. Conversely, the positive aspect of volition is that we enter into a dramatic world willingly, as we do when we watch a play or a movie, read a book or engage with any of the arts. Part of an applied drama facilitator's skill is to find ways and means to help participants engage more fully in the fictional world they wish to create.

The final component of aesthetic distance identified by Ben Chaim (1984) is an awareness that *perception*, or what we see and hear in a dramatic world, is not real. This is "a metaphorical mode of thinking, a 'seeing-as'... based on our own willingness to imagine" (p. 75). Drama, as all art forms, works through metaphor: we see something *through* something else as a way to heighten our skills of perception. A "peppermint moon" is neither a peppermint nor the moon; we perceive in our imaginations that something new has been brought into be-

Metaphor serves to illuminate a concept by stating that one thing is another. Its structure is composed of two images having sufficient in common to highlight their differences.

– Gavin Bolton, 1990, n.p.

ing. When we play a role, we are ourselves (of course) but we have agreed to see and be seen as somebody or something else (Oatley's "possible self"). Applied drama may seem to be about working with our own stories, but in fact we are crafting something new that exists beyond our individual stories, "Our-story," that is shared by everyone involved (Oatley's "possible world"). We cannot emphasize enough how crucial to applied drama practice is the safety of this perception of the fiction, or what we presented in Chapter 1 as the protection of the role.

2.3 How does the key component of improvisation function in applied drama?

Improvisation is a means for applied drama participants to test out, up on their feet, their ideas and the possibilities that lie within. Group processes can quickly become very talk-filled and one of the key advantages of improvising is to stop talking about or around a topic and to begin working on it directly through action. We can begin understanding the function of improvising in dramatic process by acknowledging that life itself is an improvisation of sorts. As Hodgson and Richards (1966/1974) define it:

> Improvisation in drama aims to utilize the two elements from everyday life improvisation: the spontaneous response to the unfolding of an unexpected situation, and the ingenuity called on to deal with the situation; both of these [are needed] in order to gain insight into problems presented. (p. 2)

The notions of spontaneity and ingenuity (creativity and inventiveness) are foundational to improvisation, whether in dramatic process, actor training or in real life. When we encounter the unexpected, we are challenged to adjust our attitudes and behaviours to this new situation, whatever it may be. An applied drama facilitator is responsible for providing participants with opportunities to encounter the unexpected through improvising their responses to fictional scenarios based on a chosen topic, theme, issue or problem.

There are many fine books on how to teach improvisation, which are listed under Further Reading at the end of this chapter; all are excellent additions to an applied drama facilitator's library. Here, for our specific purposes, we attempt to capture a few key concepts from prominent writer/practitioners of improvisation. Viola Spolin, for example, lists no fewer than 96 "Reminders and Pointers" in her book *Improvisation for the Theatre* (1963/1983, pp. 36–46). One of her key reminders/pointers is to always have a clearly defined focus in any given improvised scene or interaction. Spolin also considers the need for whole group response to

Focus… suggests to me a moving energy, like a ball in a constant state of movement, the players acutely conscious of everything going on around them while keeping their eye on the ball.

– Viola Spolin, 1963/1983, p. xvi

improvised work, and the development of an understanding that there is no one right or wrong answer. The focus always needs to be upon what is happening in the space *between* improvisers, not on the performers in and of themselves. She goes on to explain that that space is where we find "projection of the unknown, the inner self, into the visible world" (p. xvi).

Keith Johnstone, founder of Theatre Sports, also writes about this important concept of "the space between." His discussion of accepting offers and being aware of status in any given improvisation is valuable. Accepting offers means that a person in role in an improvisation is open to suggestions given by a partner or partners, or by participants. Being open is saying "Yes!" to an offer, not judging it or rejecting it but immediately and spontaneously incorporating the offer into the story that is being built and explored. Accepting offers is the opposite of blocking, which means rejecting an offer, thereby stopping an improvisation from moving forward. Status, another key concept for Johnstone (1999), "is not confusing so long as we understand it as something we *do* rather than our social position; for example, a king can play low status to a servant, while a servant can play high status to a king" (p. 219, emphasis added). There are a number of dramatic plays in which such status reversal is seen, of which King Lear and his Fool is one example. An applied drama facilitator needs to be aware of how status may be expressed differently in different cultures; a discussion of status and how it is understood by participants would be a good way to begin entering into improvisational work. Johnstone and Spolin offer many ways to explore status through improvisation games and activities. Building the skills of improvisation before using improvisation as a tool to explore a shared issue or problem is the most effective way to incorporate it in an applied drama process.

There are three main types of improvisation used in applied drama:

Dramatic improvisation is concerned with what we discover for ourselves and the group when we place ourselves in a human situation.... . Very simply, it means putting yourself in other people's shoes and, by using personal experience to help you to understand their point of view, you may discover more than you knew when you started.

Dorothy Heathcote, 1991, p. 44

1. *Spontaneous improvisation:* This occurs with perhaps only one or two facts (e.g. add 50 plus years to your own age). There should be none or almost no preplanning or "talking about" what is to happen. All discoveries are found when "talking as if." Spontaneous improvising generally is done only for a few minutes, allowing players time to talk together after each experience, to reflect on the discoveries that are being made, and to choose to use what has been found, to discard or to adapt it in the next "round." This way of working enables discoveries to be made in terms of what is working, what is not working and what could be changed. The reflecting that follows enables the improvising to deepen as meanings are made and significance takes hold.

2 *Improvisation based on a source:* This is a valuable means of exploring a written work, a painting, a poem, or object in order to discover more of its history, significance and meaning. For example, in *The Glass Menagerie* by Tennessee Williams (1944), Tom (the protagonist) tells his mother and sister about the circumstances surrounding his invitation to the Gentleman Caller. Players are then asked to improvise this unwritten scene, using the information from the script to guide them. In order for the improvisation to unfold without blocks, players will need to do some "talking about"; decisions will need to be agreed upon (e.g. What is the washroom like? Will both characters be there or will one enter? Which one will enter? etc.).

3 *Prepared/polished improvisation:* These are improvisations that are shared as part of the devising process. The scene is being "worked up" by repeated improvising until the players are secure in the choices that they will be making. While there is never any attempt to repeat a line reading or use the same words, the "plot" or "shape" of the scene is agreed upon.

Lockford and Pelias (2004) write that improvisation has five capacities upon which actors may draw: (1) Communication; (2) Playfulness; (3) Sedimentation; (4) Sensuality; and (5) Vulnerability (p. 432). *Communication* requires participants to establish a "communicative connection"(p. 434), to listen to each other, respond in the moment by incorporating new information and opening "creative possibilities for each other [to]… push against the expected" (p. 434). *Playfulness* asks participants to recognize that communication can be a tricky business, filled with miscommunications that may actually be useful and enjoyable spaces to explore, with the added understanding that "when choices are made, they are not the only choices available" (p. 435). Playfulness involves growing comfortable with unpredictability or what Lockford and Pelias call "thinking beyond patterns" (p. 436), more commonly described as "thinking outside the box." *Sedimentation* is the experience that we draw upon that derives from long and repeated practice. According to Spolin (1963/1983), this is the "X-area," the "hidden wellsprings, the unlabeled, beyond intellect, mind, or memory from which [players] draw inspiration" (p. xvii). Sedimentation, in an applied drama context, will be whatever lived experiences are brought into a dramatic process and are made available to participants as they begin to improvise together (another form of "tacit knowledge" as discussed above in terms of role). *Sensuality* is the knowledge and experience that lies in the body and is about how the body responds to sensory input within an improvisation. There are times when these bodily responses may be very strong and perhaps inappropriate, especially in relatively unskilled participants. A facilitator needs to recognize a participant who is being "swept away" by the moment and can stop the process either to reflect or to refocus. The final capacity is that of *vulnerability*, an "affective understanding as a person in an uncomfortable, difficult, or alien situation" (Lockford & Pelias, 2004, p. 438). Trained actors are most often capable of sensing and coping with their own vulnerabilities, but an inexperienced applied drama participant needs to feel safe and protected by the facilitator when entering into improvisations that may trigger strong emotions.

These five capacities are valuable touchstones for building skills with participants and they can be the means of generating work that serves a dramatic process, as opposed to the more popular cultural understanding of improvisation as comedy. Humour does have its place in any applied drama investigation, but participants may be reassured to know that improvisation can be more than a comedy skit. In fact, improvisation through role is one of the most powerful ways to engage a community in exploring issues.

2.4 What are the challenges of applied drama?

We see four main challenges that are common to applied drama practice:

- Understanding the difference between drama as *therapeutic* and drama as *therapy*.
- Maintaining a balance between the aesthetic nature of the art form and its instrumental application.
- Identifying how ethics and values inform an applied drama process.
- Managing the potential tension between honouring the group's ethics and values and the need for freedom of artistic expression.

We begin with the therapy/therapeutic challenge. All drama is about lived experience; therefore, participants in applied drama projects may find themselves risking the exploration of sensitive topics. For example, in any number of setting—prisons, war zones, or any other community struggling with an ongoing problem—things will "pop-up" during the work. How does an applied drama facilitator respond to these challenges?

The first thing to understand is that drama therapy is a discrete discipline in which drama activities are used with clients for the purposes of healing. Drama therapists are trained intensively in both the art form of drama and in counselling psychology before they are licensed to practice. It is very important that applied drama practitioners do not view themselves as drama therapists. There are many applied drama projects that may require a partnership with a professional therapist or counselor due to the difficult nature of the group and/or the work. However, if an applied drama facilitator is working independently and an issue arises with one or more members of a group, the facilitator's immediate responsibility is

Above all else [the facilitator] must use his [*sic*] professional judgment and resist the temptation to enter into the field of therapy just because he happens to be using particularly powerful exploratory techniques.

– Morry van Mentz, 1983/1989, pp. 111–112

Behavior change, skill-building, emotional and physical integration, and personal growth can be achieved through drama therapy in prevention, intervention, and treatment settings.

– National Association of Drama Therapy, n.d. "What is Drama Therapy?"

to know where to turn and how to access the support services required. The temptation to fix these problems ourselves is great, but facilitators must understand that they do not possess the skills and experience that is needed in situations where participants are emotionally triggered or disclose traumatic events.

On the other hand, drama (as in all art forms) may have substantially therapeutic effects on participants. Therapeutic in this context is closer in meaning to a dramatic process or experience having beneficial aspects, as in being restorative, productive, valuable and/or constructive rather than its more health-related application in a treatment setting. Artists and philosophers over many centuries have pondered the therapeutic effects of art, both for the artist and the viewer. For an applied drama facilitator, understanding the difference between drama as therapy and drama as therapeutic is central.

The second challenge an applied drama facilitator will face is how to maintain a balance between the aesthetic experience of dramatic art and instrumental (or practical) concerns. The field of applied drama is filled with instrumental and practical issues that are the foundation of the work (HIV/AIDS education, diversity training, domestic abuse policing, and so on). In the face of these real-life topics, how can an artistic process maintain its integrity? As noted earlier, it is crucial that an applied drama facilitator be grounded in the art form of drama. Ideally a facilitator should have a degree in drama/theatre plus education (as in a double major) or drama/theatre education. This background allows a facilitator to make for participants important connections between what they are doing and how that "doing" is part of a very long and rich history of dramatic art.

The work in drama operates like a corkscrew: in order to open up it must also spiral down.

– Juliana Saxton, 1990, p. 5

Thus, for example, in a monologue project in which participants write and share solo pieces from their own or others' lives, a facilitator may connect that dramatic form back to its application in theatre practice (as in the works of monologist Anna Deavere Smith [1997, 2003]) and even to the ancient art of storytelling around the fire. This movement between a particular activity within a group process and its larger role within the art form of drama is a key component of effective facilitation.

[I]magining things being otherwise may be a first step toward acting on the belief that they can be changed.

– Maxine Greene, 1995, p. 22

Another aspect of good practice in applied drama lies in a facilitator's ability to make metaphorical links between the instrumental focus of a project and how it might be addressed through dramatic artistic process. We will be offering many examples of how this works in action in subsequent chapters. One brief illustration here is how a group dealing with the issue of immigrant experience might consider the notions of migrations, journeys and voyages as a broader way to begin exploring this issue before moving into their own specific stories. Drawing on great stories, poems and dramas across cultures and times that are in the form of a migration, journey or voyage—as in excerpts from Homer's *The Odyssey* (2006), Brecht's *The Caucasian Chalk Circle* (2010), or the travelling songs of Woody Guthrie—is one way to bring a strong aesthetic element into an applied drama setting while still maintaining the overall agenda set for the program.

The final two challenges can be summarized as involving ethical questions of how we balance the moral and cultural values of participants (as well as our own) with the need for artistic freedom—freedom of both expression and action. One crucial step is to ensure there is enough time within a given project to get to know the group. It is also important to find out beforehand as much as possible about the community in general and about the group participants in particular. However, this may not always be possible; in a short-term half-day employee training drama workshop, for example, a facilitator may not know anything more about the participants beyond the type of job they do. That said, there are a number of warm-up drama games and activities that can provide both the facilitator and group members with a better sense of who is in the room. Many of these kinds of diagnostic games and activities will be offered in succeeding chapters. Carefully observing how a group gets

> There is a need for a continuous process of shared reflection to understand the meanings generated through the practice.
>
> – Mike White, 2010, p. 142

along, how well they work together and at what tempo, are all good facilitator assessment points of opening activities. The focus of these activities should be on something beyond the people themselves in these introductory exercises, as in the game Line-Ups. Here, a group has to organize themselves in a line according to called out categories as quickly as they can (in order of age, how long they have lived in Canada, or how they position themselves politically from very liberal to very conservative). The "results" of Line-Ups may be revealing and lead to rich discussions or debates but, to begin with, the focus for participants is simply on getting the job of lining up done in ten seconds or less.

Our next point may seem obvious: a facilitator must never assume that participants share the same morals and values as each other or, indeed, as the facilitator. Therefore, it is imperative to co-create a "Drama Contract" in which the ways that a group agree to work together is clearly negotiated (see Chapter 3). In these politically correct times, it is often considered to be polite to ignore cultural differences in public spaces and to pretend that we are all much the same. In an applied drama setting, the reverse must be the case: our responsibility to the group is to make visible and address any relevant differences in regard to gender, race, religion and/or sexual orientation.

Yet another ethical note is for facilitators to consistently remind themselves that the focus in an applied drama process is on the participants, not the facilitator. For those readers who come to applied drama with a theatre training background, this is a very different role from that of a traditional theatre director who acts as the expert, all-seeing-eye and who is very much in charge of what and how something is being explored. The facilitator provides the means for a group to engage meaningfully with a given topic or issue through drama, but keeps the process open to participant input at all times.

Finally, a facilitator is responsible for the creation and maintenance of a safe working environment. Paradoxically, a safe space is a necessary condition from which to generate the freedom to take risks required for the making of engaging drama.

All of those people bring all of their traditions to the room and then we have negotiation, and we agree on things that we can agree on, and it works just like it says in the stories that it works, in that we sit and discuss it until we figure out what everyone can live with.

– Yvette Nolan, cited in
Knowles, 2010, p. 66

2.5 Questions for Reflection, Suggested Activity and Further Reading

Questions for Reflection

1. How does understanding your own personal history in terms of role and status affect your sense of yourself and your presentation of yourself as a facilitator?
2. Identify some moments in your life when you thought something was going to happen, but something else happened that was unexpected. At times we deal with these events well and at other times perhaps not so well. How did you respond "in the moment" to these experiences? What do these responses tell you about yourself and your potential abilities as a facilitator?
3. Process often appears to be chaotic but does have an internal organization. In group work that you have experienced from a participant perspective, what roles have you observed being taken in the process that either hold the process up or move it forward?

Suggested Activity

Consider and list all the roles that you have played or now play in your life. You may find this helpful by creating a lifeline and entering the roles along it, noting how roles change as we mature. Using Johnstone's guide that roles are something we do rather than our social position, what status do you attach to the roles you have listed and how have they changed over time?

Further Reading

Ackroyd, J. (2004). *Role reconsidered: A re-evaluation of the relationship between teacher-in-role and acting.* Stoke on Trent, UK: Trentham Books. This study closely examines the relationship between role play and acting in applied drama settings. Of particular interest are the chapters that look at the work of master drama teachers John O'Toole and Cecily O'Neill and how they use role in learning situations.

Johnson, D. W. & Johnson, F. P. (2009). *Joining together: Group theory and group skills* (10th ed.). Boston: Merrill. This is an excellent introductory text that examines the stages of group process and the roles played within them. It also contains a number of suggestions for activities.

Schonmann, S. (2005). "Master" versus "servant": Contradictions in drama and theatre education. *Journal of Aesthetic Education, 39*(4), 31–39. This article provides a lot of useful thinking around the tension between the aesthetics of the art form of drama/theatre and the instrumental concerns of carrying out drama/theatre projects in extratheatrical settings.

What happens when we move from being ourselves to becoming others in an "as-if" fictionalized context such as drama and theatre? How do these transformations take place and what are their effects on both participants and audiences? What, indeed, is the very nature of drama ("action") and theatre ("the seeing-place")? Artists, theorists, philosophers and writers have wrestled with these core questions for millennia. What is important is that applied drama facilitators begin a process of addressing these questions for themselves because they underpin so much of what we do when working through drama. One of the great concerns for those who work in applied drama/theatre is that they often come from backgrounds that may not include an understanding of how theatre works. This means that the richness and depth in the ways the work can function for the needs of participants may be compromised.

> Everybody has recognized that there are exercises that are necessary for developing a group of actors. But actors who go into a piece of work with nothing to prepare them as a group will not do this work as well as if they go through all the very well known processes for forming a group.
>
> – Peter Brook, cited in Croyden, 2003, p. 90

The focus of this text is to highlight the aspects of drama and theatre that make the process work whatever the context, be it professional, amateur or community. As a means of creating a context for the next chapters, the following elements and terms are all aesthetic and artistic building blocks that can be found in any arts-based process but, in drama, they are used in specific ways and are central to effective practice.

Elements or spectra of drama/theatre

Darkness/Light

Dark and light can be literal as in how the space is illuminated or, as in photography, negative and positive, while in movement, "dark" is more often translated as "heavy." More importantly, these two dramatic terms can refer to the tone or mood of a piece of drama, which may shift back and forth between tragic and comic elements, or may stay consistently at one or the other end of this spectrum.

Sound/Silence

While we may think of drama as being driven by dialogue and in hearing the voices of characters, which is true, it can be equally as important to make use of silence. Silence can create powerful moments in drama as when, for example, a character cannot find the words to express his or her joy or despair. Playwrights Samuel Beckett and Harold Pinter were particularly adept at using the many different kinds of silence as a means of communicating feeling and meaning without words.

Movement/Stillness

Again, we think of drama as being action, which is so. But stillness, like silence, can create strong focus and highlight significant moments within a drama. The constraint of stillness, in the creation of human sculptures or tableaux (frozen group illustrations), can lend itself to a fuller reflective articulation on what is happening on and below the surface of what we see.

> When you come into the theater, you have to be willing to say, "We're all here to undergo a communion, to find out what the hell is going on in this world." If you're not willing to say that, what you get is entertainment instead of art, and poor entertainment at that.
>
> – David Mamet, 2000, p. 18

There can be no dramatic action without these elements in play. It is how you facilitate them that will enable a richness to enter the work. These elements also offer a way of processing the work and so effective facilitation will include drawing participants' attention to their power within a dramatic exploration.

There are four other key terms which can be used in combination with the elements defined above to enlarge and expand the available vocabulary of an applied drama facilitator in his or her work:

Tension

It is tension that holds each end of the spectra in relationship. How light or dark will a given dramatic work be? How filled with sound and silence? How may movement and stillness interplay with each other? Tension is fundamental to intellectual and emotional engagement in drama and acts as the bonding agent that sustains involvement. Tension is not the same as conflict, as conflict is a much more overt and less subtle form of tension. There are tensions that come from outside the drama ("I wonder how you can accomplish this difficult task?"), or from inside the drama ("How will we find our way out without alerting the others?"). An effective facilitator makes use of the tensions of *time* ("We only have a few moments before…"), *place* ("Where am I?"), *obstacles* ("You never let me do anything!"), *journeys* ("How will we get there?"), *secrecy* ("I can't tell you, I promised!"), *mystery* ("What's happening?"), *dare/personal challenge/test* ("Bet you can't!"), *dependence* ("I need you"), *responsibility* ("We need your help!") and *status* ("You think you're so great?"). These are the kinds of tensions that Heathcote says are "what keeps everyone there dealing with the situation" (cited in Bolton, 1997, p. 25).

Focus

In applied drama, role play improvisations will have two foci. One is the literal focus ("What is this scene about?" e.g. *two people having a cup of coffee together*) and the other, metaphorical (e.g. *a sponsor meeting a new AA member*). The meta-phorical focus is on how that literal experience is

> Focalization is the stress placed… on an action according to a particular point of view in order to underscore its relevance.
>
> – Patrice Pavis, 1998, p. 151

deepened by layers of meaning derived from dramatic strategies through, for example, freezing the action and speaking directly to the audience in an aside, having other actors embody the inner voices and attitudes of one or more characters, creating a still picture or movement sequence that reveals more than the words spoken (e.g. *the way in which the coffee is poured and sipped*). The guiding question is always "Why are we doing this? What are the messages we are sending?"; the multiple answers will provide new focus for participants as they move forward in dramatic process.

Contrast

Dramatic contrast involves the playing off of one or more element/s against another. This means that facilitators create opportunity for dramas to contain both serious and comic elements and verbal and non-verbal portrayals. But it also means that drama often moves from one state of being to another more contrasting one. The scene exampled above abruptly changes direction when *the two decide to go off to have a drink together*. The unex-pected, the unpredictable and reversals of direction or fortune are ways to explore contrast in applied drama.

Symbolization

The way a facilitator draws attention to a gesture, word or object within a drama can create potent symbols that give deeper significance and meaning. What objects endow power, such as cloaks, crowns or tridents? What indicates lack of power: an empty bowl, a ragged cloth, a chair turned on its side? These simple devices (*the coffee cups, now empty, are what remain*) can signify depths of dramatic meaning when incorporated with care into an exploration. The delicate glass animals collected by the fragile Laura in Tennessee Williams's *The Glass Menagerie* (1944) are a good example of symbolization at work.

A *sign* stands for something known: object; name; word; number. A *symbol* represents something known and/or unknown or inexpressible. For example, a flag can represent all three: a country (known), history (known and unknown) and our feelings about place that we cannot express.

Dramatic engagement

As useful as are all of the elements and terms described and defined above, they will have no value if the process lacks dramatic engagement for everyone involved. Dramatic engagement is a personal engagement in the dramatic world. How does each individual find his or her way into the process? How is that engagement supported and sustained? What are the different levels of dramatic engagement (Morgan & Saxton, 1987) a facilitator can both provide opportunities for and, in turn, recognize when they are occurring?

In mindful learning, it is the engagement of the self that is seen as central to the measures of impact: improved retention, enhanced pleasure, better health.

– Daniel J. Siegel, 2007, p. 243

Arousing interest

This demands the physical presence of participants and their engagement with watching, listening, responding and reacting. This initial level is centred on arousing curiosity in the group ("What is going to happen next?") Ways of arousing interest may be in the way a facilitator presents him or herself, wondering about something out loud, or posing an open-ended question, or sharing a *catalyst* (such as a word or phrase, a picture, a poem, a piece of music or a story of some kind) that captures the group's attention and holds it. Catalysts in drama are things that cause change to happen as they bring focus to a group, and may even engender tension or potential for symbolization. In Miller and Saxton's (2004) collection of story dramas, one structure begins with asking students to solve a jigsaw puzzle in small groups. The finished puzzle is a portrait of the story's central character and the question is posed, "What words would you use to describe this face to make it come alive in a novel?" (p. 117).

Engaging

This refers to ways in which participants can begin to identify personally with dramatic roles and situations. Engaging requires that each group member agrees to be involved, to operate in the dramatic "as-if" world, to relate to others in that imagined world, and to draw on personal knowledge and experience to assist in the building of belief in the imagined world. Choosing a task or action that will help participants enter into a dramatic sit-

In every drama… [participants] have to make a positive choice to join in or not, without this willingness bred of interest and engagement there can be no active drama. Both the world of professional theatre and world of… drama share this common feature that [it] has to be by choice.

– Jonothan Neelands, cited in
O'Connor, 2010, p. 140

uation is always a good way to build engagement. A troop of soldiers heading off to war need first to check and clean their equipment; sharing stories in pairs or small groups about experiences similar to the one being explored is another way to encourage engagement. Creating an image in response to a catalyst is yet another method.

Committing

This next level refers to the acceptance of engagement in the work by becoming responsible to the work and the group. Committing involves accepting the dramatic framework and the limits of the role and situation and agreeing to function within it. Here, group members are recognizing the power of the role and the freedom that each player has to change directions, but always understanding that there will be complications and implications for those choices. Participants at this stage are prepared to express attitudes and ideas that are appropriate within the context of a role. Commitment in dramatic process is demonstrated by a high level of absorption in the work.

Internalizing/Interpreting

Once participants are absorbed in the work, they are able to form points of view and attitudes in role in a way that is both personal and fictional. Personal perspectives are mediated within the context of the role in order to further the group's dramatic investigation. Often, dramatic process will involve both protagonist and antagonist roles and challenges participants to empathize with characters whose interests are in what Dorothy Heathcote calls "productive tension" (Bolton, 1997, p. 25). For example, in Cecily O'Neill's process drama "The Seal Wife" (O'Neill, 1995; Taylor, 2000), participants explore the motivations of a husband who has stolen his seal-wife's skin because he has fallen deeply in love with her and that is the only way he can keep her with him: he is both lover and thief. Conversely, the seal wife begins as a highly sympathetic character, but in the end abandons her children in order to return to her life in the sea. This internalization of contrasting perspectives enables a range of interpretations that arise as responses in the moment of the action. These multiple interpretations are not pre-determined, but are co-created through the dramatic process.

Valuing/Reflecting

A successful dramatic process offers participants opportunities for a sense of personal satisfaction in a shared significant experience. An effective process can be recognized as participants share meanings acquired

Effective questioning from the facilitator is key to successful reflection and evaluation, both inside and outside the fictional world. (see Morgan & Saxton, 1994/2006)

as a result of the process. These deeper meanings can be both intellectual and emotional and carry within them a recognition of how the fictional world may impact the personal. This empathic understanding marries insight and felt experience through the fictional role. Part of evaluation will also involve considering how the original source material was used throughout the dramatic process: How well was the integrity of the material maintained? How was it altered, shifted and changed? Evaluation can be effected in role inside the drama through such strategies as Conscience Alley or Spectrum of Difference (see Index), and through reflection out of role, by talking with a partner, in small groups or within the whole group. As we point out in Chapter 1, reflection is integral to effective dramatic process; it offers opportunities for integrating drama experiences into the mental map of previous learning. Apart from the knowledge-building that reflection generates, it also plays a role in building trust, refining communication skills and creating a safe environment which paradoxically encourages the taking on of greater risks.

It is important to note that before any of these processes can happen a group must cross an imaginary threshold from the real world in which they live into the co-constructed fictional world of drama (O'Neill, 1995). Whatever is being done in dramatic process, part of its potential strength will lie in the powerful dramatic element of *ritual*, of which a key part is to symbolically indicate the shift in time, space and self that occurs when participants join the ensemble. The drama structures follow an arc, like all good pedagogy, that involves preparing, entering, investigating and reflecting. The preparatory stage, which focuses participants' attention and commitment, is about co-creating an aesthetic space (akin to a rehearsal hall in theatre practice) which is disciplined, lacks outside distractions (as in cell phones ringing, and so on) and sets up the conditions within which the work can most productively take place. Preparatory work involves relaxing, warming-up, sensory awareness activities (such as breathing, listening, observing, etc.), and/or games which develop drama skills, moving freely to music, and so on. The stages of dramatic process that follow continue the arc through the levels of engagement and are highly dependent on how things begin. So too, a dramatic process should always finish with enough time for participants to reflect in ways that enable them to recognize what they can carry from this experience back into their everyday lives.

> How a person reflects internally [shapes] how he [*sic*] treats both himself and others [and] alters the brain's ability to create flexibility and self-observation, empathy, and morality . . . Reflection is the skill that embeds self-knowing and empathy in the curriculum.
>
> – Daniel Siegel, 2007, pp. 260–261

Chapter Three
Building a Community

3.1 Learning about participants

There are two major ways in which a facilitator may learn about participants before meeting them in person. The first is the more traditional model of having participants sign-up or register for a series of workshops because they are interested in a particular issue or proposal. For example, participants may wish to explore a community's history through drama or are united by a concern for a social justice issue. The second model is when a funding agency, organization, business or social service offers a workshop series for which participants will only show up on the day, and may indeed come and go throughout the project. This sort of irregular attendance is often the case where facilitators are working with at-risk communities or low socio-economic groups that have multiple responsibilities both at home and/or at work in which shift schedules are not prepared very far in advance. Whichever way, a facilitator should consider how he or she is going to get to know about each participant, as well as plan which "ice-breaker" activities will best help participants get to know each other. Appendix C (p. 211) provides an example of a biographical sheet that we have found useful. Information such as the kind gathered here can be a component of registration, or can be requested at the opening or closing of a first workshop. In some communities, however, this information may be more appropriately gleaned in oral rather than written forms (for example, when working with very young children, or with participants who may not have high levels of literacy in writing). We recommend asking each participant's permission to take individual digital photo portraits for identification purposes only, or to have them provide a personal photo. This is a helpful way to remember each person's name and should be done quickly as recognition is, of course, a first step in building a strong sense of community.

3.2 Entering a community/drama contract

Many participants will have never worked in drama and, as the work progresses, there will be many opportunities for individuals, groups or the facilitator to discover together the codes of behaviour.

Negotiating how an applied drama group agrees to work together is the function of what is called the *drama contract*. While we suggest that the very first activities be focused on getting-to-know-you drama games and activities (see Further Reading), from the earliest point on facilitator and participants are co-creating a contract that sets out the terms that will guide the ways in which they will work together. Whether the "contract" is actually recorded and posted (as is often done in work with young people) or only negotiated and accepted as implicit, participants should be aware that the drama contract is always open to additions and renegotiations. Although much will stand as a guide to behaviour, the contract is never static but can shift and flex according to the needs of the group as seen by the facilitator and/or the group. Jonothan Neelands (1984) insists that, whether this contract is implicit or explicit, "*it must be there*" (p. 27, original emphasis). To summarize Neelands' view of the purposes of a drama contract:

Often groups will resort to raising hands as a signal to speak. This may work in a traditional classroom but can inhibit group progress and process. If another method is preferred, then it is helpful to figure out together what signs we will look for in order for everyone to be heard.

Jonathan Haidt (2012) suggests that if we want to change ourselves and others, we need first to see others from their perspectives; we need to get used to each other if we want to work together productively.

- It establishes the terms of the partnership between facilitator and participants.
- It carries the expectation that everybody will contribute and respond.
- It acknowledges the particular demands that drama makes (working orally, physically, emotionally and cooperatively).
- It demystifies drama as an art form and guarantees that the facilitator will not ask more of participants than they are willing or prepared to do themselves.
- It provides a reference point for dealing with problems as they may arise, and guarantees a space in which people feel safe expressing how they feel about material, issues, or group dynamics.
- It initiates a dialogue that allows all group members to negotiate and reflect upon the work (p. 27).

The contract will inevitably be differently constructed by every group, but these purposes go far to ensure an effective process.

As important as the drama contract is, we do wish to echo Neelands' cautions around this negotiation. He advises not to spend too much time on this contract-building, but to see it as a work-in-progress, to remember that the facilitator is as bound by the contract as are the participants, and that the drama contract does not in itself predict successful practice (p. 28). For participants, the contract can allay very real fears around misapprehensions that dramatic process is simply another term for actor training. For facilitators with little or no experience, the contract provides support in his or her becoming a member of the group, in being challenged by and in challenging the group, in being transparent in talking about how the process works, and in encouraging participants to share responsibilities for the work. In our own teaching practice, the contract is negotiated implicitly through the drama work itself and the key terms of communication, cooperation and concentration are reflected upon throughout the process. At the same time, in the interests of refining the group process, dramatic terms such as tableaux, improvisation, dialogue and monologue are woven by the facilitator into the work in order to build a sense of expertise through the vocabulary of the art form. In some groups, for example with children in schools, a more explicit approach may be suitable and a contract may be recorded, signed and posted on the wall. However, the contract is never set in stone and can be revisited and renegotiated at any time dependent upon the needs of the group.

3.3 Creating a safe space

The creation of a safe space in which to work has a number of considerations. First, the space must feel physically safe, and preferably inviting. Whatever a facilitator can do to ensure that the area is clean, clear and well-organized will have a significant effect on participants. Ideally, a facilitator will see to having enough chairs to accommodate the group, and for use in group work, along with a few tables, or blocks for multipurpose use. A facilitator should have some supplies at hand such as chart paper, mural paper, felt pens, pencils and lined paper, tape or Blu-tack to post ongoing work on the walls, and a sound system (however minimal). We have found that an overhead projector (however ancient) with coloured cellophane placed on the glass, creates wonderful lighting effects.

The second aspect of creating a safe space is centred on making the space emotionally safe for all involved, so that people are prepared to express their opinions and feelings. This atmosphere of trust is built over time, as the tone is initially set by the facilitator and then maintained over time by the whole group. With certain groups, a facilitator may need to ensure that participants' privacy is protected, both within the group (in terms of confidentiality) and externally (in terms of ensuring that visitors or new participants will only be welcomed with the agreement of the group). There may be some situations

> In every drama class [participants] have to make a positive choice to join in or not, without this willingness bred of interest and engagement there can be no active drama.
>
> – Jonothan Neelands, cited in O'Connor, 2010, p. 140

where it is the facilitator's initial responsibility to ensure the safety of personal property. It may also be the case that certain at-risk groups require additional assurances.

3.4 Drama structure: *Investigating the Circle*

We are making use of the drama structure format designed by Miller and Saxton (2004), as it is a well-tested way in which to organize instructional strategies so that a facilitator can see right away what is happening in his or her mind's eye. The formatting is centred on *action language*, which captures the wording of a teacher/facilitator and can be used or adapted for him/herself. The wording may be used as a dramatic process begins, but over time it will change as each facilitator will find his or her own way of working. In terms of the layout: **Grouping** simply describes the way in which participants will be functioning in the activity; i.e. as individuals, in pairs or groups, etc. **Strategy** names the activity involved in each part of the larger structure. **Administration** serves as a reminder of any materials needed, such as paper and pens, boxes, photocopies, etc. **Focus** suggests the reason/s why the activity is being done and is a source for reflective questions after the activity. The Facilitator's voice is indicated in standard font, while notes on instructions are provided in square brackets and italics and comments are provided in Arial font.

In lesson planning, two types of language predominate. In "narrative" language, the lesson is described as a story and, for the purposes of teaching, then has to be "translated" into words that will put the students into action.

For example:

Narrative: Participants will choose a partner and then claim a space on the floor and sit down together. (18 words)

Action language uses stronger words and fewer of them, putting people to work at once.

For example:

"Find a partner and your own space and sit down together." (11 words)

One of the difficulties encountered by new facilitators is the tendency that too many instructions are given at once. The double spaces between instructions indicate when participants are carrying out an instruction. In the first activity given below, the facilitator is part of the action, so the pauses between instructions are opportunities to observe and consider the response to the activity in the moment and the preparedness of the group to move on. A facilitator has the choice to fully participate with a group in an activity, to slowly withdraw from participation, or to simply give instructions and observe. If a group is working, the facilitator should also be seen as active and ready to assist, rather than as a passive observer, waiting.

These structures can be delivered in one longer session or a number of shorter ones. In either case, delivery is always about keeping an eye on the clock. Twenty minutes before the end of the time allotted, it is time to stop, tidy up and then reflect. The facilitator should know what reflective questions can be asked so that the session can close with a sense of work accomplished and possibilities for the next time. It is better to finish early and leave time for reflection and discussion, rather than rush too quickly through the work, or have to stop in the middle of a task.

1. Preparing for the work

This particular activity takes place at the first meeting of a group and therefore these activities are focused on learning about each other and building a sense of community. It is not just about playing these games, as the facilitator is also going to use observation of participants as they interact as a way to begin to understand the kind of group with which s/he is working. At the same time, these activities give the participants an opportunity to see themselves and each other, and to see the facilitator in that particular role. There are lots of introductory activities available in a wide range of texts, and we offer one here that we find effective.

- **Grouping: Whole group standing in a circle**
- **Strategy: Pass the Pulse**
- **Administration: None**
- **Focus: To get a sense of the group, their comfort level and pace, and how they meet the challenge of the game**

Facilitator: Let's begin by standing in a circle, making sure you are not crowding each other. Hands relaxed at your sides.

All right, now just reach out and hold hands with the people next to you. Good.

Now I am going to very gently but firmly squeeze the hand of the person to my left. When you feel the squeeze, pass it on to the person to your left by squeezing their hand, and so on around the circle. Let's have a try. [*You might want to check that everyone knows their left from their right by asking them to raise the appropriate hand. A simple task but one that comforts the digitally challenged and is the first group activity that challenges only slightly!*] Well done. Let's see how it works going the other direction.

Good. Anybody have any problems? Just check with the people on either side that your signals are getting through.

Who'd like to start the pulse this time? Surprise us by not telling us which hand you are starting with. [*Repeat with different people and changing directions.*]

Now I'll start the pulse again and let's speed it up. This time, I'm going to count how many seconds it takes for the squeeze to get back to me. [*"one thousand, two thousand"...*] Great. Let's see if we can go even faster in the other direction.

You're doing really well. Our times are getting faster and faster. Turn to the person next to you and talk about what in life we can associate with this activity? What sorts of things that you know or can think of work in these ways? Let's share some of those ideas. [*People may talk about heartbeats, electricity, time, gossip, etc. Sometimes someone may surprise you and you may not quite understand what has been said. Acknowledge that response and say "Hmm... that's very interesting. I'll have to think about that."*]

Right, now here's the challenge. I'm going to squeeze both of my hands at the same time and let's see what happens.

How did that go? Who got the crossover and how did it go for you? [*Once the problems are sorted out, the facilitator can send out a second double pulse or even a third in the same without telling anybody.*]

Now we seem to have a lot of messages going, let's think about what that has to do with our lives. [*Here is another opportunity to discover how the group thinks and how much they are prepared to share.*]

Let's finish this activity with one more challenge. Close your eyes. Trust that you will be able to do as well as you have been with your eyes closed, even if you don't know from which direction a squeeze or a number of squeezes will be coming your way.

How was that different?

We've talked about how this activity relates to life, I'm wondering now how you see it relating to the work we will be doing together in drama? [*Here is where the group may begin talking about the conditions that make up the drama contract.*]

2. Entering the work: The Circle

- **Grouping: Whole group, then groups of four or five**
- **Strategy: Discussion**
- **Administration: Sitting in a circle, with paper and pencils available for each group**
- **Focus: To look at the circle as a symbol, signifier and metaphor**

Facilitator: Can we just sit down? [*Have them sit on the floor rather than on chairs. If someone cannot sit on the floor, they can remain standing or take a chair.*]

Just look around and make sure that it's a perfect circle. [*Keep provoking the group to achieve this perfection. Do not let them be satisfied too soon. This is the first aesthetic decision they have to make.*]

That was a bit harder than we might have thought it would be. What criteria enable us to say that this is a perfect circle? [*Everybody can see each other, everybody is included, everybody is spaced apart and yet a part of the community, etc.*]

Shakespeare's audience could understand the Globe Theatre as a "wooden O"… because the concept in their minds allowed them to think about the wooden globe as having an inside, an outside, and a boundary between them.

– Bruce McConachie, 2008, p. 122

What sort of occasions can you think of where this arrangement is used or has been used? [*Storytelling around the fire, the Knights of the Round Table, the United Nations Security Council, a reconciliation circle, etc.*]

What do circles symbolize? What is the significance of a circle? Take a minute to think.

Thank you. Some interesting ideas there. Let's get into groups of four

I would like you to brainstorm a list of things that have to do with circles. We've made a good beginning. You can probably come up with at least thirty more. Just one person will volunteer to be the scribe and report back to the whole group. About five minutes should do it.

Time's up. In your group read over what you've got and put a star beside a couple of ideas that you think are particularly rich. [*This prepares for the next activity.*]

Now we're going to hear from each group via their scribe. Scribes, check off any of the same ideas that you hear so you don't have to repeat them when you read your list.

Were there any ideas you heard that need clarification? [*Not everyone may know about crop circles, for example.*]

[*If you choose not to use the option offered below*] Thank you everyone. Let's come back to sitting together in our circle. Who would like to share some of the thoughts and ideas that came up as you worked together? What did we see in this last activity that told you more about how we work together in drama? [*Another opportunity to develop the criteria for the drama contract.*]

Option:

- **Grouping: Individual or small group**

Now I'd like you to go on a circle hunt. In two minutes I'd like you to bring back to the centre of the room any objects you can find in this space that are circular. If the object is immovable, remember it for later. Any questions? All right, let's begin.

You've found a lot of wonderful things. Let's share some of the things you have found; point to anything you weren't able to bring back.

Great. Now this pile of objects is interesting because it's made up of circles, but it does look a bit of a mess. I wonder if we could work together to arrange it in a more pleasing fashion. Thinking as art curators, how can we make this into a sculptural installation that is the first thing visitors will see when they enter a new art show called "Circles"? We only have a few minutes to rearrange the objects, and you may use other things in the room to make use of different levels or to draw attention. Remember that an installation is three-dimensional, so make sure it pleases you from all sides.

Finish up now. Good. Just step away from what we've been doing, find your own space in the room and close your eyes.

When I ask you to open them, you will be a visitor to the art gallery who is seeing this piece for the first time. Take a minute or two to look at it in your own way, then find a partner with whom you can talk about your ideas as you move around the installation. Any questions? Open your eyes. [*You may choose to participate as a visitor and offer your own reflections if participants need encouragement.*]

Thank you everyone. Out of role now. Let's come back to sitting together in our circle. Who would like to share some of the thoughts and ideas that came up as you walked and talked? What did we see in this last activity that told you more about how we work together in drama? [*Another opportunity to develop the criteria for the drama contract.*]

The first workshop may end here. If there is an opportunity for participants to bring in resources to do with circles (images, books, songs, poems, objects, fairy tales, myths, and so on) these materials may be helpful for the second session, but are not mandatory. Or, the facilitator may wish to have such resources available at this point (for example, a recording of Joni Mitchell's 1970 song "Circle Game" [www.youtube.com/watch?v=X5HXT0bn7QY]) for groups to use.

3. Engaging in the work

- **Grouping: Whole group, then groups of five or six**
- **Strategy: Tableaux**
- **Administration: None**
- **Focus: To arrive at a shared understanding of how the group sees a circle**

<u>Facilitator</u>: I'd like you to get into groups of five or six and talk about the ideas you've just heard [heard last time], particularly any ideas that have extended your thinking about circles. You've discovered many different aspects of circles, that circles have insides and outsides, that they can include or exclude, and that they can represent symbolic notions of unity, harmony and eternity. You might want to talk about how a circle is similar to yet distinct from other geometric shapes such as a square or a triangle. [*These kinds of prompts draw on what has been offered previously and may introduce new ideas as part of that reflection. Depending on your group, you may offer the above as a whole or interject each of them as separate prompts during the group discussion. Suggested time: no more than fifteen minutes, but this will depend on the make-up of the group.*]

One thing that a facilitator needs to discover for him or herself is a means of drawing the whole group's attention. You can use your voice, clap your hands, or use a signal (a tambour, a tambourine, a bell, a triangle or a cymbal) to indicate that silence is requested.

The first task is to create three still pictures, or tableaux, that illustrate the group's ideas about the circle. Everyone must be in each tableau. In creating your tableaux, you should think about the idea and where the *focus* will appear. Also consider your picture as capturing something happening in *action* and that your picture has visual interest through the use of *levels* (high, medium and low). As with the installation we created, [omit if not done] your tableaux are three-dimensional and intended to be seen from all sides.

First, you'll need to arrive at a concept for your first tableau, and I suggest you get up on your feet as fast as you can and try these ideas out rather than talking too much. [*Getting participants up on their feet is crucial and may need to be a constant prompt over the first few sessions.*] I think five minutes should be enough time.

Time in process work is really important. Drama time is elastic, but it is always better to give less time than too much time. The message here is that the work is significant; we need to get it done and it must be done both efficiently and effectively. Participants can negotiate for extra time if it is genuinely needed. There is nothing to stop a facilitator using a signal and saying, "Time's up" and asking if everybody is ready and, if not, how much more time is required. If participants ask for another five minutes, offer them three!

Let's have a look at what you've got. I'll count down from five and when we get to one you should be frozen in your tableau. Let's try that.

Just before we relax, close your eyes and memorize the position your body is in, because you will need to remember for later on. Relax. Talk together about how that went.

Let's try that again. This time, when you arrive at the freeze, someone in the group will step out of the tableau and look at it from all sides, then fit himself or herself back in. [*Groups may want to choose someone to step out, but generally this works as self-selection without discussion.*] On the signal, relax and talk about any adjustments that need to be made.

Now let's move to your second tableau. We'll follow the same pattern.

Now we have Tableau 1 and Tableau 2, and your task is to work out how you move from Tableau 1 into Tableau 2. I suggest as we're working with a count of five, that you think about that transitional phase taking five counts.

Good work. Now let's create our final tableau. Part of this task involves figuring out how to move from Tableau 2 to Tableau 3. You know how it works by now, so I'll leave you to it. Don't forget to memorize your new tableau and that someone steps out to look at it from the outside. Three minutes enough?

Of course, during any group activity you should be circulating around from group to group, observing the process and lending a hand if need be. Try not to interfere too much with what is happening, but be prepared to help a group that is struggling, or to make a suggestion that lifts the work up a level.

[*If the option is not taken up, go to *** below.*]

Option:

We're not finished yet! Now we're going to add three more things to your work: a *breath*, a *sound* and a *line of text*. These can all appear in the same tableau, or once each in your three tableaux; it's about finding where they are most appropriate. However, each of these three things may only be done once. That is your constraint. How you express them is up to you, but each may only be done once. You explore this. You've got five minutes to decide where you're going to use these three additions and how. Off you go.

Okay. Are we ready to share what we've created? [*You may wish to offer the use of some musical selections, if available, to underscore the tableaux/movement sequences.*] Would you like to have a final rehearsal? We'll all work at the same time. Do you still want me to count or are you all right to do it silently on your own?

We seem to be ready. As we share this work, I'd like you to pay attention to what comes to mind as you watch each group's sequence. What do their tableaux and transitional movements and other elements tell you about circles? What tells you this? In other words, be prepared to point to specific moments, images or parts of images that draw your interest.

*** Talk in your own group about how that went.

Each group number yourselves off, from one to five or six. Now I'd like all the ones to gather here, the twos there [*and so on*]. Talk together about how the process worked and what had the most impact for you? What do you see gave those moments their impact?

Return to your own group and share what was most significant in your conversation.

4. Reflecting on the work

- **Grouping: Whole group**
- **Strategy: Reflection**
- **Administration: None**
- **Focus: To look at the work in terms of meanings and artistic effect**

Facilitator: Let's come together into our whole circle. What advice would you give another group who is about to do this work? How can we make this process work most effectively and efficiently? More importantly, what tips would you have for making the work clearer in terms of communicating the powerful meanings that we saw in your work today?

All work will be full of meaning; there is always something you can point to as having potential, even if it is partial or incomplete. It is important that participants feel a sense of satisfaction, fulfillment and pleasure. In the reflective discussion it is participants' responses that are primary, but it is your responsibility as facilitator to build on these responses. You may ask a group (or the whole group may request) to repeat their sequence, or just a small part of it, in order to highlight something that you and/or the group felt was particularly effective.

You've worked really hard and you've done an enormous amount. All of the work we've done together encapsulates what dramatic process is all about. Nothing we'll be doing in future workshops be anything more than an extension of the things we've done together with the circle. This work involved us in using the six elements of drama (movement/stillness, light/dark, sound/silence) and we also incorporated focus, tension, contrast and symbolization. When you think about the work, where do you see these dramatic elements in action?

Action language is made more inclusive by using "We" and "Our" rather than "I" and "You." This equalizes the power relationships to help participants see the work as something created all together rather than achieved simply by following instructions.

It is these key elements that we will continue to work with and develop throughout our time together.

3.5 Questions for Reflection, Suggested Activity and Further Reading

Questions for reflection

1. What type of participant group are you most interested in working with through applied drama? What is it about this group of people that draws you to them? How might you learn more about this group through online and hands-on research? For example, where are the community resources available that could provide an entry-point into a particular community group? How are you going to identify their needs?
2. What are the most important things to consider when first meeting a group? How will you present yourself and let them know who you are and what you have to offer? What are you going to be looking for as you are working with the group in terms of who they are and what they have to offer?

Suggested Activity

Begin creating a card file of introductory and skill-building drama activities that develop the Five Cs of drama (see below under Further Reading for places to start). Some of these games and activities can be taught directly from their sources, so may simply be photocopied and pasted onto cards. Other sources may require translation into action language. We also recommend that you keep reflective notes on these cards after using each activity. Each of these activities will need to be adjusted according to the group you are working with (physical capabilities, language, age, cultural contexts) and this planning is part of your record-keeping.

Further Reading

Barker, C. (1977/2010). *Theatre games: A new approach to drama training.* London: Methuen.

Boal, A. (1992). *Games for actors and non-actors* (A. Jackson, Trans.). London: Routledge.

Swales, J. (2009). *Drama games for classrooms and workshops.* London: Nick Hern.

Swartz, L. (2002). *The new dramathemes* (3rd ed.). Markham, ON: Pembroke.

Swartz, L. & Nyman, D. (2010). *Drama schemes, themes and dreams: How to structure and assess classroom events that engage all learners.* Markham, ON: Pembroke.

Each of these texts is full of activities that can be used as warm-ups to separate participants from their everyday contexts, and/or to get groups moving physically or intellectually. These activities may be used because they have direct application to the themes and contexts of the work to be undertaken.

Chapter Four
Risking, Trusting and Being

4.1 Building trust/creating community

Jonothan Neelands (2009) has written about the importance of creating an ensemble when working together with students/participants through drama:

> Working together in the social and egalitarian conditions of ensemble-based drama, [participants] have the opportunity to struggle with the demands of becoming a self-managing, self-governing, self-regulating social group who co-create artistically and socially... The ensemble serves as a bridging metaphor between the social and the artistic [and] has the potential of reconciling the tensions between the social and the artistic. (p. 182)

In working collaboratively through drama, a group of people are functioning at two distinct levels at all times; the social level related to group process and dynamics and the artistic level focused on the making, sharing and reflecting processes of drama. A successful ensemble is capable of seeing these dual functions working within the group, and can also reflect effectively on both the social and artistic aspects of what is happening. This double functioning works through a process of constantly moving back and forth between the metaphors of the drama and the individual and group experience of engaging in those metaphors. An applied drama facilitator must be always conscious of how the group is functioning at these two levels, and should include many opportunities for a group to consider their work in ways that are sensitive to peoples' feelings yet critical enough to be of value.

[C]ommunities of identity are constructed when people recognize their own experiences in others, and share an understanding of each other's values or stories.

– Helen Nicholson, 2005a, p. 94

One way to begin to build trust within a group as a means of helping it to grow into an ensemble over time is to begin each session with a check-in of some kind. This may be as simple as asking participants to give a number between one and ten indicating how they are doing that day. Any numbers five or below may require closer attention to see how the group may support a member who is having a bad day. Then there is a more local check-in that invites participants to share any events of interest with the group, from the personal to the cultural to the political. Depending again on the nature and purpose of the group, another way is to have a check-in on a more global level, to process significant world events or issues that have had an impact on the group. For example, in our own experience, two days after 9/11 we spent a whole class processing this event. Our judgment as instructors was that talking about this event (which, oddly, students had not yet done in any of their other classes) was an emotional imperative in creating a community of identity (Nicholson, 2005a). These check-ins demonstrate that human experience is always part of what we are doing in drama. How we feel and what is concerning us will always be a part of the work. The decision a facilitator needs to make, often in the moment, is whether the event should be processed through more simple and direct conversation that meets the social needs of the group or through the work (as in dramatic forms) that offers a richer, deeper experience. For example, our colleague Peter O'Connor, working with teachers and students in Christchurch, New Zealand helped these survivors of a major earthquake process their emotions in a safe way through drama (A Teaspoon of Light, see Bibliography).

Checking-out is an equally important way to build a sense of ensemble, and is focused on reflecting on what has been done and where the work is going. This is an important weaving together of sessions, as the end of one becomes the beginning of the next. A facilitator needs to prioritize spending the last part of each session in this reflective phase, and manage the time accordingly.

Another way to continue to build a sense of trust and community in a group is to continue using drama games and activities as a way to begin each session. As we have said before, these activities must have a clear purpose and are selected to fit the work to come; for example, "word rounds" brainstorming to prepare to meet the issues that may arise (Miller & Saxton, 2004, p. 32) or, as in this chapter's example, the movement activities that engage students in exploring shapes and feelings, inherent components of Being 14. Allowing time for the group to reflect on a game or activity to see what dramatic principles underpin it (as in the Five Cs) is key and then later, seeing how these beginning activities are relevant to the work overall. In other words, all of these activities should be clearly contextualized for participants so that they can see the relevance of these activities within the context of the group's overall mandate or focus.

4.2 Encouraging risk-taking/accepting failure

There are two common misconceptions about drama. One is that drama is about conflict, when tension is a much more useful term. The second is that dramatic process involves consensus, everybody agreeing on how to proceed, rather than the more useful term conspectus. Conspectus means an overall survey or observation of a particular topic or question that includes everybody's view and involves what is called 'radical listening'—the kind of listening in which participants make an effort to understand others' standpoints without seeking to change them (Kincheloe, cited in Tobin, 2011, p. 20). Neelands (1984) writes:

Conflict: 1. to come into collision or disagreement; 2. to do battle; 3. discord of action or feeling

– Jess Stein, 1966, p. 308

Conspectus is a more accurate term (than consensus) in that it conveys the sense of a synopsis of opinions, in other words there may be a wide range of opinions (and differences) reflected in the drama… In drama, then, we are saying to [participants] that although we are working together as a group, individual reactions and opinions are still important… The [facilitator's and participants'] role is then to look for possibilities of grouping answers, to look for patterns that establish a conspectus whilst not ignoring or leaving out "rogue" answers that don't seem to fit at first. (p. 40)

Tension: 1. the act of stretching or straining; 2. the state of being stretched or strained; 3. mental or emotional intensity or excitement.

– Jess Stein, 1966, p. 1462

Encouraging participants to express their individual views, and valuing them as part of an overall process, is crucial to creating an atmosphere within which people with little or no experience in drama may begin to take risks. Prominent drama educator Brian Way (1967) reminded his students repeatedly that the workshop or classroom space for drama was one in which everyone must genuinely feel they have the freedom to fail. While this may seem to be a somewhat contradictory notion, it is a principle for successful dramatic process that reflects what another drama educator, Dorothy Heathcote (Johnson & O'Neill, 1991) termed a "no-penalty zone" (p. 130).

[Participants] must make themselves vulnerable and visible in order to participate and must know that there is protection and mutual respect for difference from within the group to match the personal and social challenges of taking a part in the action.

– Jonothan Neelands, cited in O'Connor, 2010, p. 140

47

4.3 Creating composite characters

In theatre characters are inhabited by actors who may or may not live closely to these characters in real life. Audiences have the pleasure of seeing actor and character merge into one in a successful performance. Audiences may also be "haunted", to use theatre historian Marvin Carlson's term (2001), by other actors who have portrayed a specific character, or by other characters played by the same actor. This ghosting effect is unique to the performing arts and is one of the reasons we are drawn to these social art forms.

In applied drama settings, however, we work more closely and consciously with people's real life histories, stories and experiences as material. Richard Schechner (1997) calls this "believed-in performance" when this kind of work moves into performance settings in which "people are who they perform, playing their social and/or personal identities" (p. 77). This is a more autobiographical form of applied drama/theatre that we suggest is only suited to groups with more experience and abilities built over time. In applied drama work with inexperienced participants, we recommend the creation of composite characters, as modelled in the drama structure that follows. By this we mean that characters are created in a collaborative process that includes aspects of all participants' experiences so that they belong to everyone rather than to one person alone. Another form of protection in the use of composite characters is that we fictionalize the characters, endowing them with their own life stories and sets of given circumstances. This is aesthetic distance, as discussed in Chapter 2, and is also known in dramatic art as *ostranenie* , or "making strange" (Eriksson, 2011, p. 103). When participants are freed from the burden of playing themselves, they are unshackled from what they already know and are released to imagine alternate situations, actions and outcomes, which is one of the key social functions of drama.

> [D]istancing functions primarily as *protection* for the participants against becoming inhibited by an embedment in reality, i.e. the distancing creates a protective distance between one's self and one's fictive role.
>
> – Stig Eriksson, 2011, p. 104

4.4 Drama structure: *Being 14*

1.a. Preparing for the work
This structure is focused on the continuing creation of the ensemble and developing the terms of the drama contract. This structure looks at the movement of bodies in space and the effective use of space in multiple ways, particularly sculptural ones, and offers an opportunity for the group to begin to share aspects of their personal histories toward the creation of a composite character who is 14 years old.

Throughout these structures we offer prompts for facilitators to help in the reflection of the work. However, more often than not, the prompt ideas will come up naturally in the participants' discussions. It is important to give participants time to reflect, a good starting question and time to answer before moving into additional prompts.

- **Grouping: Individual**
- **Strategy: Movement**
- **Administration: None**
- **Focus: To get people moving with an awareness of how they are using the space**

<u>Facilitator</u>: Okay, everybody into a circle. I'm going to give you a letter, so try not to forget. [*Walking around the circle, assigning each person A, B or C.*] As raise your hands. Bs raise your hands. Cs raise your hands. Good.

You can move anywhere you want to in this room and the idea is to explore as fully as possible, without bumping into anybody or getting in anybody's way. So you'll need to keep your antennae up. As, you're going to move as quickly as you can without running. Bs, you're going to move at a normal easy pace. Cs you are to move slowly without ever stopping. When you hear the signal, you are to begin, and when you hear it again, you are to stop. This is a movement exercise so try not to talk. Any questions? Standby. [*You may wish to repeat what each letter is doing one more time.*] Off you go [*Signal*].

Let this activity go for about a minute then signal to stop.

Talk to the person next to you about that experience.

Anything anybody would like to share?

Try to use responses to bring out how there were weaving patterns you could see, and that the whole space was being explored.

Right, we're going to do that again, only this time Cs you're going to take over from the As and go very fast. As will walk at a normal pace. And Bs you will be moving as slowly as possible. Everyone got that? This time really begin to play with your speeds and challenge yourself to explore and try things out. Stand by [*Signal*].

[*Signal to stop.*] That was a bit different. What was happening there?

They should be comfortable enough to respond to the whole group. Or they may need a more specific prompt like, "I could see some really interesting patterns and ways of exploring the space. What did you notice either about yourself or the people you were moving through?"

All right, no surprise here, let's do the last switch-up. So you are all doing the third of the three actions. But we are going to add something different. As you are moving, let what is happening around you begin to give you an idea of who you might be and the situation you are in. And let those impulses begin to inform what is happening to you. If you feel the need to stop, that's fine. Ready? [*Signal*]

[*Signal to stop.*] Move into groups of two or three and talk about what was happening to you and what situations you might have imagined yourself in.

Let's share some of those ideas and, if you can, what it was that prompted you to think that way. What was the physical thing that happened in your body that clued you in?

Now looking at this exercise of moving through the space overall, what does this tell you about the dramatic element of movement? [*You may want to prompt, "What might these movements tell us about people? And, if you used stillness, what is it that prompts you to stop moving?"*]

1.b. Preparing for the work

- **Grouping: Pairs**
- **Strategy: Filling in the Shape**
- **Administration: Music (Pachebel's *Canon*, Samuel Barber's *Adagio*, any other slow tempo classical music, or *Harry Potter and the Deathly Hallows: Part 2*, trailer music from the soundtrack)**
- **Focus: To see the possibilities of space in shape, to experience self-control, and to make offers to partners**

Facilitator: Find a partner and a space in the room where you're not going to interfere with anybody else. Choose A and B.

A, your job is to make a shape with your body that offers some interesting spaces.
B, your job is to fit your body into some or all of those spaces. The rule is there will be no touching because the purpose of the exercise is to be able to move in and out. Let's just try that. A, take a shape.

B, fit yourself in.

A, step away, look at the spaces that B is now offering you. You may want to move around the shape to see all the possibilities. Now, fit yourself back in with your partner in a new way.

Relax. Talk with your partner about that. [*This is a chance for pairs to connect through the experience, and share thoughts if they wish.*]

I'm going to put on a bit of music, Bs, stand-by to take a shape when you feel ready as you listen to the music. A, using the music, you'll fit yourself into Bs spaces and freeze. B, when you fill A is still, then you move away and find new spaces to fit yourself into. Remember the key is to keep offering those open spaces to each other. Everybody ready? Bs stand-by to begin. [*Play music.*]

You may want to encourage by noting some lovely or powerful shapes you have observed. Remind the group to hold still in the shape before one person steps out. Tell them to let the music inform the process. This activity can be revisited in groups of three, and in larger and larger groups. It can involve touch over time and make use of different kinds of music.

Talk to your partner about what you began to feel was going on as you did this. What sorts of ideas or images came up? Was there a moment when you felt that you had created a still image that surprised you or suggested a story or relationship?

Was there anything you would like to share with the whole group?

What kind of skills were involved in this activity? What do those skills tell us about how we work together in drama?

2. Entering the work: Being 14

- **Grouping: Individual**
- **Strategy: Recollecting**
- **Administration: Tambourine**
- **Focus: Remembering when we were 14**

If you are working with teenagers, you might want to ask them to go back to when they were 10 or 11 years old.

Facilitator: Find your own space in the room and find a comfortable position either sitting or standing. Close your eyes. [*Turn lights down.*] Begin to think back to when you were 14. Remember how you felt at that age. What were some of the things that happened? What was a place where you felt safe and had some privacy at that age? As you are thinking, find a position that as your 14-year-old self you would be comfortable in within that space. What would you be thinking about? As your 14-year-old self you are looking back at a moment that was important to you. Let yourself begin to quietly say out loud what's on your mind. I'll just rattle this tambourine so nobody needs to worry about being overheard.

It may be that you will have a participant who for whatever reason does not feel comfortable revisiting that age. We suggest that you invite him or her to remember a time being a little bit younger or older, but to choose a time that was less challenging. It may also be that the cultural contexts of your group are different from your own in terms of maturation. As ever, your role as facilitator is to create a safe space for everyone and a part of this is to make accommodations for participants in the moment.

Come back into yourself at the age you are now. Just turn to your neighbour and talk about what you were thinking. Let's share with the whole group. How difficult was it for you to look back? Is it easy or hard to recall what life was like then? Why do you think 14 is such a significant age?

Those skills and that sensitivity with which you've been working are going to be important as we move forward into the work.

3.a. Engaging in the work

- **Grouping: Groups of five or six**
- **Strategy: Discussion, followed by sculpting**
- **Administration: None**
- **Focus: To come to a collective decision and to represent that decision in an embodied way as a sculpture**

Facilitator: Get into groups of five or six and share with each other your experiences of what it was like to be 14. What did that time in your life mean to you? What do you remember? What issues were important to you then? How have things changed?

I'd like someone in each group to volunteer. [*There is no need to explain what for, but take note of who does volunteer.*] Volunteers, you are going to be the Clay on which the rest of your group is going to create their idea of what it is to be 14. Everyone in the group will contribute their ideas and, Clay, you also can have your say. We all need to be really aware of the ways in which we create this sculpture. Touch, if you use it, should be respectful and whatever positions are chosen need to be ones that the Clay can hold comfortably over a period of time. Remember this is a sculpture and needs to be interesting from all angles. Facial expressions are best mirrored, as nobody wants their face touched. Often, if you talk about the feeling behind the expression, that is more helpful to the Clay. The sculpture will be communicating a number of ideas, so you need to be really clear about your focus and the message you want to put across. You may use one or two props, if they will help your ideas. Any questions? Go ahead.

You have just another minute; you can begin to finish up.

Right everyone, Clays, hold the position you've been given. Artists, step away and look at your sculpture objectively. Remember what you had in mind, look at what you've created, are there any details that need to be adjusted or changed. Be sure to look at your sculpture from 360°.

Relax everyone, just sit down in your groups and talk about that process. Be sure to hear from the Clay.

Anything anybody wants to say to the whole group about that?
Because this is the first time participants are drawing on their own history and working together closely, there may be some concerns expressed and these should be addressed by the group and the facilitator. Again, this all about the drama contract and how we are working together.

Each group's task is now to lead their Clay into the middle of the room and arrange these statues as works of art in a sculpture gallery. Again, you need to think in terms of 360°. These are not six individual sculptures but rather six works of art that are in relationship with each other, because each one reflects the theme of this exhibition, *Being 14*.
They may ask to use a box or chair to create levels for a stronger focus. Whenever participants ask for something that has not been part of the instructions, it is helpful to the facilitator if s/he asks the reason(s) for the request. Participants' answers can be great indicators of their aesthetic development.

Step away from the exhibit and walk around it with the eyes of designers. How aesthetically pleasing is the whole effect? What sorts of changes do you think we need to make to this arrangement? Be ready to make suggestions. [*They do that and adjustments may be made.*]

Sculptures, relax, but Clays, remember your positions and stay where you are. Everyone else, move away from the centre of the space and turn your backs to the display.

Now we're ready to really have a look at what we have made. As gallery-goers, you have been attracted to this exhibition because you too were once 14 and this is an opportunity for you to revisit your past as adults. Clay, the task you are about to undertake is highly demanding because you are going to be required to hold your position as if you could neither see nor hear, yet of course you can. So your responsibility is to behave as if you cannot and remain still so that everyone has the chance to see this exhibition individually and as a whole. Take a moment to remember the meanings that underlie being 14 that you and your group decided upon. Let those feelings infuse your sculpture. Clay, into position now please. And freeze. Gallery visitors, the exhibition is now open. Please enjoy your visit.

As facilitator, you too should be a visitor to the gallery and can make comments or draw attention to something you are noticing. Be sure that the group moves so it observes from all sides.

Stop everyone now. When you feel ready, just say what you see, using sentences beginning with "I see…" or "I feel…" or "I remember…"

Okay, sculptures relax and everyone go back into your original groups. What do your sculptures have to say about their experience of being 14-year-olds? What did you as a group, see and hear in the gallery that you'd like to share? Then, talk together about that whole experience. What sorts of things that were a part of being 14 are still a part of you today?

This could be the end of the workshop in which case you might want to ask participants to share how what they have seen and heard resonates with their own personal experiences of being 14.

Thank you. We've built a wonderful resource now that we can continue to explore (or pick up for next time).

3.b. Engaging in the work

- **Grouping: Individual, then original groups of five or six**
- **Strategy: Timeline, then role playing**
- **Administration: Paper and pencil for each person**
- **Focus: To enrich the back story for the 14 year-old and to identify significant players in his or her life**

Facilitator: Take a piece of paper and a pencil and find your own space in the room. We've been exploring being 14, but we don't just appear full-blown at that age. So what I'm going to ask you to do now is to think back into that life to recall significant events and people that helped to shape who you are. These may be events that happened to you in your own life that you are prepared to share, or they may be events that occurred in the life of the 14-year-old. So these may be actual things that happened or they may be imagined things that happened… that's up to you. We don't need to know which is the real and which is the fictional. On your piece of paper draw a timeline. Mark off 14 spaces, each space to represent a year. On each of those years, mark those events that were important to you before you turned 14. No need to fill in every year, only those that you remember as significant.

Finish that up and when you have done so turn your page over so that I know you are ready to move on.

Now, on the back of your paper, draw the place you like to go to be by yourself (as a 14-year-old). Don't worry about not being an artist, this is just for you!

Write somewhere on your paper a phrase or sentence that you remember hearing quite a lot as you were growing up.

Write somewhere on your paper what you wanted to be when you grew up.

Turn your page over again, look at the events that you've marked as significant and write down beside any of them, the names of a person or persons who are connected in your mind with that event.

Now find a partner, not someone in your group, and share only those things that you wish to share. You can use your paper or not. [*By now, you should sense when they are ready to move on but you can always check by saying, "Are we all ready to move on now?"*]

Fold up your paper and put it in a pocket or a safe place and then return to your groups.

So now we've got a wealth of material to draw on. Fourteen-year-old, you've got your role already. Just move away from your group to hear this next step and listen. There are four or five others with roles to be assigned. Each person in the group is to select from the following roles; a teacher, a parent, a sibling, a best friend, someone who knows the 14-year-old on a professional basis, and someone who knows the 14-year-old personally but is not a close family member, so that everyone in the group has a role. As you are choosing the roles, be aware of the dramatic potential that any of these roles offers. [*There are more possibilities of roles than group members, so as to offer a range of choices.*]
   If you have a board and chalk or chart paper and pen, they are useful places to record lists. Then the choices can be left for everyone to see.

Clay, resume your 14-year-old shape. Make sure there is space around you for your group to form.

Each groups' first task is to create what we call a sociometric circle. That is, each role is to place themselves in a spatial relationship with their 14-year-old. For example, the mother may see herself as close to or as slightly distanced from the 14-year-old. We are not thinking about clichéd positioning here. These are your roles, so you make the choices. Do this one at a time so that you can see the picture coming together. Try to do this without talking and when everyone is in place, then relax and take a moment to re-identify your role for the group.

Right. All groups, take up your positions and freeze. Each role, you now have a chance to reflect on the distance between you and the protagonist, our 14-year-old. Your task is to begin to fill that space with what you know about the relationship between you and the protagonist. Fourteen year-old, you will be noticing where each role is placed and you have the same chance to think about those relationships.

Now everyone, including the 14-year-olds, go quietly back to your circle, taking a pencil and piece of paper as you go. Find a comfortable spot, sit down and write, *in role*, about what was going through your head as you thought about your relationship with that child. Don't talk. This is your own private time.

They should have at least five minutes for this. A useful prompt, when you see a pencil being put down after only a few lines of writing, is to say, "I see some people are taking the time to think before they go on writing." It acts both as an encouragement and also a reminder that thinking is a useful and appropriate activity.

Read through what you have written quietly to yourself and underline what you feel is the most significant sentence or phrase and commit that to memory.

Re-form your sociometric circle and someone volunteer to begin. He or she will say what they have underlined. Then hear around, listening carefully to what every role has to say.

Relax. As a group, your task now is to order those lines in a way that supports your feelings about this 14-year-old. If you want, you may repeat one of the lines. What you choose and where you choose to say it will depend upon how you create the dramatic action that lies underneath this still picture.

Sometimes they ask if lines can be changed or amended. Yes, of course, as long as the original creator agrees and the group agrees and they all have a good reason for it. Often, when explaining the reason, they all see that that is not what they want to do but something else, so these opportunities for questioning and explaining are valuable to creative work.

I'm going to give you a couple of minutes to rehearse.

That seems to be coming along nicely. Now, the next task is, for each line, you may make a movement, either before you say the line, as you are saying the line, or after you say the line. This new suggestion, may necessitate you changing your original positions slightly, but keep the same spatial relationships.

I think we are ready now to see our 14-year-old protagonists in relationship to the worlds in which they live. Which group would like to go first? We'll watch them one after the other without any comment.

It is helpful to establish that group sharing happens where the groups are situated and not by moving into an "up at the front, audience watching" theatre style. The important thing is that everyone should be able to see and hear from where they are and that the facilitator makes sure that this is so for everyone. If a group seems to be rather quiet and difficult to hear, ask them if they would mind doing it again so that we can all hear.

4. Reflecting on the work

Thank you for this work. I invite you to go back into your groups and talk about how your sharing worked for you as a group and about what you saw and heard from the other groups.

Let's share some of those thoughts together in the whole group. Would you like to move into the big circle or would you prefer to stay where you are?

I wonder if you would like to talk about what you have discovered about being 14 that you perhaps had not recognized or realized? And I wonder what implications might those discoveries have for you now at your present age?

It is interesting that although everyone was working on the same thing and in the same way, every group's response was different. I wonder what that tells us about how drama and theatre work?

This has been a pretty challenging journey that we've been on together. We've certainly learned a number of ways to work dramatically and, perhaps, we've found out a little more about ourselves and each other. Thank you.

OR

Option:

We've been through a pretty challenging journey together. Just take another piece of paper and, writing as yourself in the present, what would you now say to your 14-year-old self?

Thank you. I am not sure what you would like to do with that writing but, perhaps, you might like to keep it for future reference?

This session has been focused on building community through the sharing of personal stories in a metaphorical structure of the composite character of a 14-year-old. At the same time, we are adding theatrical skills of role playing and script writing and a more extended performance piece to share and reflect on. The major focus is still on building community, putting the drama contract into practice and learning more about how we work together.

4.5 Questions for Reflection, Suggested Activity and Further Reading

Questions for Reflection

1. What are some of the risks we enter into when we invite participants to draw on their own lived experiences as a source of dramatic material?
2. In the reflection stage of this structure, reflection is focused on the meanings and feelings of the work before discussion of how we made the work. What might be the reasons for organizing reflection in this way?
3. Working in educational settings, there are many established ways of dealing with students' work. In applied drama settings in various communities, these structures are not as clear and therefore need to be addressed. What responsibility does a facilitator have for looking after the materials that are created in a working session? Are participants to be responsible for keeping anything they've written or otherwise created (visual materials, maps, etc.)? Are you as facilitator going to gather and maintain these materials as documentation of the process? What are the implications of not taking care of these materials, particularly when working with at-risk participants?

Suggested Activity

There are two things that need to be planned in terms of documentation. The first is to plan for what supplies are required in order to keep materials generated organized and safe. If materials are not being kept, what is to be done with them? The second area asks what ways are to be employed to document this process (audio, video, photographic, etc.)? Which bits of the process do you see as most pertinent for documentation? Write a one-page plan for how the process will be documented throughout a group's project. This plan is to be shared and negotiated with participants as an extension of the drama contract. The plan will also be affected by the needs of funding agencies or institutions connected to the project.

Further Reading

Boal, A. (2002). *Games for actors and non-actors* (2nd ed.) (A. Jackson, Trans.). New York, NY: Routledge. Boal's key text is recommended as many of the exercises and activities in it are both movement-based and intended for non-specialist participants. We also recommend seeking out excellent movement texts written for educators and adapting those exercises for the ages, skill levels and backgrounds with which you are working.

Griss, S. (1998). *Minds in motion: A kinesthetic approach to teaching elementary curriculum.* Portsmouth, NH: Heinemann. Although this text is written for working with young children, it offers a lot of practical movement exercises that can be adapted for uses with groups of all ages.

Morgan, N. & Saxton, J. (1995/2006). *Asking better questions* (2nd ed.). Markham, ON: Pembroke. This text offers an array of approaches to effective questioning and reflecting in groups.

Human Kinetics: www.humankinetics.com. Human Kinetics publishes a wide array of books and other resources on movement and physical education. There are very few books written that focus on using movement with non-dancers, other than those written for use in schools.

5.1 Using role play

Role is the fundamental act of theatre, in which actors take on characters and play these roles in imaginative complicity with an audience that accepts this fictional reality. In applied drama, participants use role as a means of exploring issues, telling stories, developing themes, and so on. Unlike the theatre, which asks an actor to provide the outer clothing of the inner life (as in voice, make-up, costume, etc.), role finds its life in the attitudes, points of view, values and feelings that are characteristic of the inner life of a person. Role allows us to move from the nonfictional world we live in every day into a fictional world within which we can take on any number of different kinds of people (or animals, aliens or machines) as a way of gaining deeper understanding of whatever it is we have gathered together to investigate. Role play is more about being than it is about doing, and is improvisational rather than scripted. In a play, an actor is bound by the text. In role play, we can try out all kinds of situations with freedom to explore what stories we wish to tell and which aspects of that story catch our attention most.

The work of applied drama is always about the human dynamic; how we live, work and communicate with each other and what each of us brings to these relationships. Drama allows us to see how past history, present contexts and future dreams have powerful effects on the choices we make when speaking to each other in role. Sitting down drama which is the first extended role playing activity in this text allows us to function within a fictional world where the focus of the work is about the quality of the relationship that is created between two or more people in conversation.

> However common the [situation] ultimately the interaction will be idiosyncratically contingent [for] no two interactions will be exactly alike. Thus most role-play practice must allow for this degree of unpredictability without stretching its believability.
>
> – Gavin Bolton & Dorothy Heathcote, 1999, p. 39

5.2 Levels and dynamics of role

In real life we converse quite freely with others, to greater or lesser degrees. However, when participants move into role play, which asks them to step into another person's shoes and speak as if they were that person, they may feel uncomfortable. Self-consciousness when first entering into working in role is to be expected and should be as low risk an experience for participants as possible. Staying in a seated position creates a low-risk first effort at playing a role, as the physicalization of another person is not necessary. When a participant voices an understandable fear, saying "I don't know how to act!", a facilitator must be able to grapple with those fears and to create an understanding that role play is distinct from acting. Taking the emphasis off the watching aspect of performance within a role play, and putting the focus on the doing—that we are all inside the story we are telling—is key.

The work participants have done in the drama structures in *The Circle* and *Being 14* were group processes where the beginnings of role play were supported by others. In *Sitting-Down Drama*, the support of the group is still always available and present, but in a slightly different way. Although participants will be observing each other's work in role, the purpose of the work is not entertainment and a facilitator needs to keep the focus on the engagement with the chosen topic rather than overt criticism of any one person's contribution. Reflection on a role played dialogue, asking the question "What did we learn from this scene?" rather than the more generic and less useful question "How did that go?" or "How did that feel?", helps to lessen the performance pressure on participants. Facilitators may ask participants to repeat a scene, with different participants taking on the selected roles, to explore how a second or even a third version deepens or shifts the understanding, or provides more information.

When entering into role play with inexperienced participants, it is sometimes useful for the facilitator to take on a role as a means of modelling the process and accepting the same risk that is being asked of participants. In drama education this convention is called *teacher-in-role* (Ackroyd, 2004), and for our purposes in this text we are naming *facilitator-in-role*. The main difference between these two terms lies in the context of education, within which students are involved in curriculum in compulsory ways, and community settings, where participants should have more freedom to choose the material they will engage in through drama. An effective facilitator should be prepared to take a role in appropriate ways that do not overwhelm participants, not by "showing" or "demonstrating" how it is done but simply by being a part of the drama that is being co-created on equal terms with the group. The overarching

In teacher in role the teacher is "taking a part in the play" and at the same time monitoring the experiences of the students… releasing the power to the students when they are ready.

– Norah Morgan & Juliana Saxton, 1987, p. 38

intention carried by a facilitator-in-role is to present an attitude within a role that allows the story or situation under examination to continue to unfold itself in productive ways.

The value of facilitator-in-role lies in the fact that it is organic and enables facilitators opportunities *in-role-within-the-drama* to suggest alternative views, ideas and intentions that can move participants away from clichéd thinking and open them up to a broader creative palette.

5.3 About *Sitting-Down Drama*

Sitting-down drama developed in the practice of drama educator Gavin Bolton and is documented briefly in his 1999 book with Dorothy Heathcote, *So you want to use role-play?* (pp. 38–41). Bolton developed this strategy for use in non-classroom settings and offers his memory of how he began to invent this strategy:

> [Sitting-down drama] emerged from my work in a local psychiatric hospital where for about six years I did a weekly session with adult patients under the watchful eye of a woman consultant. I would have about 6–8 patients in the group plus one or two of my MA students (who occasionally took active part). I would take on the role of someone who is really anxious about something. I would first get them to choose the problem and I would start interacting with a selected patient (both of us still sitting down, talking across the little circle) as though the person I was talking to was part of my life; and then shift to standing up in front of a different group member to, say, knock at someone's door; and then (the next step) find myself casually saying to either the same or to another "character" "stand up to talk if you would prefer it"; and reaching the next point of something happening (a minor crisis, perhaps) so that the other people in my life needed to talk to each other for which they would automatically stand up without giving it a thought – leading to moving around and making appropriate signals. I would try to build it so that my problem got worse, reaching the point where they finally, as a group, took on the role of "consultants" interviewing me about my life and giving me advice—they tended to love this!
>
> The most important part was the sequel—the consultant was then able to use the fictitious "drama" as a shared point of reference in her own one-to-one timetabled session a day or two later. (May 6, 2011, personal communication)

Juliana made use of Bolton's sitting-down drama in her Theatre and Drama in Education degree program at the University of Victoria over many years. Her approach was to begin by asking students how they remembered the fairy tale *Snow White*. Students would share their memories in small groups and share their different versions with the whole class. Then, moving into a seated circle, Juliana would narrate the beginning of the story and take on the role of the wicked stepmother. She would turn to the person seated next to her to ask if he or she could help her to acquire some poison. This simple request, delivered differently each time ("I am your Queen and I order you to give me some poison!", "I'm so afraid of rats, what can I do to get rid of them?", "My husband, the King, has asked me if I would order the following items for him.") would continue as different students were approached. Then students would collectively decide on where they wanted to go next in the story and what roles would be needed in the new scenes (see Morgan & Saxton, 1995/2006, pp. 34–44).

The sitting-down drama we offer below illustrates the techniques a facilitator needs to be aware of when using this form. If an idea to be explored has not come from the group, we encourage readers to consider using a catalyst or pre-text (O'Neill, 1995) that is a good fit with their contexts and participants, as a way into the dramatic process. The challenge here is centred around how to improvise within a story structure that all participants fully engage with, thereby beginning to "offload" your authority so that the people role playing become centrally responsible for the content of the story.

5.4 Drama structure: *Sitting-Down Drama* [see Appendix D, p. 213]

1. Preparing for the work

- **Grouping: Whole group in a circle standing**
- **Strategy: Game of one-word circle story**
- **Administration: None**
- **Focus: To encourage focused spontaneity**

Facilitator: Let's stand and make a circle. Be sure you can see everybody, because that's going to be important. We're going to tell a story and we're going to tell it one word at a time. We'll go around the circle clockwise with each person adding a word. The challenge is to keep the story going, to keep it logical, and to keep it interesting. I'll begin and we'll go to my left. Are there any questions? [*Participants might ask about the little words like "and," "the" or "but"; these are important words, especially "but" which can change the direction of the story or add tension or conflict.*] Are we ready? I'll start.

The game proceeds and can go around the circle as many times as the story stays interesting. Stop when the story has run its course. If the group wishes, a second or third story round can begin going counter-clockwise or with a volunteer to begin the story.

Great! This second version is a little bit different. May I have a volunteer?

Your task is to stand in the centre of the circle. You are going to make eye contact and point at someone. That person will begin a new story using a single sentence. For example, "She stood at the window looking down." As soon as the sentence is spoken, you will swing your pointing finger around the circle and point at someone new. That person must immediately give the next sentence of the story. And so on. [*To the group*] What are some of the skills you're going to need to exercise in this version of the game? [*To be ready at any moment, not to plan ahead etc.*]

It is sometimes useful to sum up what has been said, adding any of these points if they haven't been raised. For example, "So we're going to need to be ready, to listen hard, to keep the story open, to keep it logical, and to see what we contribute as a kind of gift to the group to play with. Any questions before we begin?"

OK, volunteer you can begin by pointing.

A volunteer can stay in the centre for one round of this game. If the group wishes to do another round or two of the game, ask for new volunteers. In a large group, you can split the groups into groups of seven or eight with participants facilitating who goes in the middle. For the whole group story, find a place to stop then ask participants to turn to the person next to them and ask where the story might go. They can share some of these ideas in the whole group.

2. Entering the work

- **Grouping: Whole group**
- **Strategy: Selecting a pre-text**
- **Administration: Handout with three catalysts/pre-texts, either copied from below or own choice**
- **Focus: To come to a collective agreement about what the group wants to explore**

Facilitator: Let's move our chairs into a circle so that we can all see and hear each other (as we did in our first workshop on *The Circle*). I'm handing out a sheet that has the beginnings of three stories; we can choose one of them to work with today (see below). Read through these sources and then decide which one interests you the most; in other words, in your view which one has the most dramatic potential?

Now turn to a partner and talk about your reasons for choosing that pre-text. What questions come to your mind in terms of how the fragment stimulates your curiosity; what is it you want to find out based on this small piece of information?

FOR IMMEDIATE SALE

One all-inclusive Honeymoon Package at Blue Moon Resort in Jamaica. Leaving May 28th for two weeks. Paid $5000 but willing to sell for best offer. Call Nick at 555-4321.

MISSING

Police Division 27 is endeavouring to find a missing person, Dylan Kennit Horth. Female. Age: 32 years old. Height: 5' 9" Weight: 140 lbs. Last seen December 16th, 2011 leaving her residence at Matheson Avenue and Fifth Street in the vicinity of Sutton Mall and Highlands Park.

Please contact Detective Ramon at the Missing Person's Bureau at 555-1234.

FOUND

Baby in cardboard box found in mall parking lot. Newborn male. 6 lbs 7 ounces. Anyone with information please call Child Protection Services at 555-9876.

Now let's hear what you've decided on and what are the questions you shared with your partner? [*This sharing allows the facilitator and participants to get a sense of the possibilities and levels of engagement with the catalysts/pre-texts.*]

Let's choose one of these three to explore together. All of these have potential and tomorrow we might choose a different one, but this is today. [*After some discussion the group decides on one of the three pre-texts. This may be done by voting and, if so, we recommend that participants close their eyes when voting by raising their hands. After counting the numbers for each choice, the facilitator tells the group which option has been dropped and another round of voting determines the "winning" option.*]

The participants choose "Missing"

3. Engaging in the work

- **Grouping: Whole group, sitting on chairs in a circle**
- **Strategy: Sitting-down drama**
- **Administration: Whiteboard or chart paper, if available. Chalk, whiteboard, markers; clipboards with paper and pencils.**
- **Focus: To introduce speaking in role in a low risk way**

This structure allows participants to begin working in role, but also allows a facilitator to begin working on the kinds of listening required in effective applied drama practice. Careful listening to how participants are engaging with the story being developed together, without imposing an agenda is an art. Being mindful that the story may get "stuck" or may need some intervention on your part to make it coherent, are all skills that are focused on in this structure.

Active or empathic listening involves understanding the *content* of what is being said, the *intent* of the speaker and the *context* in which the message is given.

Deep listening is respectful, freed from the distractions that fill the listener's mind with judgment, . interpretation, conclusions and assumptions. Deep listening is open, curious and interested.

Facilitator: What do we need to do to begin? What do we need to find out? I wonder if it would it be useful to find out a bit about Dylan? [*They agree.*] We can do this in all sorts of ways. For example, we could see a scene that goes back in time to learn about her early life. Or we could create a scene that looks at her current life, either personal or professional. [*They choose a scene in her current (pre-disappearance) personal life.*]

All right, so we've chosen to see a scene that's going to help us understand a little bit about Dylan. That scene will be set before her disappearance and will be about her personal life. [*This rephrasing allows you to make sure you've got it right and allows participants more time to think about what they've selected.*]

Who is in this scene?

Is Dylan in it or is it about her?

We can do this more than once if we choose. [*They suggest scenes between Dylan and her boyfriend, Dylan and her father or Dylan's two best friends talking about her.*]
It keeps things simpler to stick with two-person scenes at this point. [*After a brief negotiation, they decide on the first suggestion.*]

Okay, let's begin with Dylan and her boyfriend. Now how old was Dylan in the ad?

She's 32 and she's talking to her boyfriend, so I guess we already know something. At 32 you'll have had a life. Where will this meeting take place? [*They decide on a local coffee house.*]

What time of day? If it's the morning, that's one possibility, if it's later in the day, say after five o'clock, that's another. Time is always important when we make these choices.

Right, so this scene takes place at Beans at six in the evening between Dylan and her boyfriend. Does he need a name? [*They offer Tom.*] Okay, between Dylan and Tom.

Because we're just starting why don't I take a role here? Who would you like me to play? [*They choose Dylan. Facilitator turns to person on her right or left and asks*] Would it be alright for you to play Tom for this first scene? [*This person agrees.*]

It is not necessary to have a gender match but comfort at this stage is important.

Thank you. [*To the group*] Who would you like to have speak first, Tom or Dylan? [*They choose Tom. Facilitator asks Tom*] Do you know how you want to start or would you like a first line [*He asks for a first line*]. [*To group*] What does Tom say to start the scene? [*Someone offers, "Do you want sugar?"*] Are you all okay with that?

Right, so we know what we're going to see, we know where it is and what time it takes place. And what we're going to learn from this scene is a little bit about who Dylan is. Are we ready? Tom?

Tom: Do you need sugar?
Dylan: Tom, you should know that by now. You know I never take sugar.
Tom: Sorry, it's been a long day.
Dylan: Problems?
Tom: I'm just fed up with my boss. So controlling. It's grinding me down.
Dylan: Well I don't know why you don't leave.
Tom: That's easy for you to say.
Dylan: So? Just because I know how to save money.
Tom: Dylan, you've had three jobs since we first met. You can't go on like that forever.
Dylan: But Tom, who has the money?
Tom: You may have money for day to day, but nothing for the long term. It's not practical.
Dylan: I continue to be amazed by how little you know about me.
Tom: Well it's difficult to know you when you don't tell me a lot.

Facilitator: Let's stop there. What have we learned so far? [*They offer their thoughts, suggesting that the couple have tensions in their relationship and that Dylan seems to be more of a free spirit than Tom because he's stuck in a job he doesn't like and she moves frequently from job to job.*]

Ask participants to support their thinking with evidence from the scene. Note that the facilitator's talk was less than the participant's in the scene above. Try to be as brief as possible, keeping the focus on the participants' work rather than your own.

I thought Tom did a terrific job! Just before we go on, let's talk about the role play so far. What did you notice about it? [*Somebody comments, "There seemed to be a lot of pauses."*

Facilitator could respond, "Yes, that seems to be something true to life, that we do pause in our conversations. And in this kind of drama, if we don't know what to say we can always stop and ask the group for an idea of what to say next."]

Facilitator: Here are some options we might choose to go next. We can stay with our choice to find out more about Dylan's personal life, so we could continue to explore her relationship with Tom. But perhaps this time, we could see Dylan talking to someone else about Tom to find out more about how she feels about their relationship. Or, we could take a look at Dylan in a workplace scene, to find out more about how she deals with her professional life. We had decided to look at her personal life, but as many of us know, it is hard to separate the personal from the professional. Or perhaps somebody has another idea in mind? [*They discuss the options and decide to look at her professional life.*] Good. So shall we decide what her profession is now or should we choose a setting and find out more from within the scene? [*They choose to find out from inside the scene.*] All right. Where does the scene take place? [*In a hallway.*] Who is in the scene? [*Dylan and someone in authority, some kind of boss.*]

   You may want to ask the group if they'd like you to play a role in this next scene as well or if they feel comfortable taking the roles on themselves. If the latter…

What time of day is it? [*It's early morning.*] Good, now who would like to take on the role of Dylan this time? Thank you, and who would like to try the person in authority? Thank you. And what are we going to look for in this scene? [*We want to find out more about Dylan and how she behaves in her professional life.*] Do you need a first line? [*Boss: "No, I think I've got one."*] So are we ready to go?

Boss: You're looking very nice today. New shirt?
Dylan: No, not new. But I guess you've made me see that I've buttoned it wrong. Sorry, I was running late this morning.
Boss: Actually, it wasn't the buttons so much as I would prefer it if you wore the clothing that we are desperately trying to move out of the shop. You've got a good body, you can show it off nicely in our clothes.
Dylan: I understand your needs, of course.
Boss: Good girl.
Dylan: But I do have to say that I have a couple of issues I'd like to discuss with you. Is this a good time?
Boss: No, drink after work?
Dylan: No thank you. And that is one of the things I want to say. You keep making these kinds of comments to me that I find quite unprofessional.
Boss: Well, Miss Horth, let's see how the day goes then. Good morning.
Dylan: If you don't agree to schedule a meeting…

Facilitator: *(interrupting)* Thank you, we'll stop right there.

You stop a scene when you feel there is some dramatic potential. After about four or five exchanges is a good place to stop as there is usually enough information given (hopefully something a bit intriguing). If the scene hasn't gone anywhere, you can let it go on a bit longer but no more than a minute or two, or you can stop the scene and have another go at it with different role players. To let the scene go on and on puts undue pressure on the role players to 'write' the story. With these shorter scenes, everybody has a chance to contribute to the story that the pre-text has offered and participants aren't left wondering what to say.

What was going on there? Lots of things! So what do we know now? [*She works in a clothing store. She is not intimidated by authority.*] Yes, that makes sense in relation to the first scene, doesn't it? [*She may be financially frugal but seems to have a problem managing her time—the misbuttoning.*] What else? [*She's attractive.*] Where do we see that? [*In Boss's comments about her body.*] Well, that could be one person's point of view.

Let's go back to our source again. And as we read it, let's consider what scene we need to see now to understand this ad more clearly. [*They offer suggestions. A scene with the police detective who posted the ad and Dylan's parents.*] Are there any other suggestions? [*No, the group likes this idea.*] Okay, just before we go into this scene [*Turning to participant who made the suggestion*], what do you think we might be able to discover in this scene? [*Participant: "I'd like to find out what the police know about her disappearance and also what her parents might know or want to know or assume."*] Just take a moment to talk to the person next to you about what else might come out of this scene?

These questions offer possibilities to the role players who will take on this scene.

Right, so this scene has three people in it. Do I have an offer to play a parent? The other parent? You decide between you the roles of these parents. And while you two are doing that, is there somebody who'd like to be the detective? Thank you. All right, so we've got a detective and who's the mother? And the father?

In larger scenes, it is helpful to be sure that everyone understands who is playing which role.

Who shall we have speak first? [*The group chooses the detective.*] I don't know that the time is so important in this scene, but we do need to know if it is in the parents' home, in the police station or somewhere else? [*They decide on Dylan's apartment.*]

Detective, you're going to speak first, do you need a first line? [*He declines.*] So we know what we want to find out in this scene and we know who is saying the first line. But let me just suggest, this scene takes place three weeks after Dylan's disappearance, so we've had Christmas and New Year's and it's the first week of January. Everybody okay with that? All right, whenever you're ready.

This time frame, moving the story on, may remind participants of possible things to talk about.

Detective (to Facilitator): What was her last name again?
Facilitator: Horth.
Detective: Mr. Horth, Mrs. Horth, thank you for agreeing to meet with me here.
Father: This isn't an easy place for us to be.
Detective: I understand, Mr. Horth, and I appreciate it.
Father: What's the purpose of this meeting?
Detective: I wanted to give you a chance to just have a look around and see if this is what you expected to see.
Mother: Oh Detective, I don't know if I can. You wouldn't let us in before. Why now?
Father: This is upsetting to both me and my wife, so can we please make it as quick as possible?
Detective: Of course, sir. Why don't you have a look through the apartment on your own?
Father: Where's her computer? It's always sitting on this table in the corner.
Detective: Oh! Well, we had to take it for forensics, but that is where we found it.
Father: Good. I was worried you didn't have it.
Mother: Jim, let's get this over with.
Father: Yes, dear, I know but we have to do this.
Mother: Obviously, but I can't go into her bedroom on my own.
Father: You were the last one to see her in the apartment, when you went for lunch the week before. Do you see anything different?
Mother: You know I don't see every little detail like you do, Jim.
Father: That's okay, just try to remember.
Mother: I can't remember. You're always pushing me, pushing me. If it isn't this, it's something else.
Detective: Mrs Horth, would you like to come into the kitchen with me and we'll get you a glass of water?
Father: That's a good idea. I'm going to check this bookshelf. It feels like there's something missing here, like there's a gap, but I can't remember what was here.

Facilitator: Let's stop there.

Participant (out of Father role): Oh, I was just going to say that I thought her yearbooks were missing.

Facilitator: I stopped you too soon! That's useful information, let's keep it. Thank you. That really sparks my curiosity. I wonder what was written about her in her graduating yearbook?

Would you try something with me? Just turn your chairs so they are all facing out. Think about what was written under Dylan's picture in her graduating yearbook? And you have a choice. You can write your own entry as Dylan, or you can write an entry for Dylan by somebody who knows her. Those yearbook entries are usually pretty brief, no more than 45–70 words. Now we know quite a lot about Dylan. What would she want to say about herself in this important yearbook. What would somebody else want to say about Dylan? As you are thinking about this, just go and get yourself a clipboard and come back to your chair and write that entry. [*They write for four to five minutes.*]
Sometimes you will see someone put down their pencil. It is helpful to say, "I see that some people have stopped writing to think really hard about this." It suggests that while you might think you are finished, you may find something else to say!

Put your hand up if you need more time. Good, everybody's ready. Put your pencils down and read through what you've written. Underline the phrase or sentence that for you captures something important about Dylan.

We're going to increase our understanding of Dylan by hearing the words that you have chosen. You'll need to share your voices because we're facing out and we can't see each other so our focus is on hearing these words. Put your hand up if you think you've got a beginning and then pass to the person on your right, and so on around the circle. We'll finish with the first speaker repeating his or her line.

Thank you. Let's turn our chairs in and talk about that experience with the person next to you. Who'd like to share something they heard that added to their understanding?

4.a. Reflecting on the work

- **Grouping: Whole group**
- **Strategy: Corridor of Voices, also called Conscience Alley**
- **Administration: None**
- **Focus: Reflecting from inside the drama**

Facilitator: That's very difficult and sensitive work. Well done. But we're not finished yet. We have one more thing to do. Is there somebody who will volunteer to be Dylan… you don't have to speak. Thank you.

Let's move our chairs so they make two lines facing each other. Stop there. In a moment, Dylan is going to walk slowly along this corridor we've created as if she were walking out of her apartment building on the day she disappeared.

We have met six people in this story: Dylan, Tom, her boss, her parents and Detective Ramon. Decide in your own mind which person you choose to be to speak to Dylan as she leaves her apartment on the day she disappeared. Will you give her advice? Will you remind her of something she needs to remember? Will you tell her how you feel? Or will you ask her a question? Just take a moment to think quietly of what you are going to say.

Are we ready? Dylan, is there anything you'd like to carry with you that will help you believe in your role? [*Participant may choose to pick up a book or a backpack or something else.*]

Remember to walk slowly so that you hear each voice from each side of the corridor. There's no need to rush. And we can always do it again. Shall we stand to make a corridor or shall we sit? [*They decide to stand.*]

Everybody stand please to make the corridor. Dylan, come and stand here at the head of the corridor. Whenever you're ready.

    If for some reason, the Corridor of Voices isn't going well, it's fine to have the group stop and start again. In other words, they can always rehearse! If they get too nervous, you may stop the process and advise the group to remember that what they have to say to Dylan will have an impact on whatever may happen next. When Dylan has reached the end of the corridor and everyone has had their say, leave a pause, then say…

Thank you. Let's just sit down and share some of what we heard. It may be something you said yourself or something you heard someone else say that you feel may have been significant for Dylan to hear. [*They share.*]

Dylan, can you share a little of what was going on in your mind as you walked out of the building? What stays with you as you walk away?

I wonder what this story can tell us about our own lives or the lives of those whom we know?
    Participants can often become so absorbed in the fiction they have created, they forget to consider how it relates to their own lives. Generally, they will do this relating without a prompt, in which case this last prompt from the facilitator will be unnecessary.

4.b. Reflecting on the work

- **Grouping: Whole group**
- **Strategy: Discussion**
- **Administration: None**
- **Focus: Reflecting from outside the drama**

Facilitator: We've just done our first bit of role play where we were improvising spontaneously as we made a story. Let's talk a little bit about that process and what you have discovered about it.

Note that this discussion of "how" things worked comes *after* the reflections on the meanings and significances of the possible world they were working in. It is always better to reflect on the meanings before reflecting on the artistry that created the meanings.

You may respond to participants' comments and questions to highlight key points as in; how the group was able to both watch and listen, how well the role play worked overall, what has been learned about being in role, what happened if the group stalled and had to go at the story from another angle or direction, how the story can move backwards and forward in time, how the story belongs to everyone, how the process is more about what's going on inside the people than the plot.

5.5 Questions for Reflection, Suggested Activity and Further Reading

Questions for Reflection

1. This structure asks you as a facilitator to work without a net, although within a supported structure. How did the process work for you in terms of your comfort levels and your abilities to put yourself at-risk by taking on a role and by not knowing what was going to happen next?
2. What did you learn about the participants from this structure in terms of who leads, who follows, who listens, who disrupts, who was challenged, and so on?
3. What skills do you see the group having and what skills need to be nurtured in order to move forward with role play? Would the group benefit from another session of sitting-down drama before going on to the next structure?

Suggested Activity

Prepare your own handout of three catalysts for a sitting-down drama that uses a different approach from the classified ads we provide in this chapter. We suggest that images (photos, artworks or cartoons) make very effective catalysts as do news stories. You could encourage your participants to be on the lookout for such resources.

Further Reading

Bolton, G. & Heathcote, D. (1999). *So you want to use role-play? A new approach in how to plan.* Stoke-on-Trent, UK: Trentham. Take a look at Chapter 2 of this book, "Role-work for training adults: Examples of a range of genres (2)," Section D (pp. 36–41). This section describes how to use role play in training with inexperienced players. It offers some alternative techniques to the ones we give in this chapter.

Morgan, N. & Saxton, J. (1987). *Teaching drama: A mind of many wonders.* London: Hutchinson. See pages 203–209 and 222–224 for a description and student reflection of a sitting-down drama using a gift-giving exercise as the catalyst.

Simons, J. (2000). Walking in another person's shoes: Storytelling and roleplay. In H. Nicholson (Ed.), *Teaching drama 11–18* (pp. 16–25). London: Continuum. Simons uses a powerful catalyst in this role play based on a news story in Australia of a newborn baby abandoned on a train. This chapter is available on Google Books.

CHAPTER SIX
EMBODYING THOUGHT AND FEELING

6.1 Communicating with our bodies

All dramatic process is a form of embodied experience. This chapter focuses on accessing the thoughts and feelings and experiences that are held in and by our bodies—often without our being conscious of them. For example, we can walk into a room and be transported by a smell in the air into an emotional response, memory or state

> The body of the actor, like the body of the text, stumbles into ambiguity, insinuating more than words can say with gesture, movement, intonation.
>
> – Madeleine Grumet, 1998, p. 148

of mind. When we are taken by surprise and react with instinctual response, like a flinch or a shudder, this is another way our body reminds us of its power to inform (or even control) our actions. Often the way in which we hold our bodies can be the result of cultural or societal norms, and being effective in dramatic process requires an awareness

> Our arms reach out, our knees collapse, our heads nod, our chests cave in, our backs arch, we jump, we shrug, we clench our fists, we pick each other up and push each other away. This is language as much as it is action. This is what the body has to say about need, defeat, courage, despair, desire, joy, ambivalence, frustration, love. These kinetic images resonate meaningfully in the mind because we have all, dancers and viewers alike, felt these things so purely in the body—we have been moved.
>
> – Crystal Pite, 2009, p. 128

of these norms, so as not to impede our abilities to interpret and communicate. Bodies are signs, and we naturally read what we call "body language" all the time. When we are talking, we are physicalizing thoughts and feelings. But not only does expression and gesture help to fill out the words we are saying, they often express thoughts and feelings of which we may not even be aware. Doing physical work in drama is not so much about changing body language but rather is about extending the vocabulary, the range. *Proprioception* or the body's sense of itself in space is one of our most important ways of knowing and has been described as our "sixth sense" (Sherrington, 1906/1966 McCloskey & Gandevi, 1993). This sense is not just about writing ourselves in space but it is also about reading ourselves in space—in other words, knowing not only how we affect and can affect others but also how our actions affect our selves. As we expand our repertoire of physical experiences, our neural networks begin their life-long activity of cross referencing, building a com-

> Nonverbal communications is… central to the establishment, maintenance and dissolution of relationships.
>
> – Howard Giles & Beth LePoire, 2006, p. xvi

plex and dimensional series of systems in which all information is available at any time and from any point (Hannaford, 1995/2005). Seeing how things like status and power relations can shift body language is an important tool as we move forward in exploring drama. The effective use of gesture, nonverbal cues, posture, stance, and so on, can help to illustrate the stories we wish to create and tell together. We can also begin to explore how nonverbal communication in itself can be another way of doing drama: the focus of this chapter.

6.2 Balancing the mind-body relationship

Researchers tell us that somewhere between 65% and 90% of communication is non-verbal (Verbal and nonverbal communication", nd., p. 19). Communication studies tells us that nonverbal communication can take on many forms, including kinesics (body movements), proxemics (personal space) and haptics (touch), all of which are useful no-tions to bring into a dramatic process. *Kinesics* has to do with posture, gesture and facial expressions, all of which provide nonverbal cues to reading another person's emotional state and judging whether or not the nonverbal message is in harmony with what is being said (see Birdwhistell, 1970). Facial expression, particularly in how eyes are used, involves awareness of cultural difference. Some cultures are more wary of direct eye contact, for example, and we should not always read a lowering of eyes as sub-missive but rather as a mark of respect, as it is held to be in many aboriginal cultures. How often

> The important part of bodily-kinesthetic intelligence is not the ability to rise to difficult movement but to know in a thorough way what you are doing with your body.
>
> – Donald Blumenfeld-Jones, 2004, p. 122

and in what ways people smile in various social contexts can also be misread across cul-tures. Gestures used to be thought of as distinct from speech but are now "best thought of as a single system, larger than either language or gesture" (McNeill, 2005, n.p.). Some gestures are considered almost universal, as in a shrug and upturned hands to indicate "I don't know"; other gestures can take on almost opposite meanings depending on what part of the world you are in. For example, a circle made with thumb and forefinger is read as "Okay!" in North America, as "Worthless" in France and as a rude insult in Italy.

The body itself writes in small print and in capital letters; in italics, in bold, in short sentences and long paragraphs, with a fine flowing hand or a broad, blunt nib.

– Norah Morgan & Juliana Saxton, 2000, p. 12

Like language, gestures have enormous power, to heal or to hurt, to clarify or confuse.

Proxemics involves how space is used in personal and social settings between humans for communication purposes (Hall, 1969). Hall regards how we observe the ways in which space is used as a "specialized elaboration of culture" (p. 1). There is a range of distances in proxemics from intimate to personal to social to public (notice the resemblance here to King's continuum from private to public, see Chapter 1), in which the amount of distance between people increases from zero to a number of metres. Much can be read dramatically by noting how much distance lies between players. For example, we are working with proxemics in *Being 14* (Chapter 4) when the group is asked to arrange itself in relation to the character of the 14-year-old.

Another communication term, *haptics*, focuses more specifically on how the sensory perception of touch affects human interaction (Grunwald, 2008); again, cultural differences are important here, in the varying amount of physical connection that is considered appropriate. You will notice that in the first section of this book, how little touch is required of participants and is often given as a constraint within an activity. It takes a significant amount of trust for unskilled drama participants to begin physically touching each other, and a skilled and effective facilitator will be aware of how, where and when touch can be used, dependent upon the group's sense of comfort with each other. It is also useful to draw participants' attention to the use of gesture and other nonverbal expressions, their multiple meanings and importance to the ways in which we communicate.

6.3 Exploring movement through music

All cultures both make and listen to music and, as in life, music is an important element of dramatic process. Music demands a physical response, most clearly in dance, that makes it a powerful force in culture. Rhythm, we know, is one of the very first ways evolving human beings communicated with each other (Patel, 2006).

We can learn a lot about each other in the sharing of music, and warming-up to music brought in by participants can be an effective way to build community and ensemble. Certainly, with a group of elderly participants, music can be a terrific resource for encouraging the sharing of memories (Schweitzer, 2006). The beneficial effects of music on health have a growing research record in which the release of brain chemicals af-

Music is an important resource for world making, for the construction, reinforcement, and/or reconstruction of realities and identities—not only musical but the more broadly social and cultural identities.

– Wayne Bowman & Kimberly Powell, 2007, p. 1094

fects physical and mental responses in positive ways (Levitin, 2008, pp. 97–103).

As part of a dramatic process, music can operate as a soundtrack to movement-based storytelling as we will explore below. That soundtrack can be created by the participants themselves using their own bodies and with found objects or percussion instruments, or it can be recorded music.

> Music-dance is… a cross-modal experience of movement, synchrony, sound, and perceptual organization… because music and dance were virtually inseparable across evolutionary time scales.
>
> – Daniel Levitin, 2008, p. 102

For young people and youth, creating a movement sequence (that does not mimic the official MTV version) offers the opportunity to create an original interpretation of a piece of group-selected music; an age-appropriate and effective activity. Lip-syncing should not be part of this activity; rather the challenge is to interpret the chosen song in a new and fresh way through movement-based storytelling. Although this suggested activity may use music with lyrics, for the most part we recommend instrumental music; lyrics tend to impose a story whereas instrumental music offers more openings for collective interpretations. Music from many world traditions is also a significant means of offering participants fresh and unmediated sound experiences. Western classical music and jazz offer much but they can be familiar for many; music from aboriginal cultures and from Asia Africa, Central and South America, etc. are all ideal to have on-hand for participants' use, always keeping in mind the reasons why you choose to work with music.

6.4 Drama structure: *Interpreting Music as Dramatic Text*

1. Preparing for the work

- **Grouping: Whole group**
- **Strategy: Moving to music**
- **Administration: Music player and sound system, room as dark as possible, appropriate high energy instrumental music**
- **Focus: Getting out of the head and into the body**

Facilitator: I'm dimming the lights. Find yourself a comfortable space. You can be sitting or standing. I'm going to put on some music and at some point it's going to enter your body someplace, it could be your hand or your foot, I don't know. Just let your body respond until all of your body is moving, just in your own space. Use the music to explore ways in which your body can move, think about stretching, bending and lifting until you feel your whole body is being used as it responds to the music. As you're moving, notice your body's limitations and don't overextend. The lights are low so this isn't about watching anyone, but finding yourself in the music and the music in you.

Although you are not actually observing anyone, it may be helpful if participants hear you encouraging them with comments such as "Keep exploring, try new things, see how far your body can take you, try not to fall into a pattern," as you, too, move with the music. This activity can be used regularly as a warm-up with lots of different kinds of music including music brought in by participants (instrumental only). As they become more comfortable over time, and with gradually increasing light, they can be encouraged to move out of their space and through the room, at first without any interaction, which may be added later.

[*After three to five minutes*] Relax. Take a moment to think about what has just happened for you and just talk to the person next to you about that. [*After a few moments of sharing*] Anyone got anything they'd like to say?

Participants may offer such things as feeling as if they were in an environment of some kind, or feeling an emotional connection, or that a story was developing for them as they moved.

Great! A lot of things you've shared are going to be very much part of the work we're doing today.

2.a. Entering the work

- **Grouping: In pairs**
- **Strategy: Hypnotic Hand (also called "Colombian Hypnosis" in Boal, 2002, p. 51)**
- **Administration: None (or with music)**
- **Focus: To move with a partner; to experience both leading and following**

Facilitator: Find a partner, perhaps the person you've been talking to and stand together facing each other in your own space. Choose who will be A and who will be B. A, choose either your right or left hand and hold it up, palm facing your partner. B, you are now somehow magically hypnotized by your partner's hand and will follow it, about six inches apart, wherever it takes you. All right, A you are responsible for taking your partner on a journey, so keep them safe yet make it interesting for them, for they are in your power. Don't go too fast or they won't be able to keep up with your hand. Remember that your hand can move around your body, not just in front. Let's have a try. Make the connection with your partner. Ready? Off you go.

[*After about a minute*] Just stop everyone and talk to your partner about that.

Reverse now, so B is leading A. Make the connection, and off you go.

Freeze. Have another talk with each other about how that went. Let's share some of our thoughts and ideas.

Some suggested reflective questions: What was it like to shift roles? How did you respond to leading or following in this activity? What were the challenges of leading or following? What do your responses tell you about yourself as a leader or a follower?

Option:

- **Grouping: In threes**

Let's try a variation in groups of three. Choose an A, a B and a C. A, this time you are hypnotizing your partners with both hands. Think about what you need to be aware of as you take your partners on a journey. Are we ready? Connect with your hands, and off you go.

This option also gives B and C a chance to lead. Then, reflective questions, after they've had a chance to talk with each other, could be about how this version differs from pairs. You may want to cite Spiderman's famous tagline, "With great power comes great responsibility."

2.b. Entering the work

- **Grouping: In pairs**
- **Strategy: Mirrors**
- **Administration: Music (*Trois Gymnopedies* by Satie)**
- **Focus: To follow your partner as if in a mirror**

Facilitator: Find a partner and sit facing your partner in your own space (on an armless chair or on the floor, whatever works best for participants). Choose an A and a B. Connect with your partner by looking them in the eye and raising your hands together so that there is about 10 to 12 centimetres between your palms. When the music starts, person A will begin moving his or her hands and person B will follow those movements as if A is looking into a mirror and B is the mirror image. Any questions? Right, let's begin.

As participants try this exercise, move about the space and offer side-coaching comments such as, "Move a bit more slowly so your partner can follow you at exactly the same time."

[*After one or two minutes*] Stop. Talk to your partner about that. Switch so that B is now the leader and A is the mirror image. This time, as you are mirroring, focus on moving at exactly the same time. If you feel my hand on your shoulder I'm identifying you as the leader which means you're moving too quickly and you need to adjust your pace so that you can bring your partner along with you.

The purpose of moving around as partners are working is to identify leaders, saying "Try and adjust your pace without stopping." You can do another round of A and B leading adding the instruction to begin moving the upper body and head as well as the arms and hands, still sitting. The focus is on the flow of the music that helps to create a sense of flow between partners.

[*After one or two minutes*] Stop. Talk to your partner about that.

It might be useful to share some suggestions, for example, where do you focus?

Generally, the most effective focus is eye contact with a soft focus so that the peripheral vision is engaged. It may be that some pairs will mention that there were times when they were not sure who was leading.

Option:

Focus: To move together so that the leadership moves back and forth, and potentially dissolves

Facilitator: Choose one of you to begin. The task now is to shift the leadership back and forth between you without stopping or starting or signalling of any kind.

[*After one or two minutes*] Stop. Talk to your partner about that. What was happening there? This is the true focus of this activity, when participants discover that it is what happens between them rather than who does what that is most important. It is what lies at the heart of ensemble, which is to have the sense that "I am making it happen, it is happening to me" or what actors call "being in the moment."

Option:

- **Strategy: Mirror extension: mirroring with the whole body and moving through space**
- **Focus: To work together without words**

Facilitator: You've been working really hard with your partner, so let's carry that experience into working with a new partner. If you'd like, choose someone to begin. Take a minute or two to work together.

[*After one or two minutes*] Stop. Talk to your partner about that. What adjustments did you have to make working with a new partner?

This again is about working in ensemble, and the continuous process of making adjustments.

Right. Now let's put the music on again and after you have found the flow of sharing the movement in the mirror, at some point you will move to stand. Explore the new possibilities as you are standing together. Then, again in your own time, you can begin to move together through the space, taking each other on a shared journey.

This is a good point to change the music to some other slower paced instrumental music, perhaps more generously orchestrated (see end of chapter for suggestions).

[*After three or four minutes*] Stop. Talk to your partner about that.

Is there anything anyone would like to say to the whole group?

Option:

- **Strategy: Mirroring as a whole group**
- **Focus: To work together in a whole group as one unit**

Facilitator: This may or may not work, but let's give it a try shall we? Standing with your partner, you should be able to catch at least one other pair in your peripheral vision. This time, with the music, begin mirroring with each other and at some point become aware of how your mirror is beginning to match another pair's mirror. The task is that we will all end up mirroring as a whole group together. Okay? Any questions? Take your time and remember, you can't force this; it's about all of us being in the same moment together.

Watch this very closely. At a moment when most or all of the group seems to be moving in harmony, call "Freeze."

Everyone, don't move, take a look around and see how we've done. Relax, move into a group with one or two other pairs and talk about how that went for you.

This option is one you can come back to, as you can with many activities in this handbook, in order to continue discovering and experiencing new or different ways of working. Mirrors can be done in groups of three, in a whole group circle, in lines, all of which are valuable extensions. Invite participants to offer their own ideas for variations, these are always worth trying because it gives the ensemble opportunities to see themselves as creative contributors. Remember your key role is to create a space where there is always a sense of freedom to fail; that there is always something of value to learn even from an exercise that didn't go "perfectly" well.

3. Engaging in the work

- **Grouping: Small groups of five or six**
- **Strategy: Creating a movement sequence to a selected piece of music**
- **Administration: Music player, appropriate instrumental music. Paper for each person and at least a dozen colored markers for each group. Sheets of chart paper, one per group.**
- **Focus: To create together as a group in response to a piece of music**

Facilitator: First, collect a piece of paper and something to write with. Then go and find yourself a group of five or six people and sit down together to make yourself comfortable. The work today is about how we can as a group of people who are all very different come together to make something in response to a piece of music. I have arbitrarily chosen a piece of music, which I realize may not be everybody's cup of tea. Of course, those differences in response may become part of the texture of your work.

   This piece of music needs to be more dramatic, short (no more than two minutes long) and have a range of possible interpretations within it. "Thus Spake Zarathustra" by Richard Strauss offers lots of possibilities for playing with many dramatic elements. It is highly dramatic, invites a sense of ritual, and is very "safe" in that it can go in multiple directions (including comic or serious). See end of chapter for other suggestions.

Turn away or close your eyes and just listen to the music.

As you listen to the music again, on your paper, draw whatever images or write whatever words come to mind.

Good. Listen one more time and add anything else that comes to mind.

Come back together into your group and take a few moments to share your ideas.

What of all these various ideas can connect, can come together? I'm going to give each group a large sheet of chart paper and you can use it to begin to pull together the ideas and images that you see connecting to each other. As you bring these ideas together, new ones may emerge. Good ideas breed other ones.

As groups are working, you can side-coach with a focus on encouraging the process of creating something new that comes out of shared responses. The interpretations may be narrative or abstract, or a combination of both. Groups may quickly decide on an agreed approach, other groups may struggle more to synthesize many ideas. Highlight that these experiences are all part of dramatic process, which will be distinct for each group. If groups request it, you can replay the piece of music to help them along.

[*After five or six minutes*] Terrific! I am seeing wonderful interpretations of the music on your chart papers. Now comes the next step. I'd like you to begin working together on how you as a group can translate your work so far into a sequence of movements. Everyone must be involved in this sequence, and it needs to have a clear beginning, middle and end. I suggest you begin and end with a freeze. You can make use of whatever is available in the space that might help you, and consider how using various levels (high, medium and low) can add to the visual interest in your sequence. No one is "directing" this activity; rather, you are all working together to decide how to build the sequence. Any questions?

Groups may need to be encouraged to include participants who may have difficulty moving or who are confined to chairs. They will soon all discover the creative advantages to working this way.

Right. I'm going to give you just two minutes to come up with your opening freeze. Let's begin.

This pushes groups to get on their feet and into their bodies, rather than stuck sitting and talking for too long.

[*After two minutes*] Everybody get into position, 5, 4, 3, 2, 1… Freeze. Good, this is your starting point, now how are you going to get to the middle and end? I'm going to replay the music a number of times, quite quietly at first, to keep reminding you of it. When we're closer to sharing our work, we can have a "technical rehearsal," which is a final practice with the music at full volume.

What will be apparent in this work is the different pace set by each group. Your role as facilitator is to monitor each group's progress as you circulate amongst them. Keep encouraging groups that may feel as if they are lagging, and remind them that it is a natural process for some groups, that they move slowly at first and can move faster later on. One of the main concerns is to get groups on their feet and working ideas out physically; don't let groups sit and talk for long. With a group that's stuck, ask them to show you what they've got, and offer suggestions. Even if they say they've got nothing, ask them to show you one idea and try to build from that. If a group has moved quickly and is "done," you can invite them to add some live sound or a bit of spoken text from their brainstorming.

[*After eight or nine minutes*] Stop. Is everybody ready? Good. Let's have our technical rehearsal. Everybody get into your starting position. When the music begins, go through your sequence. Really focus on your timing and concentration and also on making your movements as large and as expressive as possible, so they can be more easily "read" and understood when we share our work.

Good. Are we ready to share our work? Shall we see each of these one after the other, to get an overall view, or would you prefer to stop and reflect on each interpretation?
Some reflective questions:

- What did you see in this group's interpretation of the music?
- How did they use movement to suggest a story, or a theme or a feeling?
- What qualities of movement were present (strong, soft, bold, subtle, expressive, mechanical, etc.)?
- What surprised you or confused you in this piece?

Just before we go on, let's talk about the intentions of the presenting group. [*Discussing this after the above, allows for alternate interpretations to be shared before hearing the original intentions of the presenting group.*]

[*After sharing process*] Thank you all for your work. Let's finish by taking a few minutes to talk together about this process.
Some suggested prompts:

- How did the preparatory work we did connect with the movement piece you've just created?
- How did other groups' interpretations resonate (or not) with your own?
- What did you learn about working with each other as a group that would be helpful in future work?
- How has this work expanded your understanding of dramatic process, its rewards and challenges?
- This work has been mostly nonverbal; what have we learned about the power of movement to communicate?

6.5 Questions for Reflection, Further Reading and Suggested Music

Questions for Reflection

1. When people are working through movement, what did you notice and learn about each individual as he or she went through the work?
2. Often participant groups tend to be very reluctant to do movement; it puts them outside their comfort zone. If this is true of the group you work with, what sorts of ideas do you have to make them more comfortable in an art form that demands whole body engagement?
3. Again, often groups may have special needs or people with disabilities; how can you adapt tasks to be inclusive and not make assumptions about peoples' capabilities?

Further Reading

Arnold, R. (2005). *Empathic intelligence: Teaching, learning, relating*. Sydney, NSW: USNW Press. This book is about how teachers and students can become more closely interrelated through the engagement of empathy, a key quality of all drama and theatre.

Bresler, L. (2004). *Knowing bodies, moving minds: Towards embodied teaching and learning*. Boston, MA: Kluwer Academic Publishers. This rich collection looks at research on the body as a site for learning in a variety of educational settings. It offers strong argument for embodied teaching as an important way to get minds thinking more deeply.

Griss, S. (1998). *Minds in motion: A kinesthetic approach to teaching elementary curriculum*. Portsmouth, NH: Heinemann. Griss's practical book offers many creative movement strategies for working with young people that could be effectively adapted for people of all ages.

Hannaford, C. (1995/2005). *Smart moves: Why learning is not all in your head* (2nd ed.). Salt Lake City, UT: Great River Books. A very accessible read on the relationship of thought, feeling and the body to movement, includes a number of suggestions for participants.

King, N. (1975). *Giving form to feeling*. New York: Drama Book Specialists. Unfortunately, this book is out of print but may be available second-hand or through your library. We highly recommend this text as it is full of ideas from beginner to advanced movement projects.

Levitin, D. J. (2008). *The world in six songs*. Toronto: Penguin. Explains the evolution of music and brains over tens of thousands of years and six continents. Argues for the role of music in human evolution, particularly in how we cooperate.

Ratey, J. J. (2008). *Spark: The revolutionary new science of exercise and the brain.* New York: Little, Brown and Company. Although more "technical," this text on the mind-body connection offers an explanation for why movement is so important for thinking, mood and sense of well-being.

Way, B. (1967). *Development through drama.* London: Longman. This classic drama education text has a chapter on movement and the use of sound (pp. 65–117).

Suggested Music

"Happy Feet" by Milton Ager and Jack Yellen (on movie soundtrack for *Shall We Dance?*) – a snappy high-energy tap-dancing piece of music to get everyone moving.

Sandy Nelson's "Let there be drums" or "Birth of the beat" are terrific for getting the blood coursing!

Big band music like Tommy Dorsey's "In the Mood" (or Count Basie or Duke Ellington) is difficult to resist once it gets into your body!

Baz Luhrmann presents Something for Everybody – a collection of music from Luhrmann's movies (including *Romeo and Juliet* and *Strictly Ballroom*, both good soundtracks in their own right) – all Luhrmann's films have great soundtracks.

Vaughan Williams – "Symphony #7" – "Antarctica" – creepy music

Mussorgsky's "Night on Bald Mountain" – atmospheric.

Holst's *The Planets* – also very atmospheric and suggestive of a journey.

"Lara's Theme" by Maurice Jarre from the soundtrack to *Dr. Zhivago.*

Spartacus Suite by Katchaturian – "Adagio of Spartacus and Phrygia (suite II, no. 1)" – excellent for mirror work.

Bach – "Air from Orchestral Suite no. 3" – also good for mirrors.

Ravel – "Pavane for a Dead Princess" – same as above.

Spanish classical guitar music – Francisco Tarrega's "Recuerdos de la Alhambra" and Joaquin Rodrigo's "Concierto de Aranjuez" – Adagio – lovely music to move to.

Keith Jarrett – solo jazz piano (he also has many trio records that are more up tempo) – also lovely to move to.

Adagio Chillout, a CD by Naxos, filled with lovely, reflective, gentle music for relaxing, mirrors, filling spaces…

We highly recommend acquiring a library of world music, and to encourage participants to bring in music from their cultural backgrounds. Putomayo is a good source for world music: http://www.putumayo.com/ or www.dramasound.com is another resource for all kinds of music and sound.

Whenever and wherever possible, if you have musicians in your group, or access to musicians in the community, bringing live music into a dramatic process is ideal. A solo tabla drummer, guitarist, or any musical instrument player can add so much richness to your explorations.

In introducing the first section to this book, we provided the artistic context for dramatic activity. To set the context for the chapters that make up Section 2, we consider the importance of ethical practice for facilitators of applied drama. Participants have already been asked to draw on their own lived experience as 14-year-olds in Chapter 4. In Chapter 5 they have worked with a fictional catalyst that requires participants to consider how they might respond to a given scenario in role. Chapter 6 considered the importance of working in embodied action in which participants are asked to create and communicate physically rather than with words, where touch and respect are key components for work that is both effective and efficacious. In the next three chapters, participants are asked to draw more deeply on their life histories as dramatic sources for storytelling (Chapter 7), to investigate a theme of shared significance to the group (Chapter 8), and to wrestle with a moral dilemma through drama (Chapter 9). While the work is also focused on skill development, at the same time you are dealing with participants' concerns; their stories may include "hot topics" such as racism, sexism and other kinds of injustices, and you are hearing material that is rich with dramatic potential and, simultaneously, potential ethical traps. As the work becomes deeper and richer and as participants continue to build their confidence and commitment to dramatic process, your role as facilitator shifts and changes. Questions of ethical practice become more pressing as you invite participants to share their own lived experiences and their points of view and attitudes toward potentially sensitive, or even divisive, topics or issues.

To enter this admittedly complex nest of issues, we define ethics and ethical practice as follows:

> "Ethics" refers to the principles or values by which a culture or group agrees to function, as in professional codes of conduct. "Ethical" refers to the ways in which someone functions in accordance with the cultural values or standards of the group. ... All of us, whoever we are and wher-

ever we live, conduct our lives by a set of standards [that we inherit from our families and develop or create as we mature]. The standards under which we operate—often without even thinking about them—may be very different from those that govern the lives of the people with whom we are working. Applied theatre practitioners work with groups in their cultural contexts all the time and that "being inside" means that the ways in which facilitators conduct themselves are open to scrutiny. ... Even before you begin this work, you need to be clear about your own understanding of what is important to you, what it is that you value and see as fair, what it is that you are prepared to give up. You need to create a sense of safety for yourself and others that will free you and them to work at optimum. (Prendergast & Saxton, 2009, p. 193)

We offer here key questions to consider with regard to ethical practice in applied drama:

- How have others defined ethical practice in the fields of applied drama and applied theatre?
- What does ethical practice mean to you as a drama facilitator committed to working in community settings?
- What are the values, standards and principles that underpin and inform your work?
- What challenges could you face, and how might you address them, in settings in which your own ethics and the ethics of one or more of your participants are in tension or outright contradiction?

Helen Nicholson (2005a) offers her perspective on ethics in applied drama/theatre:

Writing about the formation of citizenship as an identity, political theorist Chantal Mouffe has argued that, in pluralist societies, neither ethics nor morality is insulated from wider political concerns... and challenge the traditions of liberal thought in which morality has been thought to be based on universal principles and thus outside the public sphere of politics. ... [E]thics are inescapably tied up with questions of power—what is recognised as ethical depends on values, moral judgements and political principles. (p. 124)

Nicholson (2005b) uses the metaphor of gift-giving to define the ethics of the process that occurs between a facilitator and participants. She cautions that, "there is always a need to be vigilant about whether the practice is accepted as a generous exercise of care or

I see drama, its potency and its effectiveness, as ambiguous, at times risky, and regard the whole idea of understanding and working with values as at once inescapable but deeply problematic.

– Joe Winston, 1998, p. 173

whether, however well intentioned, it is regarded as an unwelcome intrusion" (p. 160).

Joe Winston (1998) writes convincingly about the role of drama in moral education, but also cautions about the problems to be faced (see text box). That caution aside, Winston offers that: "Through drama, the classroom [or applied drama workshop] can become this communal, public stage where the virtues can be problematized, played with, subverted, reframed, or brought into conflict with one another" (p. 176).

It seems clear from reading Winston and Nicholson on ethics that an applied drama facilitator should attend closely to questions of power and be open to investigating moral issues through drama that is not prescriptive, that can and should contain multiple dramatic tensions.

As a drama process unfolds and the participants reflect, they often realize more clearly and understand more fully the true reality of their own situations. Amanda Stuart Fisher (2005) points out that facilitators work best when they, like actors, allow themselves to be in those moments of discovery with their participants. It is only through this ability to put aside one's own interests, by "decentering" (Greene, 1995, p. 31), that the often unvoiced and unrealized communal concerns of the participants can be discovered as they emerge through the work. When these concerns do not align with or disrupt expectations, facilitators come

Our attempts to meddle or intervene in people's lives and communities must therefore be informed by an ethics of practice that can be responsive and responsible to each of the different contexts in which we work.

– Amanda Stuart Fisher, 2005, p. 119

face to face with their own personal investment in their practice. Ethical practice raises many questions and for those of us who work with such a variety of communities, thinking deeply about how they might be answered lies at the ethical centre of who we are.

Bruce Cockburn (2005), Canadian singer and activist, says that being an artist is "to tell the truth about what it means to be human in the world" (n.p.). It is, Stuart Fisher (2005) suggests, when facilitators sense that that truth is being betrayed that they recognize they are faced with an ethical choice. For example, what happens when an applied theatre facilitator becomes aware that the needs and wants of her immigrant participants are being compromised by the agenda of the funding body? The funding body expects that the work will be about the group's experiences on arrival in their new country; the group feels they have left those times behind, and are more anxious to explore the challenges and successes in their new lives (Kandil, 2012). Liselle Terret (2009), facilitating learning disabled clients, was told by her group's sponsors what to do next:

> I started to become aware of a divide between the ethos of the drama
> group we had developed over the past eight months, and that of the ethos
> of the committee, which seemed to see the group as more of a show-case
> opportunity for the organization. (p. 343)

In both these examples, the facilitators recognized that participants' wants and needs—their "truths"—were less important than the expectations of the sponsoring agencies. Ethical practice in both these cases requires that facilitators act on behalf of their participants, in spite of the difficulties that may ensue.

We are aware that this introduction to ethical practice in applied drama may seem somewhat daunting to a facilitator who is new to the field. Working ethically in drama does demand a lot from both facilitator and participants; a continual process of negotiating the terms of the drama contract is just one way of keeping these issues present and under close examination. Another strategy is to make use of Frank Barron's (1988) delineation of the behaviours needed for creativity, as we see these characteristics having valuable ethical implications for practitioners in applied drama. These five characteristics of creativity are:

1. A preference for complexity, balanced by a need to find simple and elegant order
2. A tolerance for ambiguity and the parallel tension that comes from not knowing
3. The ability to accept that there may be a multiplicity of right answers
4. Independence of judgement that requires us to think critically and creatively; to suspend judgement and make up our own minds
5. Ego strength: the ability to remain open to input without fear of being overwhelmed, to rally from setback and not to succumb to discouragement (pp. 76–98)

A mindful applied drama facilitator will reflect often on how well he or she is living up to this challenging yet significant set of characteristics that support working in dramatic process in both creative and ethical ways. However complex the ethics of practice may be, it is comforting to be reminded by Ross Gray and Christina Sinding (2002) that, "it is also an ethical stance to assert that people can and will take care of themselves" (p. 115).

7.1 Fostering communication

What does communication consist of? We are living in a so-called "age of communication" yet do we actually know what it means? And how do we sort out meaningful communicative messages from the almost overpowering *noise* generated by our contemporary society with its cellphones, iPods, Facebook chat and tweeting? The root of the word derived from the Latin is "common sharing," which fits well within the dramatic process. Communication is key to all professional success, the transmission of ideas, and the manner in which we rub our ideas together to generate new ones. Talking together as we share ideas is like developing a rough draft or rehearsing—a safe place to try things out, to test the waters and to have your thoughts reflected back by someone who may be talking from quite a different perspective.

Communication studies is an academic field in its own right, and an applied drama facilitator might want to seek out a course and/or some key texts and journals on this topic as a means of professional development.

Active/empathic listening is a method of listening that involves understanding both the content of the message as well as the intent of the sender and the circumstances under which the message is given.

Yet dramatic communication is unique in its heightened awareness and embodiment; we put our ideas into action to find out if they have resonance or potency, if they have legs to stand on. Performing actions with others can be inhibiting for inexperienced participants so this chapter focuses more on listening and verbal communication and more subtle forms of non-verbal communication. The tasks in this drama structure are about listening deeply to another person without imposing your value judgments or your responses on what you are being told. It is a human tendency to consider, as you listen, what you will say in response—something of which facilitators need to be aware as it means you are only half listening. The figure we have included here (see Figure 1) outlines some key skills involved in deep and active listening that are developed in this

Deep listening is not defensive, argumentative or intrusive. It is not about interpreting and analyzing, it is about recognizing that we are connected. In deep listening, we allow ourselves to be touched by the other, to hear the essence of what he or she is saying. Deep listening is respectful, freed from all the distractions that fill our minds with judgment, interpretation, conclusions and assumptions. Deep listening is open, curious and interested.

Key: Listen as if you had not met this person before.

chapter's workshop structure. Participants will be challenged to listen closely rather than simply hear, and to actively support a partner's communication by attending, questioning and clarifying. The dramatic aspect of the work is to take on a partner's story, to transfer and transmit another's story with the same degree of commitment and sensitivity you would possess as if it were your own. (Figure 1)

These communicative skills are essential as a group moves into the transferring and taking on of other's personal stories. Finally, the best way you can transmit these skills to your participants is, of course, to model effective listening throughout your own facilitation.

FIGURE 1: Listening/Responding

- **Be present.** Now's the time to really listen, not wait to talk. Completely surrender to the moment as being the other's time to talk. Maintain eye contact. Pay attention to nonverbal clues, like tone of voice and body language.
- **Reframe what you hear.** One of the best ways you can show that the other is being heard is to summarize and repeat back your understanding of what is being said and felt.
- **Ask questions.** Your questions reflect how closely you've been listening and show your true interest. Open-ended questions can deepen and further the conversation.
- **Try not to give advice.** It's tempting to immediately offer your take on how to "fix" the problem. Unless you are directly asked for your opinion, participants need to feel heard and understood first.
- **Stay focused on the speaker.** Try not to relate a story of your own (*"That's just like the time I ..."*), unless you can quickly bring the conversation back to the speaker. Donald Schön suggests that in offering "advice" it is helpful if you offer your experience for the other to "graze through" and perhaps find something useful that might apply to his or her situation. (Adapted from *Tips for Listening*, www.carepages.com.)

7.2 Drawing on personal histories

Stories and storytelling lie at the heart of who we are as human beings. Stories in dramatic process are not fixed, as are those found in books or other texts (although even these printed stories may shift and change over time). We can play with stories through drama, even stories from our own lives, by playing and replaying them, taking different positions and points of view that may allow us to see that even the most simple of stories has complexity. A

> Story telling is an attempt to deal with and at least partly *contain* the terrifyingly haphazard quality of life.
>
> – Robert Fulford, 1999, p. 14

story is both the act of the storyteller and the story listener. The audience will affect how I shape my story and the feedback loop that occurs between teller and listener will necessarily change the story and how it is told. The unfixedness and fluidity of a story offered and received in a drama process needs to be accepted by all involved. These stories are not privileged, even though they must be respected, as they are being moved from a single storyteller into a group process. In other words, context is all important when sharing personal stories within an applied drama setting. What kinds of stories are most appropriately shared in the group? What kinds of stories should be avoided, or if told, should be dealt with care? How does the group feel about transferring personal stories from one person to another? About taking on someone else's story as if it were his or her own? About having someone else perform one's personal story? These are key questions you will see are posed for reflective purposes as you prepare to enter into this chapter's drama structure.

7.3 Distancing through narrative voice

Listeners read meaning more accurately and more healthily when they are not being placed in a voyeuristic position. Counter to the status quo in our surveillance society—where voyeurism sells us peoples' stories in the form of reality television or sensationalistic "journalism"—the use of story in dramatic process is otherwise. As Adriana Cavarero (2000) writes, "[i]n the heart of everyone beats the question 'who am I?' and… it needs as a response one's own story narrated by another"(p. 136). When we give the gift of our story to another, and accept their story as a gift in return, we are opening ourselves up to learning something new about who we are. In this chapter's drama structure, the focus is on sharing a life story through which a significant

> Narratives are fundamentally social in nature in that almost all stories concern relationships between people; understanding stories thus entails an understanding of people, and how their goals, beliefs and emotions interact with their behaviours.
>
> – Raymond Mar et al., 2006, p. 696

and valuable lesson was learned. These stories are told and retold in dramatic process, and may eventually be shared in monologue form. In these dramatic ways, participants will gain the necessary distance from their own stories needed in order to see them afresh. And they will also have the experience of any actor who is challenged to step into a story and to make it his or her own through the process of interpretation.

7.4 Drama structure: *Life Lessons*

1. Preparing for the work

- **Grouping: Whole group**
- **Strategy: Game, Cocktail Party**
- **Administration: None**
- **Focus: To begin to share personal information**

<u>Facilitator</u>: Today we're going to be working with personal stories. To begin, I'd like you to close your eyes and think of three things that you would be prepared to share with other people about yourself. These three things should be both interesting and help people to remember you. When you are choosing, remember that you may have some interesting things in your life that might make other people uncomfortable to hear; so keep that in mind. Just take a minute to think about and plan what you are going to say.

Think of this next part of the activity as happening at a cocktail party where you don't know anyone and no one knows you. Your task is to meet as many people as you can, everyone if possible, and exchange your name and your three pieces of information with everyone you meet. And, of course, you need to listen and remember the names and information of everyone else. Any questions? Anything else? Off you go.

[*After a couple of minutes*] Stop everyone! Just look around, note whom you've met and think of their name and information and see whom you haven't met yet, whom you still need to meet. Just one thing: before we begin again, you may—if you wish—change one piece of information using the same rules. Remember, it must be interesting, memorable and not make people uncomfortable. Begin again. [*Depending on the size of the group you may want to do this one or two more times, each time offering participants a chance to change a piece of information as above.*]

Let's make a circle. I'm going to ask ____ on my right to introduce us to the person on his/her right, and so on around the circle. Each of you should use the person's name and as many pieces of information as you can remember. We are standing by to help you if you need it.

Just talk to the person next to you about that activity. What were some of the challenges that it presents?

Let's open that conversation up to the whole circle. Anybody have something to share?
    During these pair or small group conversations it is important for the facilitator to move around and listen in to get the tenor of the conversations. Then, when it gets to the large group sharing, you can say, for example: "I overheard a number of people saying that names were easy to remember but it was much harder to remember detailed information, others vice versa." This kind of prompting of reflection is useful at all times.

Option:

- **Grouping: Small groups of three to five, depending on your time**
- **Strategy: Game, Two Truths and a Lie**
- **Administration: None**
- **Focus: To develop observation and listening skills**

Facilitator: This variation of Cocktail Party is called Two Truths and a Lie. This time, one of the three pieces of information you will be sharing is intentionally untrue. [*It is sometimes useful to model this to the whole group first.*] Can you quickly move into small groups of five or six?

Will someone in each group volunteer to begin? You are in the hotseat and your task is to tell your group three things about yourself, in any order. The trick here is to make your lie believable! After you've presented yourself, the rest of the group will decide together which piece of information they think is false. If they are successful, they may want to tell you how they were able to guess. If they fail to guess, you may want to tell them how you were able to pass off a lie so well. Then the game moves on to the next volunteer. [*After a full round of turns.*]

Great! Let's reflect on this in our groups. What are some of the reasons that we regularly tell small untruths in our daily life? I wonder what the advantage of this is for us? And what does this fact of human behaviour tell us about drama and how it works? There are no set answers to these questions other than the ideas raised by your group as you talk about them. [*It might interest them to know that drama and theatre has been referred to as The Big Lie and that the "Antitheatrical Prejudice" (Barish, 1981) that has plagued this art form for centuries is really rooted in a mistrust of actors because they are seen to be such good liars!*]

2. Entering the work

- **Grouping: Individual then pairs, seated**
- **Strategy: Pilot/Co-pilot storytelling**
- **Administration: None**
- **Focus: To tell a personal story, to listen and question, and then to give it away**

Facilitator: Find your own private space in the room. Sitting or standing, whichever is most comfortable, close your eyes and think of a story from your own life. This can be an experience that you have had from any time in your life when you feel you learned a valuable lesson of some kind. We often experience life lessons when we go through significant change. For example, we may learn many things if as a child our family made a major move from one city or one country to another. You can probably think of other examples. [*They may offer some ideas to share.*]

This prompt helps participants in thinking about ideas from their own lives.

Again, as in our first activities, choose a story that you are comfortable with sharing and that others will be comfortable in hearing; this time a story that has something that you see as a life lesson.

Is there anybody who needs more time? [*If so, say, "Just one more minute."*]

Right, now I'd like you to find a partner and bring your chairs together facing each other. Choose an A and a B. A, you're going to begin by telling your story to your partner. B, your job is to listen intently to A's story. I think it will help both the listening and the telling if you agree to either close your eyes, or have B turn away from A so that the storytellers can simply tell their stories and are not influenced by the listeners' responses. You are storytelling, not performing your stories. B, your challenge is to listen deeply to the story, to try to be in the story with the teller. No verbal or visual responses please. Put aside your own responses or agenda and listen supportively. The story should be no more than three minutes long. When it is finished just sit quietly with your partner and think about what you have said and heard until everyone is finished.

This technique of getting everyone to remain quiet until everyone is finished is intended to maintain focus on the task and the growing silence encourages the more verbose tellers to finish up the task.

Everybody ready?

Good. Now turn back to face your partner or open your eyes. I expect Bs you may have a number of questions that you might like to ask that will clarify the story. Perhaps you need more detail about the setting? More description of what was going on around this event at the time? Anything you didn't quite understand? Were any of your senses beyond listening engaged? In short, what does the movie in your head need to come more clearly into focus? You might also want to consider how the dramatic elements of light/dark, sound/silence and movement/stillness are working in the story. Take two or three minutes to ask and have these questions answered.

Now we'll switch roles. B, you are going to tell your story to A. As, remember to close your eyes or turn away and to listen as deeply as you can. Ready? [*Repeat follow-up questioning as above.*]

Before you leave your partner, just talk for a moment about what it was like telling a story in this way, when neither of you as listeners were making visual contact nor giving verbal cues? How, when the focus is only on the words, does it change how you listen or how you tell the story?

Lots of good conversation there. Is there anything you'd like to share with the group?

The next part of this workshop will ask each of you to carry the story you have been told to another partner *as if it were your own.*

3. Engaging in the work
Facilitator: Everybody has been given the gift of their partner's story and had the chance to ask questions, add details and bring it into focus. The story you have been told is now your story. But it is important that you respect its origins as if they were your own as you carry this story forward to a new partner. As please stand and find a new B to join.

All right. As, you're going to begin by telling the story to B in first person, as if it were your own. One change from last time is that you may look at each other. Again, try to capture the dramatic arc of the story for your listener and use as much detail and description as you can remember. You may find yourself subtly shifting things a little bit to make the story your own, which is perfectly acceptable. Any questions? Again, when you have finished, just sit quietly and think over what you've said and heard until everyone is done. Off you go.

Now we're ready for the questions. But As, it's possible you may not have a ready answer, but your task is always to reply as if it is a story that really happened to you. Therefore, your answers will have that authority but in life, we are often uncertain about things that have happened to us. And Bs, you're listening for the story and asking the questions you need in order to understand and to make the story your own.

Good. Now let's switch so that B is the storyteller and A is the listener. This time, rather than sitting quietly until everyone is finished, you may begin asking your questions right away. Just make sure that you are not interfering with any other groups. Ready? Begin.

Right everyone, here are some questions you might like to think about as you talk together about that experience. Storytellers: what was it like telling a story as if it were your own? In light of the experience, what might you have changed? For the listeners, what did your partner do to help you to believe that the story belonged to him or her? How did knowing that this was not really your partner's story change the way you might have listened? How different is it to tell a story when you can see your listener and their non-verbal responses?

   This would be a good place to end a single workshop session with a general sharing built around the reflections questions above. If you have time to continue, the structure carries on from this point here. But if you are coming back to it, we recommend you begin with a warm-up activity such as a storytelling game of some kind (see Further Reading) or some sort of movement activity before returning to pairs.

[*If ending*] Each of you now has a new story. Keep it in mind until we meet next time.

[*If beginning a new session*] Everyone, find your partner from last time and sit down together. Take a minute to review the story you heard last time and, maybe, you need to ask a question or two. You might consider how you will begin and what words you will choose to say in order to attract your listener's attention. You may have a couple of minutes only.

[*If continuing*] Right, now I'd like all the Bs to get up and find a new A. Remember you are taking your partner's story with you, so let that be running in your head as you find a new partner!

There's a chance at this point that your listener may have created the story you are going to tell. If this turns out to be so for some of you, an additional task as listeners will be to put aside that recognition and to listen deeply to this story which is no longer just your own. This time we are going to retell our new stories in third person. This means that the narrator tells the story about the events, not in first person, but using "He" or "She". So you have some options: the narrator may take on the viewpoint of some other person in the story who watches and follows the characters—in which case, you need to think about which character would benefit the story's dramatic arc; or you may choose to take an omniscient viewpoint in which case, the narrator may tell us what's going on inside someone's head. Any questions about that?

As will begin and Bs your focus is on listening intently and supporting the storyteller. Again, storyteller, you may find that telling this story in the third person demands more from you as the interpreter of the story. As before, talk together and question each other about the story then switch over when you're ready. Remember that we are looking for stories of no more than two or three minutes. Your partner is not listening to a novel but only a brief excerpt, so be aware of time. Again, be aware of the words you say to open the story and how you're going to finish it off. Remember, this is not a first person story.

[*When both partners have told and unpacked their stories*] Let's think together about how different third person narration is from first person. What changed for you as both listener and teller? Was there anyone who heard his or her own story? If so, is there anything you have to tell us about that experience?

- **Grouping: Individual; whole or small groups**
- **Strategy: Whole group sharing**
- **Administration: Paper and pencils ready for drafting ideas**
- **Focus: To explore "storying" from other points of view**

Facilitator: You now have three stories to work from (we're not including your own original story): two that you heard and told and one that you've just heard. Choose the story that you enjoyed the most or found the most fascinating. You have a number of choices to make as storyteller:

- You can decide whether you're going to tell your story from the point of view of another person in the story,
- You can tell it as an object in the story, or
- You can tell it from a different vantage point in some future time

For example, the story could be told by, say, the villain of the piece or by a secondary character who witnesses what happens but may not have all the details. Objects that are part of the setting can become animated and tell the story that way; for example, the clock on the wall that sees all, or as if the teller were the car involved in the accident that happened to the protagonist. Any questions about these instructions?

You'll need a few minutes to go away on your own and figure this out. There is paper and pencils there, if you would like to work that way. Remember to think about the implications of your chosen point of view and how these choices affect your story. Also, how your story begins and ends will make a difference to what happens in the middle.

You now have some experience with the elements of effective storytelling, so you might want to consider how to bring some of those elements in. The story should only be two or three minutes, not too long. Any questions? Remember, the point of view you've chosen to speak from will be revealed as you tell your story. [*They go away and prepare for five minutes then share their stories in the whole group.*]

If you feel the group would work better sharing in smaller groups, do that, and circulate quietly to be aware of what is going on and, perhaps, noting the more confident storytellers whom you could invite to share with the whole group later.

4. Reflecting on the process
Facilitator: Let's talk a little about that process. What sort of things did you notice that the storyteller used to help you understand, retain your attention, signal important moments? How do shifting perspectives open stories up? Or perhaps close them down? Or can they intensify a story in different ways? What might be some of the advantages of telling stories from unexpected perspectives? What are the advantages or challenges of using your story as a gift and giving it away to others?

7.5 Questions for Reflection and Further Reading

Questions for Reflection

1. As part of preparing for a presentation, how might you now take one of these stories and build it into a two or three minute monologue? How might groups of five or six participants arrange a collection of monologues to share with others? What ideas might they use to create a thread to connect the stories?
2. In your own practice, what sorts of story content would you want to avoid? Dorothy Heathcote called decisions like this "teaching thresholds" and noted how important it was for facilitators to be aware of such things (such as content, noise, language…) before embarking on the work. To understand beforehand why these thresholds may cause discomfort, rather than making these discoveries in process, is ideal (although, of course, it is impossible for facilitators to prepare for all eventualities!). This is a useful question to discuss in a group as everyone will share some thresholds but also offer different ones.

Further Reading

Barton, R. & Booth, D. (1990). *Stories in the classroom: Storytelling, reading aloud and roleplaying with children.* Portsmouth, NH: Heinneman. A great compendium of ideas, stories, tales and fables that is a seminal text for classroom teachers and anyone else who wants or needs to tell stories.

Fulford, R. (1999). *The triumph of narrative: Storytelling in the age of mass culture.* Toronto: Anansi.

King, T. (2003). *The truth about stories: A Native narrative.* Toronto: Anansi.
Both of these books above, based on CBC Massey Lectures, examine the power of story in modern and traditional contexts.

McWilliams, B. (1998). Effective storytelling: A manual for beginners. Retrieved May 25, 2012 from http://www.eldrbarry.net/roos/eest.htm. This brief and informative page of suggestions and techniques is useful for both facilitators and storytellers.

Randall, W. L. (1997). *The stories we are: An essay on self-creation.* Toronto, ON: University of Toronto Press. Looks at life review and personal autobiography as self-reflection and self-understanding.

Note: The Centre for Interdisciplinary Research on Narrative has an excellent website that directs readers to any number of texts on the "countless aspects of human life" and the means of accessing and valuing those stories: http://w3.stu.ca/stu/sites/cirn/index.aspx. A good resource for practitioners working in a variety of applied theatre genres.

CHAPTER EIGHT
TOPICS, THEMES, TALK AND ACTION

8.1 Generating ideas and material

We have been generating ideas and material for dramatic exploration in every chapter up until now. Participants have been working creatively and spontaneously to create their own ideas and stories and have had opportunities to select and choose what they wish to share. The work to this point has been about keeping participants comfortable and in processes where the risk-taking has been somewhat controlled by safe circumstances. In this present chapter, we begin to challenge participants to move more deeply into the work, to broaden their imaginative experiences and dramatic vocabulary. The focus in this drama structure is to look beyond ourselves and to expand our collective understanding of a chosen topic or theme of shared interest. Working through image, particularly in the form of tableaux, employs the dramatic elements of silence and stillness, and this built-in constraint is intended to provide participants with a paradoxical challenge that gently pushes them to find imagistic ways to say what they want to say.

The famous drama question, credited to Dorothy Heathcote, is, "What shall we make a play about?" (Three Looms Waiting, 1971). The answer to that question usually comes in one or two words: "A murder," "A mystery," or "An adventure," all of which are essentially genres, or perhaps the answer might be a location like a circus or a haunted house, or even an object like "cars." Heathcote's genius as a drama educator was how she was able to take children's natural dramatic interests and mine the thematic potential of those choices to make the work both educational and meaningful for all involved. Facilitation is about being able to draw out from participants what it is that intrigues them about the topical ideas they have put forward so that whatever it is they choose to explore, it is because they themselves are invested in it. When participants tell you, for example, they want to do a play about gangs, the first questions we need to ask might be, "What is it we might want to say about gangs?" "In what ways could a gang change people's lives?" "What might be some of the reasons that drives someone to become a gang member?" "How do we as members of society react and respond to gangs?" These questions offer a number of perspectives that invite a range of responses that generate conversations that will follow, which we call "priming the pump." Participants can then build on these questions, and begin to focus in on what it is they wish to explore. One of the most powerful ways to activate these opening questions is through images, which we focus on as our key activity below: "When we think of gangs, what sorts of images come to mind?"

Once we have an image we can begin to use a wide variety of strategies and techniques to animate these images. Animation may be through movement, improvisation, writing or sequencing; all of which we cover in this chapter. Animating the circle images in Chapter 3 was an early introduction to ways of expanding the potential dramatic power of an image, which we take further here.

8.2 What is a theme?

"Theme" has its root in the Greek word "thema" meaning a place, a standing point (we note that "theatre" has the same root—a "seeing-place"). Theme is therefore not what the plot is about, nor what ideas we see presented, but which of the ideas interest us and what it is about those ideas that is important. What we deem important helps us to see the relationship of the events of the plot of a story to each other and to the deeper meanings of the plot as they may effect/affect our personal world views. The identification of the themes becomes the firm ground from which we build our conceptualizations into action. We see these interrelated concepts layered in this way:

First level: What is the *topic*? For example, gangs.

Second level: What *ideas* are generated through various images of the topic? Victims, violence, macho behaviour, bullying, crime, loyalty, belonging, money, conflict with others (other gangs, the law, family, etc.).

Third level: Which ideas do we see as the most important ones? The ideas that intrigue us as individuals and as a group and can sustain us? Loyalty and belonging are chosen as the most intriguing.

Fourth level: As facilitator, you also need to think about what ideas intrigue you so that you can offer your own perspectives which may open up further possibilities for investigation.

When you have identified in which direction the group wants to begin its exploration (for example, the need to belong within a gang can compromise loyalties in challenging ways: loyalty to family, friends, church, past relationships, etc.), you have articulated the theme. Thematic exploration of loyalty and belonging in gangs could involve a number of dramatic activities/processes:

- Creating a ritual greeting only known by gang members.
- Creating the image of the gang that subtly indicates power relations (such as who is the gang leader, second in command, etc.).
- Exploring through role play the moral dilemma of a recruit who is required to prove his worth to the gang by some rite of passage (is it going to be a crime, or something subtler that puts this character at-risk … what would it be?).
- Moving back in time and showing a photograph of a young child on a tricycle and asking what events might have caused this innocent-looking child to grow up to become a member of a gang?

Once the group is able to articulate the themes that underlie the chosen topic, then one begins to understand what will drive dramatic action. Dramatic action will involve making the kind of choices that frame and contain the examination and presentation of material. As a facilitator, your role is to move a group from choosing a topic to identifying a theme, as it is in the latter that the art form of drama flourishes. The theme will also help everyone to keep on track and, sometimes, to discover that that is not really what the work is becoming. At that point, the group will have no difficulty in identifying the more appropriate theme although the old theme should still have relevance.

8.3 Tableaux and Image Theatre

Tableaux, as a theatrical genre, has had a long history. It became fashionable as a genre alongside the rise of proscenium arches in theatres in the 18th century that allowed the notion of the arch becoming a frame of a pictorial representation. Actors would be arranged into complex visual depictions that would be revealed to an audience when the curtains opened. *Tableaux vivants* that became popular at this time, were focused on "an evocation of situations and conditions rather than of actions and characters" (Pavis, 1998, p. 377). They were especially popular in English melodramas that played in minor theatres restricted from presenting "spoken dramas" (see Booth, 1991, p. 151). This form of theatre practice fell

A well-composed tableau is a whole enclosed according to a point of view, in which the different parts work towards a single goal and form.

– Denis Diderot, cited in Pavis, 1998, p. 376

out of favour in the early 20th century—no doubt in part due to the invention of both photography and film that rendered such stylized moments in time less engaging for theatre audiences—but over time tableaux became a key strategy in drama education.

Tableaux, also known as still pictures, freeze frames, depictions, statues or sculptures, involve the dramatic elements of silence and stillness. Having students/participants illustrate their "concretized thought[s]" (Morgan & Saxton, 1987, p. 110) in tableau form allows a facilitator to immediately see how understanding is being shaped in response to a prompt. Aesthetic elements of tableaux are akin to those in visual arts, in that a still image should have some of the compositional elements present in any image; a clear *focus*, most often an *action* that is being caught, as in a photograph, and the visual interest of a number of physical *levels* taken by individuals within the group picture (as in high, medium and low). Tableaux work is very safe work for generally unskilled participants, as it only requires holding still, although there is a significant challenge in this in regard to physicality and concentration. It is always wise to advise participants that they will have to hold a pose for some time, so the position taken should not be overly physically demanding, such as balancing on one foot.

"Tapping-in" to tableaux is a drama education technique for unpacking a tableau in which a facilitator touches the shoulder of one figure within a tableau and asks what is going on in their mind at that moment, or poses a question. This process, as participants become familiar with it, may involve viewers also weighing in with their own questions. This begins to build roles within a still depiction, and a deeper understanding of what is going on.

Image is a language. All images also are surfaces and, as such, they reflect what is projected on it. As objects reflect the light that strikes them, so images in an organized ensemble reflect the emotions of the observer, her ideas, memories, imagination, desires …

– Augusto Boal, 1992/2002, p. 175

Image Theatre is Augusto Boal's adaptation of tableaux work within his system of Theatre of the Oppressed. Boal (1992/2002) began his image work with "The image of the word":

> It [image of the word] consists of choosing a word that is meaningful for the particular group with whom we are working, and asking the participants to make an image of it, using their bodies; the word can be the name of a country, a region, a political party, a profession, a state of mind, a historical character, a recent event; it can be a noun or an adjective; a word which represents something or someone relevant to the group.
>
> The group forms a circle and all members show their images simultaneously; then they regroup in families of images which resemble each other. Each family, in turn, vocalizes the words inspired by the image. (p. 87)

For Boal, images are a way to illustrate the reality of how things are, and the oppressions present in participants' lives. The focus then becomes shifting these images into how things could or should be and considering possible pathways to change. There are many ways of using images dramatically to generate ideas, view multiple perspectives, suggest solutions, and as we explore below, a means of developing a narrative based on a theme.

8.4 Drama structure: *Exploring a Theme*

1. Preparing for the work

In general discussions about an area the group might explore in more depth, four ideas have been identified: Housing, Parenting, Community History and Health and Wellness. The task then is to decide which topic will become the focus of their work.

- **Grouping: Whole group, standing in a circle**
- **Strategy: Magnets**
- **Administration: Four topics each written on a separate piece of chart paper**
- **Focus: To select the topic to be explored**

Facilitator: As you look around the room you will notice that the four topics you have expressed interest in exploring further are written on each of the four pieces of paper that I have laid out in the corners of the room. It's always a challenge in a group to agree on a topic… sometimes it is easier than other times. Your task is to walk around the room and visit each corner and its topic. You may walk by yourself, if you wish, or you may choose to walk and talk with a partner or a small group. This is a time for generating ideas and for thinking about which ideas are pulling you more strongly. When you have visited all four corners, come back into the centre so that I'll know when we're ready to move on.

It's always useful for you to move around and listen in to what participants are talking about as they do this activity.

I could hear a lot if interesting ideas beginning to bubble. Now your task is to imagine that each of these topics has become a magnet, but the topic that interests you the most will have the strongest magnetic pull. When I say go, you will move silently toward the topic that pulls you. Go.

[*If the group is fairly evenly divided amongst the four topics*] Great. We can see that there is shared interest in all of these topics. But we do need to make a choice. So I'm going to ask some of you right now to move to the topic that pulls you almost as strongly as the one you have first chosen. This will help us see if there is one clear topic we can all work within together. Be mindful that if you are moving to another topic, in order to help the group, that you are indeed taking something of interest from the topic you are leaving and bringing it to the new topic. This is very important, to see that you are not abandoning your ideas, but are offering them within a new frame.

This process may need to be repeated once or twice more if there is no clear consensus.

[*Once the group has arrived at a clear majority grouping*] Yes. We can see which topic has more pull for this group right now. It is still important for those of you who are going to be pulled now by the magnetic force of the largest magnet, that you bring your ideas and their possible connections to this corner.

2. Entering the work

The group decides on the topic of "Housing" as being of primary interest. It is useful for a facilitator to think through how the other three topics are not abandoned, and may be woven into the selected one. For example, "Parenting" and the idea of family are closely related to notions of house and home. As well, "Community History" and "Health and Wellness" can all be drawn into the chosen topic.

- **Grouping: Small groups of four or five**
- **Strategy: Brainstorming**
- **Administration: Four or five chart papers with sayings written in centre from list below; felt markers; masking tape**
- **Focus: To build collective understanding of the chosen topic**

The quotations below were selected by the facilitator but there is no reason why participants can't be invited to contribute any sayings from their own experiences and cultures. It is wise to have more chart paper ready. If there are many contributions, the maximum number is around six or seven, you may have to scrap some of the ones that you have chosen.

Facilitator: Find yourself a group of four or five. With your group please gather around one of the pieces of paper on the floor. [*Sometimes participants feel they need to choose one at this point, so say*] It doesn't matter where you choose to sit at this point, as you are going to move to every piece of paper as we brainstorm. On the chart paper, write down any thoughts or draw any images that come to mind as you look at the words on your paper. It doesn't matter if you have ideas that are different because they present ways to

Home is a name, a word, it is a strong one; stronger than magician ever spoke...

~ Charles Dickens

Home is the girl's prison and the woman's workhouse.

~ George Bernard Shaw

Home is the place where, when you have to go there, they have to take you in.

~ Robert Frost

A house that does not have one worn, comfy chair in it is soulless.

~ May Sarton

Where thou art—that—is Home.

~ Emily Dickinson

The strength of a nation derives from the integrity of the home.

~ Confucius

build on other's ideas. I'm going to ask you to work quickly. [*There may be talking and the talking may generate ideas, but be sure the ideas get down on the paper.*]

If participants have difficulty in reading, it is often enough to spend a little time at the top asking them to think about what the quotation means to them and what ideas come to mind which allows you to repeat them. You might want to paste an image as a prompt (for example, a picture of a well-used chair).

[*After a couple of minutes*] In a moment I'm going to ask you to move clockwise on to the next piece of paper. When you get there, look at what the previous group has written and add your ideas, thoughts or images. Any questions? [*Each group moves on after a couple of minutes of reading and adding. You may need to give a bit more time as groups keep rotating. The rotation is complete when each group returns to its original sheet of paper.*]

Look at the new ideas that have been added by other people to your original comments. Talk about this, about how your ideas have been expanded, and of course you may add anything that is newly generated by this conversation. Five minutes or so should be enough.

3.a. Engaging with the work

- **Grouping: Same as above**
- **Strategy: Tableaux**
- **Administration: A working space for each group; sentence strips (may be purchased from teacher supply store or can be made by cutting 10 cm strips from chart paper), one per group; felt markers**
- **Focus: To use their bodies to convey the core meaning(s) synthesized from their page of ideas as embodied in a still picture**

<u>Facilitator</u>: I'd like you to create a still picture or tableau with your group that captures the essence of the ideas that are on your page and your discussion about those ideas. We did this before with the circle, but perhaps I should remind you that we're going to be reading these pictures, so you need to be comfortable holding these positions for us. Also, it may help to remember the power of connection between people through physical touch. This is another way that helps us tell a story in a still picture, although not everybody needs to be connected, it can be a strong aesthetic choice. You can represent a person in this image. Or, if you wish to be more abstract, if that is a more powerful way to represent your ideas, then you can choose to work with a quality, an idea or feeling. But, you cannot be an object like a door or a window. You'll need to work quickly… you've got about three minutes. [*Participants may need more time, and this can be negotiated, but it is always better to limit time allowed. When the groups seem to be ready, arrange them in a circle so everyone can see.*]

Before we begin, let's hang up our brainstorming papers so they can be a resource for us now and later. Let's do a rehearsal all together before we share. I'll count you down to your freeze position, 5, 4, 3, 2, 1 … Freeze. Someone step out of the tableau, and take a look from the outside … are there any adjustments you want to make so that your tableau is saying clearly what you want it to? Relax, and take a moment to get some feedback from your outside eye. [*Groups may ask to have another rehearsal, perhaps with a different group member stepping out to take a look.*]

Good. Now our tableaux are set, but before we share them I'm going to give each group a caption strip. I'd like each group to decide upon a title for their tableau, as if it were the title of a story. The title should help us to understand the thinking and feeling in what you are showing us. Make sure the title is printed in large letters, so we can see it with the tableau.

Is there a group that will volunteer to start? Thank you. We'll then move to the right to the next group, and so on. While the first group is getting ready I'd like everyone else to close their eyes. When I see the tableau is ready, I will read the words that caption this image. When I say "Open," you can open your eyes and begin to read the picture. [*As each tableau is presented, about one minute per tableau, ask*] What do we see? Where do you see this? What tells you that that feeling is there?

[*After the initial round*] Let's go back to the first group and go around again. Before we do, any questions or thoughts?

[*The second round of sharing goes more deeply into interpreting the tableaux.*] How does the image connect to the caption? To the original statement? To your own ideas when you were brainstorming with this statement? [*This time each group can relax and respond to what they've heard.*]

Right, everyone in this group relax and shake out from your freeze. What did you hear that may have either deepened or maybe even contradicted the ideas you were conveying?

[*After second round of sharing*] Good. Everyone relax now and sit down with your group and talk together about how your own understanding of what you were doing has been enhanced by the feedback you heard. Also, how has your understanding of the topic been shifted or challenged by seeing and sharing ideas from the other groups' tableaux?

This next round of sharing could replace the second round we've just done or could be an extension.

[*Summarizing*] Up to this point we've discovered a number of things from looking at and discussing what we can see in these tableaux, from an outside point of view. Now, we can begin to consider a more inside point of view. Is there a group that will volunteer to try this next step with me? [*The George Bernard Shaw group volunteers.*]

Good. Take your tableau position and before we begin I just want to reverse what we usually do and ask the people in the tableau to close their eyes and think for a moment about who or what each of you represents and what you are thinking and feeling and doing within this tableau. [*To the group*] Is there someone in this tableau that you'd like to hear from? I'm just going to move into the tableau and place my hand gently on that person's shoulder and ask them, "What is it you are seeing right now?" or, "What are you looking forward to most on your day of rest?" or "Who or what in this life says home to you?"

There are any number of questions to ask. Sometimes tableaux figures/characters will only answer with a word, or give quite predictable answers, but what you look for here are deeply engaged responses that move understanding forward. The kinds of questions modelled above invite more reflective and metaphorical responses than the more common, "What are you thinking?" or

"What are you feeling?" or "What are your doing?" It might be necessary to do this tapping-in two or three more times in the volunteer tableau before asking for a volunteer from the group who has a question to come up and tap-in. A few things to remember: (1) when you move into the tableau, try not to block the view of the person from the viewers, (2) be sure to leave your hand in place while that person is speaking as this is a way to offer support, and (3) remember that questions should be delivered in a spirit of genuine curiosity as opposed to a police interrogation. The goal is to discover new things, or confirm our intuitions about what is going on in each image. This tapping-in process can be repeated with each tableau, with increasing numbers of perspectives on the key topics of housing and home.

3.b. Engaging in the work

- **Grouping: Same as above**
- **Strategy: Finding a narrative structure by building a tableaux sequence**
- **Administration: Have available chart paper and pens; handouts of Appendix E (p. 215)**
- **Focus: To teach traditional narrative structure as a framework for realizing the narrative potential their tableau holds within it**

Facilitator: Let's just take a moment to think back over what we've done so far. Take a look at the brainstorm pages tacked on the wall and remember the ideas that came to your mind as you worked on that brainstorming process. Then, consider how you and your group translated some of those ideas into the tableau that we first viewed from the outside, and then went inside to find out more about what was going on. But what we still don't know is where did that tableau appear in the story: Is it the beginning? Somewhere in the middle? Or is it at the end? And that, of course, is where we need to go next.

In the copy of this handout that I'm passing around, you'll see what is considered to be a traditional western narrative (or plot) structure. The first thing I want you to do is talk to the person next to you about what this image reminds you of. What does it look like? [*They share some ideas; a witch's hat, a financial statement, a lopsided mountain, etc.*] It's interesting to consider that it is not a circle, not like the circle we started out with (in Chapter 3). And yet we know that many stories may end where they begin, and have a kind of cyclical structure. This structure is more linear and takes us on a journey where the end is removed from the beginning. Can you just share with a partner a story you know of where the end is very different from the beginning?

But stories can take on many possible shapes, and sometimes a story itself changes its shape, especially when it is being created collectively. Can you share with your partner any stories you know that are non-linear, perhaps cyclical, spiral and/or open-ended in form?

For now we'll work within a linear narrative structure, as it is one way to develop the narrative potential of our tableaux.

Now, take a look at the three-part comic strip on your handout. This represents the three main parts of a story: the beginning, the middle and the end. Decide with your group where you think your tableau sits: Is it showing the beginning, the middle or the end of your story?

This may take some time, as they are imagining what their story might be about and sequencing the events in what is their first draft of their story.

Good. Now your task is to create the two missing tableaux so that you will finish with three tableaux that tell a story because we will be able to see the beginning, the middle and the end. I'm going to give you only three minutes to brainstorm some ideas around the narrative you are building from your tableau. You can jot down ideas on some chart paper if you wish. This is the only time you're going to get to work just out of your heads. Off you go.

Groups that are working with an abstract tableau—a state of mind or emotion—may need to be encouraged to see its power as integral to the emerging narrative of the other two tableaux.

[*After three minutes or so*] Now let's begin to work those ideas physically on our feet. Depending on where you've placed your tableau as A, B or C in the sequence, you'll be creating two new tableaux that are moving forward and backwards in time, or perhaps both ways. You need to consider how much time you want to move forward or backwards between the tableaux, as these three images do not need to happen in real time one moment after the other. In other words, you may choose to go backwards some years, move forward some weeks or months, whatever you like. Life itself follows this general pattern of birth, maturity and death, so there's lots of room to play with time. And of course, we can also play with space, in that your tableaux don't all need to happen in the same location or setting.

[*When you see that they have an idea of their three tableaux*] Let's just check that we've got our place in all three of the tableaux firmly in our mind. We're just working technically here, because knowing these things will help you to put the feeling aspects of the story in later. So, when I snap my fingers [*or shake my tambour, etc.*] I'd like you to snap into your first tableau. Snap!

Close your eyes and memorize the position your body is in, right down to your fingertips and toes. Now be ready to move quickly and cooperatively into your second tableau. Snap!
Repeat instructions for third tableau.

Great! Take a moment to talk about any adjustments you might want to make.

Good. Your final task is to add a tableau that appears between Tableau 1 and 2, that corresponds to the Rising Action of the story [*on the handout*], and another tableau that goes between numbers 2 and 3 that corresponds to the Falling Action of your story. In other words, these new tableaux will tell us more about how you get from the beginning to the climax of your story, and from there to the end of your story. Any questions?
They will need a few minutes to develop these two new images.

Right, now you need to be really sure about your positions in these five tableaux, so I'd like you to go through your sequence on your own using the snapshot technique we did earlier with the three, but this time you decide what signal you need to use. Your focus here is to remember each tableau and your position in it in detail, plus how you move from one to another.

Your final task is to create the movement that supports the flow of the story by how one tableau flows into the next. This may mean that you are going to have to develop a timing signal so everyone knows when to move. You may choose to have certain people move at different times and at different speeds if it supports the storytelling.
A possible extension here is to have participants use a piece of music to play behind this storytelling sequence. It may be useful to remind participants as they are working of the activity Filling-in-the-Shape they did in Chapter 4.

We've been working technically for some time, solving a lot of aesthetic problems of timing and shaping and flow and keeping the storyline developing. What we must now pay attention to are the intentions and feelings and attitudes that each one of us is representing as we move through this story. So you'll need to take a few more minutes to go through your sequence focusing on how you are letting the feeling and intentional aspects of the story be fully revealed in both your frozen positions and how you move from one to the next.

Now we're almost ready to share our stories. We have a choice: your group may choose to simply share the work or your group may choose to use the caption you wrote earlier as the title of your story; or you may choose to write a new caption that introduces your story to us.

Are we ready to begin? Let's make sure we are in our groups and spread out evenly around the edges of this space, so that everyone can see each other. Is there a group that would like to go first? Great, thank you. Let's continue clockwise from here. If you'd like me to read your caption, please place it on the floor in front of you, and I will read it before you begin. If there is no caption, you will begin when you are ready. Anything else?

We've been through a long process and we need to have a chance to reflect on the work. You need to talk about your own work first, and how you felt that affected your audience. Then, you'll want to share your responses about the other work you saw. Finally, you might want to discuss the process itself, and how it challenged and/or fulfilled you as an individual and as members of a group. [*These three reflection points could be put up on the wall on chart paper.*]

As these small group discussions are going on, it is useful for you to circulate amongst the groups for a number of reasons. You can bring points forward to a whole group discussion. If a group is having difficulty talking together, you can offer assistance, usually by offering a reflective question. However, small group discussions should be self-directed as much as possible.

Now let's talk together in the whole group. This is your chance to share responses to each other's work. We also have the opportunity to repeat a sequence, if we wish, simply because it was so pleasurable and we wish to see it again, or because something might be clarified if we saw it again.

What is it that shifts and changes as we look back at our original sources of this work, the quotes on houses and homes? How do we understand this chosen topic in new ways as a result of this process? What makes for successful storytelling in this form? What was it that we appreciated? What are the sorts of things that we learned here that will help us as we continue to work together? What happens when we hear others interpreting our work in ways that do not necessarily "fit" what we had in mind? How should we respond to these differing interpretations?

Western theatre traditions tend to be language-based, although newer physical and performance art forms are pushing those boundaries. The work in this chapter has been image-based and challenges participants to tell their story in nonverbal ways. The next chapter will continue this work by focusing attention of developing role through improvisation.

8.5 Questions for Reflection and Further Reading

Questions for Reflection

1. What kinds of capacities for generating and developing collective stories does embodied work such as this promote?

2. In terms of personal capacities, how are the abilities outlined below, taken from Richard Deasy's (2001) "Personal Dispositions" and Frank Barron's (1988) "Characteristics of Creativity" (see conclusion of Section 2, p. 94), developed in this work? Where do you see them happening?
    Personal dispositions:
    - Persistence and resilience.
    - Risk-taking.
    - Focus and discipline.
    - Respect for authentic achievement; that is to say, "junk" is not easily accepted.
    - A great sense of joy in the challenges; a delicious sense of achievement in the effective completion of the task (see Morgan & Saxton, 1994/2006, p. 10).
3. In what other ways could these personal characteristics be useful within an applied drama project as either tools for planning and reflection, or as potential tools for assessing a project?

Further Reading

Booker, C. (2004). *The seven basic plots: Why we tell stories.* London: Continuum. The author outlines seven plot forms that he argues are found in all types of storytelling. At 728 pages in length, this book is very long but worth reading.

Saxton, J. & Miller, C. (2009). Drama: Bridging the conversations between our inner selves and the outside world. *English in Australia, 44*(2), 35–42. In arguing the case for drama to bridge all kinds of literacies and as a way to integrate curriculum, this article includes an example of using tableau and how it develops students' sense of self.

Tarlington, C. & Michaels, W. (1995). *Building plays: Simple playbuilding techniques at work.* Markham, ON: Pembroke. Searching the index of this book on "Still Image" will lead you to useful applications of tableaux in playbuilding processes.

Worvill, R. (2010). From prose peinture to dramatic tableau: Diderot, Fénelon and the emergence of the pictorial aesthetic in France. *Studies in Eighteenth Century Culture, 39*, 151–170. An interesting read for anyone who wishes to know the history of tableau in European theatre practice.

CHAPTER NINE

IMPROVISATION

9.1 Learning to improvise

We have already been improvising throughout the drama structures in previous chapters. When language is necessary, people speak in spontaneous ways; this is how we live our lives. However, up to this point, the ways we have improvised have been somewhat constrained and always shared. With role play, the work is generally done without an audience, or with the audience in role itself and therefore inside the story being explored and told. That sense of being observed is heightened with improvisation, which can make people feel inhibited as the sense of the fourth wall, of separation between improvisers and spectators, is present. What can get lost in the move from whole group role play into improvisation is the more natural sense of spontaneity, as participants feel the performance pressure to be entertaining and engaging, which can often come across as false and unconvincing. Now we can pay more attention to the need to speak as we develop the stories begun in Chapter 8. The theatrical skills called on when improvising will guide the applied drama process in this chapter.

The natural communicative urge for most people is to speak, but in drama the paradox is that speaking spontaneously and effectively is a complex task. Skilled improvisers, such as we see in shows like *Whose Line is it Anyway?* (http://www.youtube.com/watch?v=gaFQyJySGJ4) or other similar kinds of improvised performances (such as jazz ensembles) have most often spent many years training and practising the particular art form of improvisation. For an actor, the skills of improvisation are called on within the memorization and performance of a given text, because it gives him or her the ability to stay present, to focus in on what is happening in the moment, and to listen closely and respond to an acting partner in a scene. In applied drama contexts, we are dealing with participants with no inclination to perform publicly, who perhaps may be challenged with the more performance-like aspects of improvisation. Therefore, it is useful to know a little bit more about how improvising works, and how it can be adapted successfully for non-performers. The trade-off with moving into a more challenging performance form is that improvisation allows us:

- To explore relationships from a variety of perspectives
- To lose self consciousness
- To sharpen powers of observation
- To heighten imagination
- To develop clear thinking on multiple levels
- To practise concise, orderly expression
- To allow for spontaneity
- To investigate in a safe environment
- To search for meaning

All of the structures we have been working on have had their own challenges; the ability to improvise such that participants feel good about the work, brings with it a tremendous sense of achievement and joy in the process.

9.2 Vocabulary of improvisation

The two building blocks of theatre are *mimesis* and *poiesis*. Mimesis is "the imitative representation of nature or human behaviour" ("Mimesis," 1986, p. 979) hence the words mimicry, mime or the mime (an old word for actor), or imitation. Mimesis is what anthropologist Victor Turner (1982) calls the "faking" (p. 93). Poiesis is the act of creating ("Poiesis," 1986, p. 1183)—hence the words poet, poem, poetry and poetic. This is what Turner (1982) calls the "making" (p.

> In the improvisation of telling, we make hundreds of literary choices: which specific details are critical; which are not directly relevant but add good colour; which symbols evoke just the feeling we wish to elicit; which elements can be cut. We shape those textual choices with promptings from intuition and memory, from our personal tastes and previous experience.
>
> – Eric Booth, 1999, p. 151

93). While both mimesis and poiesis are part of theatre, they are not equal. For once the "faking" has been polished in rehearsal, it is *being in the moment as the action is happening* that is what gives a performance its "live" quality. Poiesis is what "frees us into invention" (Bolton, 1989, n. p.) so that each moment is lived through on stage as if it were happening (or being made) at that moment (which, in point of fact, it is). It is poiesis that makes the faking true, and is what we are making and doing as we improvise.

Other terms important to introduce as part of the vocabulary of improvisation (all of which are used in action in the workshop structure in this chapter) are:

1. The Givens: The Who, Where, When, What, Why and How: the building blocks of any dialogue
2. Status: The power relationships between two or more people that can fall anywhere between very high to very low status (and can shift within a scene)
3. Space: Space is something waiting to be filled; it can also refer to the energy field that surrounds people, so space is intimately connected to status
4. Offers: The moves, gestures and/or words that are made and/or said by others in an improvisation
5. Blocking: Refers to the tendency to refuse offers (refusing to speak, saying "No" to a suggestion made, etc.) that are made and will shut down even the most enthusiastic and positive improviser

It is good practice as facilitator in instructing these tools to offer a task that the participants can expand upon in reflection, to find their own definitions. For example, if you ask participants to decide upon where they are (the setting), including details such as time of day, season of the year, and so on, they will grasp the notion of the given circumstance of setting as they reflect on how the choices they made affected the work. In addition, the fluidity and flexibility of improvisation is such that any one or more of the "givens" can be changed, which will in turn shift what happens in the improvisation every time it is revisited.

9.3 Ways to improvise

It is a natural human tendency to want to plan before doing, particularly so in the initial stages of improvising, as everyone likes to have some control. However, too much planning can kill an improvisation before it begins. It is sufficient to say, "Two people meet in the dead of night." Those givens of Who and When are enough to begin an interesting improvisation, with no prior planning. Still, within each of the six Givens, lie worlds of possibility. So, when improvising, players may work with any one, some or all of The Givens. Each of the first three Givens offer a range of possibilities upon which the player may draw. For example:

WHO: (The **Role** or **Character**) may include such biographical details as:

- age
- language (both socio-cultural and vocabulary)
- attitudes
- points of view
- profession

- experience
- status (in the public eye)
- status (one's own sense of self, values etc.)

There is nothing to prevent participants from playing roles that are cross-gender, cross-cultural, cross-generational, because we are in an as-if world; the only task is to make these choices believable.

WHERE: (The **Setting**) can be considered in the following ways:
<u>Specific</u> Where: Exact location (e.g. in a chair)
<u>Particular</u> Where: Locus of placement (e.g. in a chair on a front porch)
<u>Situational</u> Where: Relation to surroundings or "the view from here" (e.g. a busy street)
<u>General</u> Where: In what surroundings are we placed or "the view from above" (e.g. this chair is on a front porch that looks out onto a busy street in a largish town in the interior of British Columbia)
The moment we decide upon something like "British Columbia," we know a great deal more about the Where in its more universal sense.

WHEN: (The **Time Frame**) is an extremely important component of improvising in that it will provide a "here and now" that can be related to "what happened back then" and "what may happen (sooner or later) next."

Public
<u>Clock time</u>: The hour of the day or night (e.g. just before noon, which is almost lunch time)
<u>Week time</u>: The day of the week (e.g. Tuesday is Visitor's Day)
<u>Annual time</u>: The calendar year (e.g. 1939 holds different experiences from 1999 or from 2399)
<u>Historical time</u>: The era or age in which we are placed (e.g. the Renaissance, The Dirty Thirties)

Personal
<u>Simulated age</u>: The age of your role or character (e.g. the age of your "who" may require additional years of which you (as yourself) have no experience, it may require you to take away years of experience that you (as yourself) have had but your character has not yet had.
<u>Time of life</u>: The period of your life (e.g. these are your "golden years"; the Queen's "*annus horribilus*"

Personal time: When do you function best—or worst? (e.g. I really am a morning person!)

Physical time: The age you are by the age you feel (e.g. don't be deceived by the way you think you see me. I have the appetites of a young man!)

Time before: Experience and history of the role (e.g. Oh, I know all about that! Been there, done that!)

Time after: Possibilities, hopes, dreams for the role. Also your own knowledge of the future from the script, story or plan (e.g. that which must be withheld as one works in the moment but may be implied in a subtle way—what the Greeks called foreshadowing)

Simultaneous time: Those events and happenings that are occurring within the present (e.g. he is already packing the car, even as we speak)

Note: In both the Where and the When, there can also be the realization of one's length of life span in terms of the whole of time as it has been constructed since the birth of the universe. The recognition of one's place in terms of the view from space may be useful when considering one's status—both in life and in improvising!

WHAT: (The **Plot** or a **part of a Plot**) is about what is happening in this improvisation or scene (e.g. we are talking about the weather as we wait for visitors—the physical action will be apparent as we go about our "waiting.") Every improvisation will have a What. In spontaneous improvising, the What often emerges only in reflection after the initial improvising has stopped. In improvising on or from a source or script, the What is readily apparent (or at least, it should be).

WHY: (The **Meaning** or **Theme** that lies beneath the What) is what drives the improvising and the situation. This is the subtext of the scene that is being created or explored (e.g. "Are they going to come this Tuesday? They didn't come last Tuesday. I don't want Bill to know that I am worried about this. I'll talk about the weather.") As a play develops and the actions accrue, the deeper Why begins to emerge; this is what Bernard Beckerman (1979, p. 141) refers to as "the dramatic action": a river of meaning that flows along gathering power and contained between the banks of the playwright's (or improvisers') greater meanings (e.g. the extraordinary loneliness of those who are "warehoused" in facilities for the aged and the importance of caring)

HOW: (The **Method** by which something is achieved) appears to be a directive that would mediate against spontaneous improvising. It is, however, often a great stimulator to creative work because it acts as a constraint (e.g. you are very worried but you must not allow this to show in any way; you have a hearing problem in your right ear; you are in pain in some part of your body; as you improvise, you will discover where the pain lies). Often, in improvising, the How may be a technical instruction (e.g. improvise without using words; move on with the improvisation but look for opportunities for silences). Not all the Givens are required for an improvisation. Indeed, the purpose of improvisation is to discover one or more of these when provided with only some of them.

We have often struggled with students in our educational drama teaching practice who are unwilling (or even unable) to get on their feet and dive into an improvised scene without pre-planning ("I'll say this, then you do that"). The goal of the structure we offer below is to build participants' confidence in jumping into spontaneous improvisation with a degree of pleasure, rather than frozen by anxiety. One technique that we rely on is to have improvisations happen simultaneously by pairs or in small groups, all working at the same time. This relieves the performance pressure that happens when two participants are put in front of a group and watched closely as they try to improvise. Another technique is to keep improvised scenes quite short (see *Sitting-Down Drama*, Chapter 5). It is enough for improvisers to go for a minute or so, but not to feel they need to keep pushing and pushing, which often becomes both unproductive and uncomfortable. While you may feel you are interrupting the process, in fact your participants will be grateful to have the chance to step in and out of improvising, to reflect as they build their skills. This is not unlike children's dramatic play, where they will pop in and out of the dramatic situation with regularity to adjust the direction of the story they are making.

9.4 Drama structure: *Improvising from a Source*

The dramatic process offered in this structure is designed to be quite technical at first, in order to help participants understand how working with the Givens can shift what happens when layered into a simple improvised dialogue one at a time. We then move into small group improvisations around the theme of unhappy families, drawing on the work of our colleague Warwick Dobson. Dobson uses the opening line of Tolstoy's 1877 *Anna Karenina* as a powerful source for dramatic investigation.

1.a. Preparing for the work

- **Grouping: Whole Group in a circle**
- **Strategy: Game, Pass the Object**
- **Administration: An object such as a pencil, a scarf, a ball**
- **Focus: To be able to transform a recognizable object through imagination into something it is not, yet is equally recognizable; to accept offers**

<u>Facilitator</u>: I am holding something I'm sure you all recognize. Using our imaginations, we can turn this into anything we wish. Watch carefully as I transform this object; if I do this well enough, you should be able to tell me what it is I have made. How I use the object is an important part of how you will be able to recognize what I've changed it into, so be sure to use your object when it comes to you.

Let me know you understand what it is I've done by nodding your heads for Yes, or shaking them for No. If one person is shaking his or her head that means I need to do it again and do it better until everyone sees what it is. [*Demonstrate two or three transformations.*]

Now I'm going to pass this object to my left and you will change it into something else and the person to your left will nod when they know what it is, or shake their head if they are confused, in which case you'll try to make it clearer. And so on around the circle. Any questions? If you can't think of an idea, you may of course simply pass the object to the next person. Off we go.

Variations on this game can be to add a sound to the action in a second round. Another variation is to work with a different object. Again, you might want to demonstrate once or twice before passing it on. It is sometimes useful to change directions, or to cross the circle to begin at another point in the circle. If the group is large, you might want to establish the game and then break the group into two smaller circles. Of course, if you are working with a group of people who don't share your language, this is a great game which can be done without any instructional words at all, but simply by demonstrating.

What does this game tell us about what we need to do to help others see what we see? What is it that people do that helps us believe that the object has been transformed?

1.b. Preparing for the work

- **Grouping: Whole group in a circle**
- **Strategy: Game, What R U Doing?**

- **Administration: None**
- **Focus: To concentrate on passing an activity on while maintaining a different one; to accept offers**

Facilitator: This game needs a little preparation. I'd like you to think of a simple daily activity that you can show us and keep repeating for a bit of time. Pick something you feel comfortable doing in public. Can someone give me an example? [*Stirring a pot, washing your face, vacuuming, walking the dog, etc.*] Now, I'm going to go into the middle of the circle and begin an activity that I will keep doing until someone is brave enough to step into the circle and ask me, "What are you doing?" [*Mimes swinging a baseball bat, participant steps in and asks the question.*] I'm shopping in a grocery store. As soon as I say this, you must immediately begin shopping in a grocery store, and keep shopping until someone else comes in and you have answered the question "What are you doing?" by offering them the daily task you earlier prepared in your mind and kept ready to pass on. So, the challenge of the game is a bit like rubbing your stomach and patting your head at the same time, as you need to be doing one thing while saying another. Try to keep doing whatever task it is you've been given while you answer the question. Don't let the task you are doing drop until the person replacing you has begun doing what you've told them to do. Any questions about how the game works? As we get better, we should be able to go a bit faster as well, which makes the game all the more fun.

Play the game as long as there is a volunteer who steps in. Be sure to encourage participation but keep it voluntary.

Talk to the person next to you about the challenges of this game. Two things we work with when we improvise are power and respect. How does this game help us see and negotiate those notions?

2. Entering the work

- **Grouping: In pairs**
- **Strategy: Improvisation**
- **Administration: Chairs for each person**
- **Focus: To explore the possibilities that become available for improvisation when using any, all, or some of the Givens**

Facilitator: Please find a partner and take you chairs to a space in the room where you can work together without interfering with anybody else. We're going to look at some of the ways in which we can become more effective improvisers. So I'm going to begin by asking you to have a conversation with your partner. [*If anyone asks, "What about?"*] You may talk about whatever you like. Ready? Begin.

[*After 30 seconds or so*] Stop. Just talk to your partner about that experience. Good, we won't talk as a whole group about that yet. Next task: add fifty years or so years to your present age. [*If working with seniors, ask them to take off thirty or forty years.*] I'm going to ask you to talk to your partner again, but this time as if you were fifty years older [*or thirty or forty years younger*] than you actually are. All right?

[*After about a minute*] Stop. Talk to your partner about how that experience was different from the first one. Any thoughts you'd like to share with everyone about the differences between talking as yourself and talking as if you were a different age?

What you are looking for in reflections is that pairs had more to talk about when their age changed.

So who you are, just in terms of your imagined age, provides conversational material. Let's see what happens now when I ask you to keep that "as if" age and let's give ourselves a Where. You and your partner are sitting on the porch. You might want to rearrange your chairs, or think of them differently in some way. Now you have a view in front of you, and this Where also gives you something behind you, some kind of structure. I'm not going to ask you to decide together the details of this Where, but to listen to the offers each of you is making in this improvisation, which will give you a clearer idea, probably about a number of things. Ready? Off you go.

Stop. So, talk together about where you are and what you learned about where you are. Come to an agreement about where these conversations are actually taking place. This will of course depend on what you talked about in terms of your view. Perhaps things will become clearer as I give you a time When this conversation is taking place. Let's say it's five o'clock, an interesting time of day. If you're in a hospital, that may be when you are served your dinner. On the other hand, for others it may be cocktail hour, or when someone comes home from work, and so on. Just before we begin, think about who you are, where you have agreed to be, and now what time of day it is. When you are ready, continue your conversation.

Stop. At this point you should have a beginning sense of who you are in this situation, and who your partner is as well. The three Givens we've been working with—the Who, the Where and the When—have probably begun to give you a sense of who these people are by adding [*or subtracting*] years. Talk to each other out of role about how you are seeing each other, what are you noticing about each other that's different from the norm? In improvisation, all these things help you develop your roles. We could have come at this work in another way by starting with the time of day (or season of the year), the When, or a location (a Where) and let those decisions determine Who is speaking.

Let's shift away from the Ws of the Givens for a moment and look at How operates as a Given in improvisation. I'm going to tell you how you're going to do something while maintaining everything else we've established. But one of you is hard of hearing, whatever that may mean, but not stone deaf as that would block the improvisation. Take a moment and decide which one of you will be this person. Got it? Right, I'd just like to remind you that the degree of your disability is a matter of choice, and we all know there are people who can hear perfectly well and choose not to.

Stop. Talk together about how that went.

Anybody want to add anything they discovered or that they want to say to the whole group?

Let's do the same thing again, but this time at some point you will get out of your chairs and we will discover that the other person in each pair has a mobility issue of some kind (arthritis, bad knees, lack of balance). By the end of this improvisation, only a couple of minutes as usual, you will both be up and moving.

Stop. Talk together about what happened this time. Now here in preparation for what is to come, I'd like you to find another pair and arrange your chairs so that you are all together on that porch. Share your Where with each other and choose one of them to continue working with.

This time, I'm going to tell you What your conversation may be about, because whether you choose to talk about it or not, this will be what is in each person's mind. You have been told that there has been a new pill created that will prolong life, certainly by 20 years, if not more. This pill will not make you any younger than you are, and will not cure anything that is a present health issue, although of course the gift of extra time may provide chances to find cures in the future. Each of you has been invited to be a part of this clinical trial, and the application forms to join the trial must be signed by tomorrow at noon. Any questions? [*If someone asks, "Are there any side effects?"*] Not as far as we know, but it is a clinical trial. Hopefully, no one is offering you anything that is not good for you.

Your job here is to remain quite neutral but to not diffuse the tension of this situation. Be sure not to take too many questions, just enough to prompt some possibilities.

Facilitator: I'd like you to begin without feeling like someone has to talk right away. Try to let the conversation build out of a silence as you're looking at the view. As we did in *Sitting-Down Drama*, someone may want to volunteer to speak the first line, or you may choose to just let that happen. It's up top you. Everybody ready? Begin.

[*After three minutes*] Stop there. Just talk together about that.

Is there anything anybody wants to say to the whole group? Did you hear something or say something yourself that surprised you or concerned you?

Let's talk in your groups about the experience as improvisation. You might want to discuss how your role has grown and changed or how the Givens have affected what you improvised and the ways you did so. You might want to talk about the challenges and the pleasures of improvising: what were the moments that were working really well and what were things that seemed to get in the way?

Let's open this conversation up to the whole group. What came up in your group that you'd like to share?

3. Engaging in the work

- **Grouping: Groups of four**
- **Strategy: Improvising from a source**
- **Administration: Chairs in groups of four and small tables or boxes if available and/or needed**
- **Focus: To further explore spontaneous improvisation, working with the Givens, to explore a source**

Facilitator: Now we've got the tools with which we can improvise [*you may want to review them*], so let's first make new groups of four. Try to form a group with three other people you haven't worked with yet. Take your chairs with you.

Right. This improvisation is a little bit different because we're going to be working from a source and because we're going to do a little pre-planning before we improvise, just to make sure we're all on the same page. Listen to this quote:

"The other night I ate at a real nice family restaurant. Every table had an argument going."

I'm going to read it once more, for the last time, so be sure to listen very carefully. [*If someone asks for the source of this quote, it is from George Carlin. Avoid identifying him as a comedian, as that may shape the improvisation too much.*] The first task is to arrange your chairs so you can believe you're in a family restaurant; it could be a booth, a round table, a square table. Make that arrangement now.

Now I'd like you to stand together away from those chairs and make the following decisions. It's a family restaurant and the four of you are members of the same family. Decide who you are – what role you are taking on. Remember there are many different kinds of families and family members may be from different age groups and relationships within a family, so that the four of you might not all live together. What is the occasion that brings these four people together? What time of day is it and therefore what meal are you having: breakfast, brunch, lunch, dinner, afternoon tea or a late night supper?

Just move a little bit further away from your table and the improvisation begins when you start to move toward your own table. As you approach the table, remind yourself of the quote we're working with [*you may want to repeat it*]. Let's see how things develop.

Stop. Whatever that family argument is going to be about, the seeds may already be there, let it develop form this point on. Remember that every family is present in this restaurant at the same time and that you can see and hear each other. It is a public place. Continue from where you left off.

Stop. Step out of role for a minute. Talk to each other about what's happened so far. What do you now know about this family that you didn't know before? How authentic, true to life, was this scene as you look back on it? What made it so, or not so? How did the status of the various relationships in this family work in this improvisation? Were there any shifts in status (if, for example, a family secret was revealed)? In an argument, when the tendency of people is to want to block the dialogue, how did you keep the scene going? How was silence used as a dramatic element, if at all?

We're almost out of time. I have one more task. In a moment I'm going to ask you to go back into your scenes and, without talking, to take a position that reveals as much as possible the truth of this family argument and how you, in role, feel about it. Counting down from 5, 4, 3, 2, 1 … Freeze.

Repeat the quote and have groups look at each other as snapshots of the family arguments going on in this restaurant.

Now we know the tools that will help us to improvise. We've seen some pretty powerful ideas at work. Has anybody any further comments or questions to add?

It is useful, if the opportunity arises, to point out that none of the work we did here provided solutions or resolutions to the tensions, problems, or decisions that were being explored. Closure is not necessary in improvisation, what is important is that participants see the values of exploring without the necessity to find answers. It is the questions that are raised about human behaviours (the Why) that are essential, rather than finding "neat" endings.

9.5 Questions for Reflection, Suggested Activity and Further Reading

Questions for Reflection

1. What have you learned about improvisation after conducting this work-shop? What else do you need to learn? Where are you going to go to find out more?
2. People often see improvisation and theatresports as one and the same thing. However, there is an enormous difference between the two. What are these differences? Why is simultaneous improvisation, as seen in this workshop structure, arguably the more appropriate form in applied drama settings?

Suggested Activity

Quotations can be a powerful resource as catalysts for dramatic process. You can begin to create your own compendium of sayings, quotations, images, poems, songs, etc., from which participants can improvise. You can also encourage participants, especially if they come from diverse backgrounds, to bring in sources with which to work.

Further Reading

Barker, C. (1977/2010). *Theatre games: A new approach to drama training* (2nd ed.). London: Methuen. This new edition of a classic text comes with a DVD video of Barker teaching some of his games. Filled with great and effective activities.

Christensen, C. A. (2005). Crossing boundaries and struggling for language: Using drama with women as a means of addressing psycho-social-cultural issues in multi-cultural context in contemporary Copenhagen. In P. Billingham (Ed.), *Radical initiatives in interventionist and community drama* (pp. 55–70). Bristol, UK: Intellect. An excellently laid-out drama process with improvisation as its key strategy. The chapter addresses the issues of working in an NGO-funded context where language, self-identity and self-efficacy are the goals.

Foreman, K.J. & Martini, C. (1995). *Something like a drug: An unauthorized oral history of theatresports* Red Deer, AB: Red Deer Press. A lively history that speaks to the original non-competitive use of theatresports for training purposes.

Frost, A. & Yarrow, R. (2007). *Improvisation in drama* (2nd ed.). New York: Palgrave MacMillan. This text surveys the key practitioners in the field of dramatic improvisation and how these practices are used in actor training.

Spolin, V. (1986). *Theatre games for the classroom: A teacher's handbook.* Evanston, IL: Northwestern. A valuable companion to Spolin's *Improvisation for the Theatre* (1963/1983) that is organized to be teacher-friendly.

Note: Many practical improvisation activities may be found in a range of drama education texts. A valuable list of key texts is available here:

http://www.theatrebooks.com/drama_education/improvisation.html

Theatrical vocabulary

The final group of drama workshops in this section expands the perspectives around what is possible when working through dramatic process. Here, we are inviting participants to take their individual and shared interests and issues and move them into processes that involve crafting monologues, dialogues, and simple yet effective presentation pieces. Our focus here is to move a few more steps along the Drama ←→ Theatre continuum by consciously beginning to employ a slightly more theatrical vocabulary throughout these structures. The use of language employed by the facilitator in this section highlights how the refining processes of devising and rehearsal, akin to theatre practice, help to instill a sense of artistry in participants. The very process of refining, honing and making artistic decisions often generates within participants an interest in sharing the work with others beyond the group itself. While none of this work needs to be shared beyond the group, the option becomes available to invite a selected audience in to view what has been created. So, this section aims to begin the lifelong process of developing an "artistic eye" that can discern what is more dramatically effective out of the material being generated. Up until now, things like finding the focus, knowing when to stop, that anything has a beginning, middle and an end, have been informally indicated in the workshop structures. And one of the facilitator's questions has often been, "How might we make this different? Better? Shift it into a new direction or point of view?" Now we begin to focus more on the How of What we are doing, and to begin to explore the Why in ways that make the meaning and the sense of it even more powerful. All of the work done so far has most likely had moments that everyone felt were working well, when a shared sense of emotional power or changed understanding was experienced. The structures in this section aim to assist participants in developing their abilities to both create, and recreate, such moments. This is the heart of dramatic process wrought into theatre.

Dealing with challenges/personal dynamics/material

At this point in the process, a facilitator needs to reflect on the social health of the group before moving forward into more challenging work. From a skills perspective, any or all of the previous structures may be repeated as variations on a theme if it is felt by a facilitator that the group still needs to build basic skills in dramatic process. One of the pleasures of working though drama is that a process will never be, can never be, exactly the same way twice! However, from a social health perspective, this stage in the workshop process is most likely a very good time to carry out an assessment on how well the group is functioning. Some questions for reflection along these lines are:

> When you come to make a play, you will not want a group that biases its investigation. Each situation will have its own ethos, its central spring. A sensitive group will respond to this, a biased group will twist it and bend it to itself.
>
> – Brian Clark, 1971, p. 48

- What kind of conduct do I see in the participants?
- What is my response to this conduct; in other words, what kind of conduct tends to delight or irritate me? For what reasons?
- What is a list of things that I find "comfortable vs "uncomfortable" and how do I address these personal biases?
- How can I build on what I see to be effective and change what appears to be conduct that is disruptive or even harmful to the overall social health of the group?
- How much of any behaviour that I am not comfortable with has to do with me? What challenges do I need to address in my facilitation as a result?
- How much negative behaviour has to do with situations or contexts beyond my control? And, if I feel things are beyond my control, how do I engage the group in working on these issues before moving forward? From whom might I need to seek help (sponsoring organization, support institution, partners)?

People become involved with an applied drama group for all sorts of reasons. There are of course those participants who have been told they are participating; i.e. somewhat less than voluntarily as with incarcerated youth, for example. In those cases, collaborating with an assistant facilitator skilled with working with this population is always best practice. Occasionally, however, you may encounter a voluntary participant whose own issues can create disruption or even serious emotional upset within a group. If you are working independently as a facilitator and this situation arises, our recommendation is to deal with the problem with as much additional support as you can locate. Dealing with someone who may have mental health challenges, or who may be seeking a more therapeutic experience than you are willing and able to offer, needs to be handled with great sensitivity and care. Some situations, with the best effort in the world, can only benefit in the end from the departure of a participant. Whether this participant chooses to leave him or herself, or is asked to leave, the facilitator will probably feel guilty or a sense of failure. However, if the situation has been handled with tact and care, the better social health of the group is what is important.

One more consideration in terms of dealing with the group dynamic is to be aware that the presence of a co-facilitator or assistant from the sponsoring organization might alter how a group, or an individual, expresses themselves. For example, a youth social worker involved with a group of juvenile offenders can be seen as being in a "power-over" relationship with the participants. How does that person's presence affect the group and their perceived freedom of expression? What might their absence accomplish? These quickly become complex ethical questions as well as practical ones. The effectiveness of the work is always reliant on the space created and maintained by the facilitator whose responsibility is to maintain a safe, open, respectful and non-judgmental space for participants' ideas, interests and needs.

Yet another level of challenge is in the material generated by an individual or the group. The old mantra of speech communications courses was that students could talk about anything they liked, as long as it did not involve religion, sex or politics. In applied drama contexts, this is never the case! How does a facilitator develop tolerance for diverse perspectives, including ones that may challenge or contradict deeply held beliefs? How does the drama contract (Chapter 3.2, p. 32) assist both facilitator and group members when encountering challenging material? The facilitator's skill lies in being able to ask the kind of questions that help participants to dissent in ways that are respectful and useful. This approach both models and asks participants to think critically about their dissent and to take the responsibility to articulate what it is that concerns them. Often, moments of difficulty can evolve into powerful dramatic moments, but the process required to move from a negative to a more tolerant response cannot be skipped. The journey through the careful discussion and processing of these challenges can be the destination itself.

> Through the discipline of theatre we can practice acting rationally rather than reacting emotionally when our buttons are pushed. The more we understand just what triggers our emotions, the better equipped we are to stay in control of the situation and ourselves at all times.
>
> – Patricia Sternberg, 1998, p. 40

In the chapters ahead, as we make artistic choices, we are also engaging in the process of valuing. With valuing comes devaluing—we always warn our students that up to 90% of their improvised input in a playbuilding process will end up on the cutting room floor—and therefore the issues we have raised in this introduction will definitely be a part of what is to come. In Chapter 10 we break out of our workshop structure somewhat to present a range of possibilities in taking research materials and working dramatically with them. In Chapter 11 we return to a workshop structure that builds monologues from a literary source as a model of how to create monologues. In Chapter 12 we focus on how to develop scenes and Chapter 13 looks at the process of polishing, presenting and engaging with invited audience members. To create a through line connecting these chapters, we have chosen the topic of crime in the community, as this issue could be of potential interest to many participant groups. Of course, any group will need to determine its own focus, and we point the reader back to Chapter 8.4 (pp. 111–119) for an effective way to select a topic or issue.

10.1 Deciding to share the work

Devising, also known as playbuilding or collective creation, is a dramatic process. However, it is a process with a product in mind, that of some kind of shared performance as an outcome. That outcome may be as limited in its audience as one or two invited guests—perhaps funders—and a few scenes. As the continuum moves from dramatic process toward presentation, it is never disengaged from the process of drama which is akin to the rehearsals that precede performance. Devising is very demanding work, asking participants to wear many hats as actors, directors, designers and playwrights. Facilitators have the most demanding job of all, in juggling these many roles and supporting and guiding participants as they begin to piece together monologues, scenes, movement sequences, sound, light, costumes, props and perhaps even sets, into some kind of theatrical event.

This chapter tackles the research and exploration phases of a devising project. Participants will be asked to conduct some kind of research and bring materials into the workshop to explore together through drama. We offer multiple ways to explore different kinds of materials and invite facilitators to pick and choose amongst them.

It is our experience that as participants begin to understand how drama works, and specifically how it is working for them, they may begin to show some interest in wishing to share their work. There is also often a growing appreciation in participants that watching the work of others can be as engaging and informative as doing their own. This creates an opportunity for a facilitator to begin to focus on the artistic development of participants. Such questions as, "What did you like so much about that?" invite participants to begin to develop an aesthetic appreciation of dramatic process. With this development, artistic criteria for success also can be explored in terms of seeing what elements and qualities make the work more effective. Critical responses need to be carefully facilitated such that creator/performers can hear opinions without feeling overly vulnerable or judged. When speaking about something that created discomfort or offense, facilitators can assist participants in expressing difficult opinions in constructive ways. A facilitator dealing with participants who may wish to air negative responses may wish to remind respondents that comments should assist creator/performers toward improvement of their work.

10.2 Conducting research and the RSVP Cycle

Unlike students in schools and universities, who are motivated by the need for grades and credits, community participants may not do their "homework" and often for very good reasons. Participant groups have busy lives, and may have little access to or knowledge of community resources. Therefore, our process here begins with addressing that challenge. Inviting guests in to speak with the group about the issue under investigation may be good option, with the condition that participants are comfortable with the presence of outside visitors. Other resources such as web-based information, film, video, and so on, may also be valuable to draw upon. Photographic and other visual images make terrific catalysts for dramatic process, as do objects of various kinds, some of which may become essential props along the way. For an investigation centred on crime in the community, as we will be working on here, objects such as handcuffs, a prop knife (that is, plastic and not dangerous), a rape whistle, a liquor bottle, a spray paint can, and so on, may all be useful for a facilitator to have on hand. However, keep this open as once participants see the possibilities, they will often bring in other materials.

As the facilitator and group gather research and materials on their chosen topic, exploration can begin. Facilitators have many options available at this point. Circling back to some of the structures and skills from earlier workshops, but repeating them with a new focus, is one option. So, for example, a group may wish to conduct a sitting-down drama based on a news article, or an image, or even an object. Or, they may wish to create tableaux sequences based on a source. Taking a close look together at the gathered resources, and discussing the possibilities that participants see in them, is also a valuable activity. Groups can often get bogged down in this discussion, however, as people easily begin to talk at cross-purposes, with very different points of view. This can lead to a feeling of frustration that nothing is being accomplished; yet these conversations are vital to the process. That said, a facilitator must handle these preparatory discussions with dexterity and diplomacy, valuing all input and mediating carefully when opinions are at odds with each other. Knowing when to pause the discussion and to move back into dramatic process, is key. Talking can feel safe and comfortable for participants, and they can talk ideas to death without ever putting them on their feet. Facilitators need to resist this risk of inertia and encourage participants to get up and put their ideas into action—not with a view to polishing but rather as exploratory sketches.

The RSVP Cycle, developed by dancer/choreographer Anna Halprin and her husband Lawrence Halprin (Halprin, 1995, pp. 48–52), is a very useful model for groups to guide their discussions and the resulting processes. This model allows creative process to move forward, rather than get bogged down, and helps participants see more clearly what it is they are talking about. Here is our adaptation of the RSVP Cycle for an applied drama context:

> **R is for Resources,** whatever materials are available and under consideration by a group, including human resources. Discussions on Resources are discussions and examinations of the potential that lies in the materials gathered. This may include a sorting process of selecting resource materials by noticing which ones have particular dramatic possibilities. Focusing on each item's dramatic potential is more productive than whether everyone "likes" it or not. It is quite possible that a participant may choose to shift to Valuing for a moment, because they have an idea about how a resource might be useful dramatically. Understanding and identifying when a participant is moving to a different point on the RSVP Cycle makes the discussion clearer for all involved.

> **S is for Scripting/Scoring,** and focuses on ideas the group has around how to use Resources as dramatic material. This may involve labelling materials and organizing them into possibilities (monologues, scenes, movement sequences, choral chants, etc.), or, conversely, looking at one resource and unpacking all the possibilities that may lie within it.

> **V is for Valuing, and** is about sorting, ranking or prioritizing materials so that the group is invested in as much material as possible, and is also willing to set some (eventually most) material aside as a necessary part of the process. In many ways this is the hardest part of devising, as people understandably are attached to their own ideas. A skilful facilitator will learn how to value each person's contribution which also helps individuals and the whole group to see the "big picture."

> **P is for Performing, and** is to be used judiciously, as a way to put material on its feet for examination and discussion of its potential. The risk with performance is that it can pull the focus away from the RSVP Cycling process, which should be a continuous one. Participants can easily get caught up in the performance phase and want to begin polishing and perfecting. And it can be a trap for the facilitator who may be looking towards "proving" the work to the funders. However, keeping the focus

firmly held on the dramatic potential of the materials is a way to continue the sorting and valuing processes already underway. It is also a productive means to avoid letting either yourself or the group be "seduced" by the end results or by the tyranny of time.

The RSVP Cycle is a global plan for devising, within which groups can gather resources, figure out how to use them, decide on which ones are most effective in what order and then move the material toward some sort of presentation, if wanted. It is also an integral model for effective discussions and decision-making within a devising process. If a facilitator can help participants "see" what phase of an RSVP Cycle they are in, and when they may be working at cross-purposes, this can help move a group forward in productive ways.

It would be wise to remember never to throw anything out. Materials that all agree are not useable should be kept available because they may become the very things needed to bridge scenes, or within which there may be an idea that could be right. Working on a piece means that participants and facilitator will have filed it away mentally and when it is called upon, it is helpful to be able to be able to lay your hand on it!

10.3 Sharing research through drama

In order to anchor the work more firmly, we use "crime in our community" as the topic for the range of strategies that follow. We offer a broad selection, from which a facilitator can pick and choose to assist a group in accessing and exploring research opportunities through drama. We begin with the group itself, using a variety of strategies to uncover the prior knowledge and experience, attitudes, opinions, concerns, stories (and so on) within the group toward a chosen topic. The next level of exploration is locating resources within the community itself; local experts, articles, events, interviews, local radio and television broadcasts, etc. The final level to explore is larger, more global aspects of the chosen topic or issue. This may involve tapping into films and TV shows, documentaries, research reports, lectures, journal articles and historical perspectives. Considering future possibilities in the light of past and present discoveries is also an important aspect of research that should not be neglected.

One of the concerns that arises in devising processes is the need to talk. There is a tendency in an inexperienced group to get so engaged in the talking phase that the process can suffer, and even may die. The facilitator's task is to know when to move the group out of discussion and encourage them to begin dramatically exploring materials. As noted above, this exploration can happen while accumulating resources, sorting them for their potential and how valuable they are determined to be. What we offer here is a multiplicity of ways material can be explored that keep the RSVP Cycle in motion.

10.4 Drama strategies: *Working with Research in Dramatic Ways*

Resources within the group

These series of strategies aim to get at experiences, opinions and attitudes within the group toward the chosen topic or issue under exploration: "Crime in Our Community." Of course, how a group approaches this topic is entirely dependent on their make-up; youth, senior citizens, new immigrants, and so on, will all have very distinct attitudes and ideas on this important topic.

What do we know?
1. Storytelling
- Stories can be told from the perspective of instigators, victims or witnesses.
- Stories can be told from past, present and/or future perspectives.
- Stories can be told in large or small groups, or in pairs.
- Stories can be told by an individual or can be co-constructed in pairs, or in small or whole groups (using one word at a time, or one sentence at a time).
- Stories can be retold by other participants from protagonist, antagonist and other points of view available within the group.
- What expertise is available within the group? How may that expertise be shared? Experts may be interviewed by the group, particularly in response to a story or stories that have been shared. (*Note: The facilitator's expertise and perspectives should be included here.*)
- Listeners respond with questions with a focus on eliciting detail for clarity (not valuing, just generating resources). Sensory details (sights, sounds, smells, textures), emotional details, details of step-by-step actions and events are all useful approaches.

2. Writing
- Stories can be written out in first, second and third person points of view.
- What expressions do we have about crime, including clichés?
- What songs or poems do we know that refer to crime?
- What books, TV shows or films do we know and how they might help us understand our topic?
- Writing can be done collaboratively as well as in individual ways. Try writing one word or one sentence at a time, passing the paper from on person to the next (or in small groups or pairs). Instructions could be to write a suicide note, or set of instructions to carry out a crime, or from a posted notice, or a few lines of dialogue from a story that has been shared.
- Imagine a library shelf filled with books on crime, fictional, nonfictional or combined genres. What are the titles of these books? Brainstorm and list these titles

with the group. How can these book titles be used for writing, storytelling and other drama activities?

3. Image Work

- Stories may be translated into tableaux.
- A tableaux sequence can be created on "Crime" and then on "Community." How do these two notions come together in a blended version?
- A group image exploration, repeated as many times as deemed valuable, involves one person entering the circle and taking a frozen position in response to the topic or issue (or to a story that has been shared). Other group members enter and become part of this image in any way they choose. Facilitators can tap-in to these images, as with tableaux, to discover inner thoughts.
- Storyboarding, creating a comic strip or cartoon, and other visual art activities can lead to image work as well.
- Comic strip "bubbles" that reveal thoughts ("I knew I shouldn't have come here!") and/or nonverbal responses (Bleahhh! Sigh. Pow!!!) can be made and incorporated into images, movement sequences and/or improvisations.

4. Movement and Sound

- Stories are retold with improvised movement, like a silent film with narration.
- A movement sequence can be created on "Crime" and then on "Community." How do these two notions come together in a blended version?
- Small groups are each given an object that may signify some aspect of the topic of crime (a prop gun or knife, or some fake money, a spray paint can, a key, a purse, a laptop or iPod or cell phone, etc.). The object is incorporated into a movement sequence that tracks the 'life' of this object from the moment it is acquired.

5. Improvisation/Role Play

- Stories are played in Story Theatre style, with a mix of narration, dialogue and action.
- Stories can be created by a Story Conductor who volunteers, with a small group or in the whole group, to stand facing the group (in a line or circle) with a baton of some kind. Conductor points at one person at a time who begins and the next person must carry on the story without interruption when the baton is pointed at them, and so on.

Resources in the community

1. Storytelling

- Who do we know who has experienced crime first-hand who might be useful to our investigation?

- Interviews carried out with community members of all ages and backgrounds on their experiences and views on crime in the community.
- Family members, colleagues, friends and acquaintances could all provide valuable information.
- Professionals such as police officers, social workers, lawyers, judges, crime reporters, corrections or prison officers, security guards, business owners, and so on, are all good sources for information through interviews.
- Interviews across a broad spectrum of cultural, gender and age diversity will create a fuller and richer understanding of the issue.
- Talking with local artists will also bring an interesting and perhaps very useful point of view to the table as well.
- What questions are to be asked? How are these questions to be developed and agreed upon?
- How will interview materials be used? If there is an intention to use any material from interviews in any kind of public performance, a release form should be drawn up and co-signed by interviewee, interviewer(s), facilitator and (if appropriate) a signatory from any funding agency involved. See Appendix F (p. 217) for sample template.
- How are these interviews to be documented? Options are note-taking, audio-taping and video-taping. How does each option shift the possibilities?
- How does each interview subject present him or herself in terms of what they were wearing, their movement or gestures, manner of speaking, overall impression?
- What was most memorable about an interview? What made those moments memorable?
- Another option is to invite community members to visit the group and share stories about their experiences with this issue of crime. Who will the group invite? What questions can be prepared in case a guest needs some gentle prompting to tell their story?

2. Writing

- What newspaper stories can be gathered, in print or online, that deal with crime on a local level?
- What other written resource materials can be found? A visit to the local library will no doubt be well worth it in this regard. A search for blogs created by community members that may address crime issues is an option.
- Interview material can be written up in monologue and/or dialogue forms. How can you use the various ways interview material has been gathered (notes, audio or video) to craft dramatic writing? How might audio or video interview material be incorporated dramatically? For example, a video or audio clip could be used

as one side of a dialogue with an actor. Clips can be paused and responded to by an actor, who can choose to agree or disagree with positions presented, or offer another perspective. It is very important to have interviewees' signed permission to make use of their voice and image in these ways.

- Interview materials can be collaged together into a choral voice activity that juxtaposes voices from the community on the topic of crime. Each participant can select quotes that are meaningful and the facilitator can invite the group to share these quotes in a number of ways. The first option is a simple hearing of all quotes around the circle, without comment. Second, ask if there is a quote that feels like a good starting and ending. Other group members add their quotes as they feel they follow in some kind of both logical and artistic pattern. Quotes may be repeated for choral effect, even by the whole group.
- Quotes may be written on strips of caption paper (long narrow strips of paper) and then organized by the whole group or small groups into dialogued scenes. This process of random scripting is very playful, yet often yields surprisingly effective results.

3. Image Work

- Use a camera to document public notices, including in the local police station (ask first!), dealing with crime issues. Graffiti is worthwhile to capture as an indicator of community.
- Documenting safe versus unsafe spaces within the community, as perceived by group members and/or interview subjects, is another good option.
- Mapping invites participants to draw their community with an eye to marking safe/unsafe locations, locations where crime has occurred, locations where people gather, and so on. This mapping can be done by either layering words and images onto a pre-existing map of the community, or can be wholly created by the group. Options for mapping include birds' eye view (from above), or street front view.
- Interview material can be processed with an eye to where in the interviews were moments that had a visual element. How might these moments be pulled out and sculpted? What gestures, facial expressions, body language can be more closely examined in still picture form?
- A collection of artefacts gathered in the community could be displayed and responded to through image, as in tableaux in which an artefact is included. These artefacts can then potentially become props in a later stage of the process.
- Interviews and/or newspaper stories can be read out loud by the facilitator, or a volunteer, with the group in a standing circle. One at a time, either going around the circle, or whenever someone feels like it, participants can step into the circle and take a frozen position in response to the stories being told.

4. Movement and Sound

- Walking maps can be created in which individual or paired participants use either a tape recorder or video camera and take a walk through the community, capturing their thoughts, stories and feelings as they travel. The focus of the walk can be on safe/unsafe locations, or some other predetermined focus, and each map becomes a "guide" to the community in a unique and personal way. These walking maps may be used as theatrical elements later on in the devising process.

- Songs that say something about your community, by local musicians, could be edited together into a sound collage that can become the soundtrack for movement sequences. Alternately, a song can be chosen that resonates well with the topic at hand and used in a similar way.

- How might some of those sculptures, created above from interviews, be moved into action?

- There are many drama games that make use of movement and contain metaphorical connections with the topic of crime. Here are some examples:

> **Hunter and Hunted**: Group is in a seated circle. Two people volunteer. One is designated the Hunter and the other the Hunted. Each person is blindfolded and moved to the inside edge of the circle, as far apart as possible. When the facilitator signals to begin, the task is for the Hunter to find the Hunted. The game may take in silence, which focuses on listening, or the group may use sound to indicate when the Hunter is getting closer to the Hunted. This sound can be fingers drumming on the floor or hands patting the thighs at various volume levels. This game raises many issues, one of which is dramatic tension. What causes the tension to build and dissipate? How does listening function in the game? With whom do your sympathies lie, and do these sympathies change and if so, how? And from the players, what was going on for them as they played the game? Finally, how does the game relate to community and crime?

> A variation of this game is called **Rattlesnake** and adds a shaker for each player protagonist, with the group in a standing circle. Shakers can be maracas, or just yogurt containers with a few dried peas or beans or corn in them. The Hunter is given only three shakes, to each of which the Hunted (Rattlesnake) must respond. In this version, the whole group remains silent but as in the original game, must be responsible for keeping the two players safe at all times. If a player strays to the edge of the circle, they should be gently turned back into the centre. If the Hunter cannot find the Rattlesnake after the three shakes are used up, the facilitator calls a stop and new players

are chosen. Reflective questions here can follow those above with the added level of how the sound created by the players changes the game.

Boal's **Enemy and Protector** (1992/2002, p. 82) game also works well with the topic of crime. The whole group walks in the space at a medium pace with the instruction to explore every part of the open space as possible. As they are walking, the facilitator asks each person to pick someone—without letting them know who is to be their Enemy. They keep walking with the focus on keeping as much distance between themselves and their Enemy at all times, without indicating who their Enemy is. After a couple of minutes, the facilitator adds the instruction to choose a second person who is their Protector. Again, this choice is secret. Now, the challenge becomes to keep walking while keeping their Protector between them and their Enemy. After another couple of minutes, the game is stopped and reflection questions can include: What strategies did you use to keep yourself safe? How did having a Protector help or hinder your sense of safety? What did you notice about how patterns of walking were shifted by the game? What does that tell us about the effects of fear in our communities and ourselves?

5. Improvisation/Role Play

- An improvised extension of Hunter and Hunted is to ask the group to pair up and to recreate as accurately as possible the search of the Hunter for the Hunted but to do it with their eyes open. The challenge is to make the tension as real as it was with the blindfolds. These tensions are going to be useful in the devising process. See Clive Barker's *Theatre Games* (1977/2010, pp. 57–61), for his description of a similar exercise he calls "The Fighter in the Dark," based on a scene found in Chinese opera.
- Based on all the research carried out in the community, participants in small groups decide on an issue that interests them, they then can choose what is, for them the most appropriate context in which to improvise: a talk show, a press conference, an academic conference, a medical consultation, a parole board hearing, a courtroom trial focusing on victim impact statements. Other possibilities can be brainstormed. Groups are then invited to share two or three minutes from their improvisations that they feel might be useful. It becomes important at this point to record what is shared in some way, through note-taking or audio/video-taping, as this material may become important as the group moves forward.
- Improvisations may also move into different genres such as a ballad, a poem, a rap, or a series of e-mails or tweets or Facebook postings.
- Role play structure: Group is seated in a circle. Facilitator has a lifelike baby doll wrapped in a blanket. Facilitator talks about the wonderful resources the group is exploring and that we're going to use these materials in a different way. The role

play begins with the facilitator passing the baby around the circle. Each person holding the baby offers a gift to the baby to help it through its life. This could be something concrete, like wealth or beauty or fame, or a quality bestowed, like courage or wisdom. The baby is returned to the facilitator who summarizes all the gifts that have been given. S/he then tells the group that this child grows up to become a criminal. Is it more likely, based on what we know, that this child would be male or female? Drawing on the materials at hand, in groups of three or four, what can we see that will help us to understand how this happened? What sorts of things might have changed the direction of this young person's life? What events in this child's life were significant in shaping the future? The task is to find an event, based on information available, that might have been the tipping point that steered this child, later in life, toward criminal behaviour. These improvised scenes can be selectively shared with the whole group for reflection and response. Again, every scene should be captured for future use.

National and international resources

1. Storytelling
- What stories can be gathered beyond the local context, at provincial or state levels, national levels and international levels? Sources can include news stories, television programs (both fictional and nonfictional), documentaries, magazine articles, websites, and so on. Websites of national and international organizations can be very useful as are such groups as Amnesty International, or other similar non-governmental organizations dealing with issues related to crime and imprisonment and human rights. Groups dealing with restorative justice, a ban on capital punishment, Mothers Against Drunk Drivers (MADD), and so on, are also good sources.
- Fairy tales make wonderful sources for stories about crime! Hansel and Gretel are abused and sent off to die by their stepmother, Rapunzel is kidnapped and imprisoned, Cinderella is enslaved and, in some versions, tortured by her stepmother and stepsisters. These stories can be retold with a focus on the element of crime. Updated versions, in which the victims seek justice from their perpetrators, is one option.
- Novels and short stories and plays are rich resources for material on the topic of crime. While all groups will have their own cultural sources to share; Dostoevsky's *Crime and Punishment*, Charles Dickens's *Oliver Twist* and Truman Capote's *In Cold Blood* are three well-known examples. In plays, *Twelve Angry Men* by Reginald Rose, *Death and the Maiden* by Ariel Dorfman and *Macbeth* by William Shakespeare, or Caryl Churchill's *Serious Money*, all tackle various aspects of

crime. For a more female dominated fictional source on crime, we note that many of the best crime writers in the world are women (Agatha Christie, P.D. James, Ruth Rendell/Barbara Vine, Sue Grafton, Donna Leon and Kathy Reichs).

- A search of video sites such as YouTube and TED Talks using the word "crime" as a search term could yield some interesting results. The number of YouTube hits on the search term "crime" is over one million. As facilitator, your job is to help your participants bring a critical eye to sorting through this mountain of material. What is being said about crime, from what perspective and with what goal in mind? How trustworthy are these sources? How does what we have found inform our local context, which is our main focus? It is easy to get pulled out into larger contexts, so it becomes the facilitator's role at this stage to keep the focus sharp and tight. In contrast, a search of TED Talks yields a much more manageable number of 20-minute videos on crime, from a very broad number of international experts in diverse fields. Selections of these videos can be used in similar ways as described above, for participants to engage with in dramatic ways.

2. Writing

Global transmigration means that most countries have very diverse populations. This diversity offers a rich and deep well of resources that will become part of any dramatic process if it to be of benefit to its participants.

- What newspaper stories can be gathered, in print or online, that deal with crime on a national and international level? What kind of relationships can be drawn between criminal activity at the local, national and international level?
- What kinds of research would intrigue participants about these potential parallels? For example, a local crime issue might be bike theft. How does this kind of crime relate to car theft on a global scale?
- What statistics on crime can you locate, and in what form are they represented? Percentages, charts, tables and graphs all present information in diverse ways. What writing could be done that responds to statistical material? How can some personal writing bring a more human context to this factual information?
- What other written material might you bring in that speaks eloquently to what it is you want to say? Sharing and selecting quotes from these additional sources can add a lot of material for the group. A facilitator can ask each group member to share a quote that resonates for him or her with the whole group. Then, the group can create a free-written response to each quote for a few minutes, timed by the facilitator. This writing can then be shared and selectively polished into potential monologues or dialogues for further development.
- Another research option is to seek an informant through social media or websites with whom participants might have an ongoing opportunity to correspond. Finding

experts with various perspectives on crime who are willing to engage with the group's process could be invaluable in terms of lending a different view on the issues.

3. Image Work

- Create a portfolio of powerful images from national and international sources. These could be newspaper photographs of actual events, or visual artworks that tackle aspects of crime and punishment and, of course, historical images from the visual arts are valuable for their very distance from our contemporary world. These images make very effective visual backdrops for monologues and scenes, with viewers making connections between the local and the global as they watch and listen.

- Screen these images for the group and devote a session or two to exploring group images created in response to the images gathered. These images can be done by the whole group or in small groups, which then share their work. The facilitator's focus is to encourage how participants can show their thoughts and feelings prompted by each image, and to also guide meaningful reflective discussion on shared images. What can be seen in the image? How is that idea made clear to us? What questions come to mind as we engage with an image? What's missing in the image that we might want to add in? Or, conversely, is there something present that we wish to make absent, to erase or take away? What is that something? What does it indicate or represent as a tension or problem, or hope that the group is carrying in regard to the topic?

- Creating a context for the work can make use of the space in new ways. This is where the work of a designer comes into play. How are we going to use the space available as a way to reflect what it is we want to say? Imaginative use of simple things such as boxes, ladders, swags of material, and so on, can carve out some key locations or settings for the dramatic material the group is generating. Even a large pile of used newspapers and rolls of masking tape can create amazingly powerful spaces. This activity of creating spaces leads to the beginning of also thinking as directors as well as designers. Costume and prop design can become an element to consider at this point as well. For example, the group might want to create a space that is confined, like a prison or detention centre. How might the group use a reconfiguring of chairs and a pile of newspapers, markers and tape to accomplish this task?

- A visual activity that also generates design material is the creation of a group collage. Each person has a large sheet of craft paper and markers or paint. The facilitator asks the participants to draw, either realistically or in abstraction (or a mix of both) their responses to the research and emerging understandings in their applied drama project. When these images are complete, the facilitator asks each person to look at their image with one hand held like a telescope, to focus in on one part of their image that captures something powerful about crime. These parts of images can be either cut out or torn away and then pieced together with everyone else's in a group collage that is displayed and can provide yet another potential backdrop.

4. Movement and Sound

- Music from beyond the local context can now be brought into the mix. This music can be responded to through movement. Be aware that mimicking music videos is never the most creative of options; rather, invite participants to interpret a piece of music in their own original way.

- A session focused on listening to a range of music from around the world, both instrumental and songs, can be discussed with a focus on how some of this music could be used as linking devices as the work goes forward.

- If there are group members with an interest and ability in making music, some time can be devoted to creating original music for the project. Participants can write song lyrics that are then composed by those who play instruments. Music can be easily recorded, even onto a computer using a program like Garage Band, if available. That said, live music is almost always preferable whenever possible, and could become a strong element of the piece the group is putting together.

5. Improvisation/Role Play

- As described above, there are many options available for the group to both improvise and role play in response to national and international stories and events that have been gathered. The facilitator should encourage the use of many kinds of dramatic genres, particularly those that may at first seem to be in tension or even direct contradiction with the topic. For example, a story of a crime can be told in a way that helps us see who may *benefit* from this action, rather than keep the focus always on who suffers as a result. This shift in focus, and resulting interesting choices of dramatic genres to show these shifts, make for a richer and less one-sided investigation.

- Second, third or fourth rounds of improvising a scene can focus on genre-shifting, or can shift the focus from one character to another. What happens when the story is replayed from the "victim's" point of view, the "bystander's" point of view, or the "criminal's" point of view? This is known as the "Rashomon effect," so-called from a famous 1950 film by Akira Kurosawa of the same name in which a murder mystery is retold three times by the three survivors, each with his/her own opinion.

All of the various options we have offered here, like a long list of recipe items to pick and choose from, enable the facilitator to keep things in motion, and not to let choices be made too prematurely, in a "set it and forget it" kind of mentality. Inviting participants to keep exploring, examining lots of creative options and opportunities, is the facilitator's main function at this stage of the process. It is important to be aware of the group's level of both energy and interest at all times.

10.5 Questions for Reflection, Suggested Activity and Further Reading

Questions for Reflection

1. How are you as facilitator going to archive what has happened and is happening within your group's process?
2. What may be the ethical implications of using archival material beyond the personal use of those involved in the project?

Suggested Activity

The discipline of maintaining a log of activities and your reflective responses to the log is an invaluable professional practice for any applied drama facilitator. How you have set up and run each session as a plan, followed by reflections on what actually happened, what worked and what didn't work, and how so, will help you move your own practice forward. You might wish to gain your group's consent to photograph moments in the workshops as part of your archive. Be sparing with the use of a camera, either a still camera or video, as it can tend to make participants "perform" for it, rather than keep their focus on the process. Judiciously used, however, photos and videos can become valuable archival elements. This is particularly important if your project is being funded by an organizational partner in terms of materials that can be drawn upon when writing a final report.

Further Reading

Billingham, P. (Ed.). (2005). *Radical initiatives in interventionist and community drama.* Bristol, UK: Intellect. Critical essays and practitioner accounts on a range of projects from a number of different countries.

Cohen-Cruz, J. (2005). *Local acts: Community-based performance in the United States.* Piscataway, NJ: Rutgers. An excellent survey of community-based theatre practice and projects carried out in the United States from the early 20th century to the present.

Cohen-Cruz, J. (2010). *Engaging performance: Theatre as call and response.* New York: Routledge. Cohen-Cruz surveys and analyzes "socially-engaged performances" that aim to respond to community needs.

Common Plants. (n.d.). Retrieved March 12, 2012 from http://www.yorku.ca/gardens/html/. Website for York University multidisciplinary intercultural performance and visual art project.

Community Arts Network (1999–2010). Retrieved March 12, 2012 from http://wayback.archive-it.org/2077/20100906194747/http://www.communityarts.net/. A multidisciplinary US-based website that is a wonderful resource for community-based artists of all kinds. News items, events, research reports, essays, and many practical resources can all be found on the Community Arts Network archive.

Goldbard, A. (2006). *New creative community: The art of cultural development.* Oakland, CA: New Village Press. Goldbard draws on her many years of social activism through the arts to envision creative communities bound together through artistic processes.

Greig, N. (2008). *Young people, new theatre: A practical guide to an intercultural process.* Abingdon, UK: Routledge. Although this book describes an international theatre exchange program, it is full of excellent ideas, activities and exercises for developing work with young people. Adaptable for most ages, it also raises the value of international exchange as a means of broadening perspectives.

Kuppers, P. (2007). *Community performance: An introduction.* New York: Routledge. This very useful resource offers a practical approach to entering into and engaging with communities through performance. A companion volume of related readings is also recommended.

McAvinchey, C. (2011). *Theatre & prison.* Basingstoke, Hants: Palgrave MacMillan. Athough this small book is directed to prisons, it is a fine example of a short, comprehensive text that offers both useful theory of "life on the other side" and is full of resources that provide a helpful model for any facilitator.

Naidus, B. (2009). *Arts for change: Teaching outside the frame.* Oakland, CA: New Village Press. Naidus writes an impassioned and well-documented case for teaching social change through the arts.

Note: For recommended books on devising, see Further Reading in Chapter 13.

CHAPTER ELEVEN
CREATING MONOLOGUES

11.1 Collaborative solo speech

In the first chapter in this section, we looked at how participants could build an extended process into a presentation that would reflect their interests. With that overall understanding, we now step back to ask participants to create monologues as an initial activity in a process that will add in scenes and transitions (the next two chapters), toward the possibility of some kind of culminating shared experience. In many ways this chapter connects to Chapter 7's focus on storytelling in that monologues are role-based stories addressed to imaginary and/or actual listeners (on stage and in the audience).

Monologues, in which one person does all the talking, are longer speeches than participants have experienced so far. This does not mean that a monologue expresses only one point of view; its interest lies in the variety of perspectives that the speaker may present as part of the argument. Monologues are valuable components in the devising process and can serve as introductions, reflections and/or as links between scenes. Perhaps one of the most powerful monologists in contemporary theatre, Anna Deavere-Smith (see citations under Further Reading) sustains a whole evening by the ways in which she weaves a whole series of differing points of view and opinions on the same subject or issue. However, here we are exploring how participants can develop their own monologues in a non-threatening and supportive collaborative process.

11.2 From the personal to the political

The intention in this monologue workshop structure is to move a group beyond personal storytelling to address larger ideas or concerns of interest to the group. As a result, a group has the opportunity to come to know more about a chosen topic than when they began. This makes the intention as pedagogical as it may be political—political in the "sense of the word as having to do with power relationships, not the narrow sense of electoral politics" (Hanisch, 2006, n.p.). Another set of intentions is to offer what is most likely a very new experience for the majority of participants: the challenge of discovering what you want say and finding a way of saying it through a sustained and shaped one-person monologue, in which the responsibility for its development may be shared. Self-efficacy is a key goal of applied drama work and the experience of moving into more theatrical modes of presentation, such as monologues, is an important step in developing a sense of one's voice—either as a group or as an individual.

Although monologues are solo-voiced, in their theatrical representation there is a need for a more dialogical reality, with a real or imaginary "listener" to whom the monologue is directed. In this kind of work, a monologue is not the product of one person alone, but is processed and shaped within and by the group, which is a political act in itself.

11.3 From nonfictional to fictional representation

All art springs from a personal place and is powered by a desire to share experience in a public space, moving from the semi-private to the semi-public to the public on the King (1978, p. 205) continuum. It is important to recognize that relatively unskilled applied drama participants understandably may wish to explore and present their lived experiences in quite a nonfictional way. That said theatre has a history, transculturally speaking, as a fictional narrative art form. Therefore, a facilitator's challenge is to support the desires of participants to tell and share their own stories, but also to offer them theatrical and more fictional modes of representation. Fictionalization will begin organically with the telling of a supposedly "truthful" story, as storytellers are subject to "the filters of memory and personal editing" (Govan, Nicholson & Normington, 2007, p. 6). A facilitator's task is to make visible to participants this process of shaping narratives in relation to our perception of the narratives of others. We adjust our stories in response to the stories of others. A facilitator sets the focus for these stories, such that participants feel more and more comfortable with moving their nonfictional narratives into more composite, imaginative and fluid co-constructions.

Aesthetic distance becomes a key concept at this stage in the dramatic process. Frozen stories, which are regarded as precious objects no one is allowed to play with or alter, are not the kinds of stories useful to this process. If a

Distancing is seen as both an aesthetic device but also as a political act—one that can enable participants, not only to be protected into imagining in ways never before thought of or considered, but through reflection on that imagining, to recognize what it is their lives are at the moment but [also], with action, could be in the future.

– Maria Zannetou-Papacosta,
2002, p. 390

story feels too close, or too "holy" or "sanctified" by a participant or the whole group, we recommend a facilitator suggest that this story be set aside. For example, a story that discloses an abusive relationship may indeed be powerful but too private and too painful for the storyteller and group to process into a dramatic monologue. A sense of aesthetic distance is required to work with a story through drama, as a sculptor works with a lump of clay. If the storyteller is at a distance, such as the distance of time, from the narrative of abuse, then the story may become a possibility for theatrical adaptation into a monologue. An effective story is open enough to allow for the layering of some fictional elements onto the story to make it feel more alive and in motion as opposed to fixed and incapable of changing its shape. We see these latter types of story as holding within them dangers of becoming narratives of victimization only, resistant to reframing or alteration. A better story, in our view, lives in the present moment but is also open to a depth and breadth of exploration, across time and space and potentialities. The collective dramatic process becomes, as a result, a way of thinking and working creatively and collaboratively to find ways of weaving multiple stories together into drama with its roots in reality but its branches, leaves and flowers fictionalized.

The political and social power of storytelling in monologue form is less about the participant and his or her story and more about how these stories, framed and presented in theatrical ways, do some work in the world.

11.4 Drama structure: *Generating and Working with Monologues*

1. Preparing for the work

- **Grouping: Whole Group, sitting in a circle**
- **Strategy: Choral Reading**
- **Administration: Copies of Raymond Souster's poem (see Appendix G, p. 219) and pencils**
- **Focus: To invest in the story presented in the poem**

Facilitator: I'm handing out copies of a poem I'd like you to read on your own in silence. Read it through two or three times so that the story of this event is clear to you.

Read through once more and this time, just take your pencil and underline those words or phrases or lines that for any reason resonate with you. I'm not going to ask you for your reasons, they are yours alone. Take a minute or so to do that.

Good. Now, we're going to read this poem out loud together. I'm going to read the whole poem at a storytelling pace that will allow you to join in with me whenever I speak a word, phrase or line that you have marked. So this is a very organic way of doing a choral reading, as everybody will have his or her own part, as we'll discover. Are we ready?

That was pretty good! Anybody got any thoughts or suggestions about how that was working? Based on what you heard, you might want to make some changes to the words you have scored, which is fine. Let's try it again. [*This can be repeated as many times as the group wishes.*]

Now let's discuss some of the ideas that are in the poem in relation to our interest in exploring the issue of crime in our community. What came up for you as we read the poem together?

This is an opportunity for the facilitator to hear some of the interests and responses that are particular to this group. Keeping all interpretive options open, not synthesizing and offering a group interpretation, is key at this juncture.

Let's make some notes on our first impressions. Just jot down in the margins or the back of your paper your responses to some prompts.

- What sort of sounds might you be hearing?
- What smells are in the air?
- What time of day or time of year is it? You might like to think of this in terms of the light and how it carves out shadows or points of focus.
- What feelings are resonating around this event? These feelings might be in the poem or could be ones you feel yourself as you read through it.
- What do you see in your mind's eye? What is the image of the event? Create a quick sketch if you wish.
- Where do you see yourself in this scene? Who else is there? Are you inside the shop? Are you outside looking through the window?
- Who are some of the people you see involved in this event? [*Let participants generate this list, do not offer these … we list options here in case participants need help: Son, Shopkeeper, Father, Shoppers, Passersby, Police Officer, News Reporter, Mother, Sibling, Friend, Grandparents, Other Family Members, Teacher, Social Worker, Counsellor, etc.*]

2. Entering the work

- **Grouping: Whole group sitting in a circle**
- **Strategy: Constellation of roles**
- **Administration: Chair and found objects to represent Boy or Father**
- **Focus: Generate inner thoughts as the beginning of monologues**

Facilitator: Whom do we see to be the protagonist in this story? [*The Father and the Boy are suggested, and one person suggests the Shopkeeper. It is agreed it is the Father.*] I'm going to place this chair in the centre of the circle to represent the Father. I wonder what we could use to help us accept that this chair stands in for the Father? [*A dark coat is hung over the back of the chair, or flung onto the chair. The group decides which option works best, and notes the difference.*] What other objects might help us to believe that the Father is here? [*Group decides if they are happy with what's there, or might add a pair of shoes, a cellphone, etc.*]

Now I'd like each of you to have a look at your list and choose one of those people that you think might be interesting to explore. What is that person's relationship with the Father? Lots of rich choices here! We've got family relationships, business relationships, friends and neighbours, and so on. Where do you stand in relationship to the Father? Just come and take this position in the room, as we did in *Being 14*.

Imagine that we are part of a constellation of planets orbiting around the Father as he is speaking with the Shopkeeper. The kind of relationship you have with him, will determine the type of orbit. In other words, you could be like the moon and have a tight, close orbit that shows an intimate relationship. Or, you can be far flung and keep your distance which tells us you might not know the Father personally at all. Or you may have a relationship that shifts, that is more like an oval than a circle, that draws you in close at times and pushes you further out at other times. Without moving, just decide for yourself the pattern of your orbit. Everybody ready?

We rarely choose to demonstrate for participants, but in this case it may be helpful. You could take on the role of the Mother in this story. If she is a caring wife in a happy marriage, her orbit will show this and she will move in quite a tight circle around the chair. If on the other hand, she and the Father are divorced and she feels bitterly toward him, her orbit will show this by the distance from him that she chooses, mindful that like him or not, they co-parent the Boy.

When I say go, just begin walking your orbit, taking care that you don't bump into others. Your speed may change depending on where you are in your orbit. What's driving you are the thoughts you are having as you either are witnessing the scene or are thinking about what's happening. Let's give that a try ... Go. [*Leave enough time for orbits to become established.*]

Good. Just stop there. Talk to the person closest to you about how that worked for you. What did you notice? Any concerns before we move on?

OK, we're going to do that again, but this time as you orbit, put yourself more firmly in the shoes of your role. As you orbit the Father, what's going on in your mind? What are you thinking about him and this situation? Let the thoughts float and you'll find that the movement will help. After a minute, I'm going to start shaking my tambourine and when I do you can let your thoughts become thinking aloud. [*Start shaking tambourine after a minute or so…*] Try to keep your thinking aloud going. Let your orbit affect your thinking.

[*After a minute*] Right, just stop where you are for a moment. I just want to layer in another level of possibility. Is there a particular memory that is triggered by this encounter with the Father? Does this event conjure up a memory for you about when you were younger, perhaps, or when you yourself had a difficult emotional experience similar to this one? When I start shaking the tambourine again, let those memories feed in to whatever it is you are thinking about out loud.

[*After another minute or two*] Good, let's stop there. Go back your own space after picking up a fresh piece of paper. As you're doing this, just begin to think back over what you've said. What do you consider to be the most significant thoughts you had? The memories that came up, or comments you made? Try and get those down on paper.

[*After five or six minutes*] Reread what you have written and you may want to choose four or five sentences, consecutive or separate, and put them together into one short passage.

3. Reflecting on the work

- **Grouping: Small groups of four or five**
- **Strategy: Editing and weaving monologues into source material**
- **Administration: Paper and pencils**
- **Focus: To work as playwrights to create a new version of the poem**

Facilitator: Find a group of three or four people to work with, and a space of your own. One at a time, share the passage you've crafted from orbiting in role. Listeners, remember how the co-pilot worked on our storytelling workshop to take in whatever is being offered by listening openly? You may ask any questions you need to in order to clarify and understand each person's short monologue. Speakers, you may wish to make changes or additions to your monologue as you listen to the feedback.

When you have heard and responded to all the monologues, just take time to reframe your monologues on the basis of the feedback and your own sense of how your presentation went—you may need another piece of paper. You'll probably need a bit of time for this, and I'll come around to listen in to see how you're getting on.

[*After twenty minutes*] How's everybody doing? Who do you still need to hear from? How much more time do you need? [*After another five or ten minutes*] Stop there please. Now, turn again to Raymond Souster's poem, and go back to your group. Your first task now, after hearing these four or five monologues, is to decide where are the breaks in the poem where you would insert each of these monologues? Each monologue needs to be fitted in. It might help to number the monologues and then decide which number fits best where in the poem.

[*After ten or fifteen minutes*] Right. Now we've got that sorted, let's try a rough read-through. You may decide how you want to read the poem, perhaps using your original scoring, or perhaps dividing the poem up using your voices in various ways. What's important is that these monologues become part of the fabric of the poem and are not seen as add-ons. There might be a line in the poem that you select to repeat chorally as an echo or an underscore.

[*After another ten or fifteen minutes*] I think we're probably ready to hear what each group has done. Just arrange your chairs in each group how you would like to have them in order to share your work. Is there a group that would like to go first? What we're interested in is hearing the different monologues that you've created and how each group has fitted them into the original poem.

[*After all the expanded Souster poems have been heard*] What have we learned about how we feel together about crime after this process? How closely does this work that we've just heard fit into our ideas about crime in our own community? Just talk to the people next to you about how our inserts worked with the poem.

What have we learned about monologues as a specific kind of theatrical speech? How are they different from stories and storytelling?

Optional extension

This extension can work on its own as a way of exploring written resources. Invite participants to bring in a newspaper or magazine article on crime of personal interest (or any other topic of shared interest). Each person chooses from whose point of view he or she will tell their story, and to whom they will tell it (to a spouse, across the fence to a neighbour, to a group of police recruits, or office colleagues, etc.). Direct quotes from the story should be incorporated into the monologue version. The improvised parts adapt the monologue to suit the imagined listeners. Each person then writes a brief intro for the facilitator to frame their monologue and to give the audience a sense of who they are. Hot-seat interviews may be carried out between the listeners and the speaker after each monologue (the facilitator may take part as a panel chair might do). Passages from fictional sources, nonfiction texts, research articles and other kinds of sources would also work well in this preliminary devising process. The original source material and monologue adaptations can be displayed or catalogued and remain available for development.

11.5 Questions for Reflection, Suggested Activity and Further Reading

Questions for Reflection

1. The word "monologue" is closely associated with a theatrical activity and it is often the bane of an actor's existence to find a monologue for an audition. But, in fact, we encounter monologues quite often. Where do we encounter monologues in our daily lives? Consider things such as newscasts, political speeches, teaching, stand-up comedy, judges' rulings, sometimes parenting, reporting on our day to loved ones, etc. And of course the world of writing beyond plays has plenty of monologues, as does the online world in its so-called "blogosphere"!

2. In this workshop, we are actually using two kinds of solo speech, *monologue* (public speech to another person or persons or directly to the audience) and *soliloquy* (private thought overheard by an audience)? Where can you point to examples of each of these types in this structure? How would you categorize the poem itself? What is the value of either of these forms as part of a performance?

Suggested Activity

The trick to making a piece of text into a monologue is to move it from a narrative past into the immediate present. Using this Aesop's fable, below, rewrite it not as a story that happened to you, but rather as a story that is happening to you as you tell it. The first sentence might then read something like this: "So here I am walking along this dusty track with my old friend George. Do you hear something, I say."

The Bear and the Two Travellers

Two men were travelling together, when a Bear suddenly met them on their path. One of them climbed up quickly into a tree and concealed himself in the branches. The other, seeing that he must be attacked, fell flat on the ground, and when the Bear came up and felt him with his snout, and smelt him all over, he held his breath, and feigned the appearance of death as much as he could. The Bear soon left him, for it is said he will not touch a dead body. When he was quite gone, the other Traveller descended from the tree, and jocularly inquired of his friend what it was the Bear had whispered in his ear. "He gave me this advice," his companion replied. "Never travel with a friend who deserts you at the approach of danger."

MORAL: Misfortune tests the sincerity of friends.

[www.aesopfables.com]

Further Reading

Beckett, S. (2009). *Krapp's last tape and other shorter plays.* New York: Faber & Faber. The first play is an post-Apocalyptic extended soliloquy, one of few in dramatic literature, that presents an elderly man who is audiotaping and listening to a collection of these tapes as the world ends.

Bennett, A. (2003). *The complete talking heads.* London: Picador. A set of 13 monologues by one of England's best playwrights. Also available on DVD from BBC Films.

Brave New Voices. (n.d.) Retrieved April 5, 2012 from http://www.hbo.com/russell-simmons-presents-brave-new-voices/index.html. This series from HBO features North American youth spoken word artists competing in regional and national competitions. Their voices are indeed brave, poetic, angry, hopeful and articulate. A marvelous model of monologues in spoken word form, especially for younger participant groups, but inspiring for all. Many videos from this series are also available on YouTube.

Deavere Smith, A. (2006). *Letters to a young artist.* New York: Anchor Books. Anna Deavere Smith is a North American monologist who has created a series of powerful theatre pieces based on in-depth interviews with hundreds of people for each performance project. This book is a series of letters about her work. Scripts of two projects are also available, *Fires in the Mirror* (1997) and *Twilight: Los Angeles* (2003). Deavere Smith presents different people with divergent points of view on an event, issue or topic. *Fires in the Mirror*, about tension between black and Jewish communities in Brooklyn, is available on YouTube [http://www.youtube.com/watch?v=hnkrUJny0CE]. Her most recent project, *Let Me Down Easy*, aired on television in January 2012, is available on the PBS website: http://video.pbs.org/video/2186573615.

12.1 Panning for gold

Scenes in plays are akin to chapters in books; scenes and chapters put together create an overarching plot structure, but also should have a beginning, middle and end in and of themselves. Crafting an effective dramatic scene from improvisations prompted by research is the focus of this chapter. This next stage of development in dramatic process invites participants to shape a satisfying scene that attends to theatrical qualities such as setting, exit and entrance points, dramatic arc and blocking. The challenge is to translate mostly prose material gathered as research on a given topic into dramatic text. The facilitator's role is to encourage participants to improvise as much as possible out of the research material and then select only those improvised scenes that participants feel have something to offer. This improvising is not done in front of the whole group, but rather is being done simultaneously by all group members. We recommend this approach as it takes away the performance pressure of improvising for an "audience"—however integral—encourages risk-taking and can generate multiple perspectives. That said, the process is a noisy and somewhat chaotic one, as everyone in the space may be talking at the same time. If you are working with a group that may not be open to this level of noise and creative confusion, you may need to strategize around finding some extra space to accommodate them.

The metaphor of "panning for gold" may be a useful way to frame this process for the group. Gold miners had to pan through plenty of sludge and mud in order to find one or two small nuggets of gold. The devising process is the same; much material will be generated that will not be used, and everyone needs to be clear that this is to be expected. At this stage although props, costumes, sound and light should not be a concern, using what is available and on-hand should be encouraged. A few sturdy black wooden boxes are ideal, as this creates opportunities both for seating and different levels. A music player will also allow participants to add background music, or even improvise to a particular song or instrumental piece of interest.

12.2 Understanding dramatic structure

This chapter introduces some new terms with which participants may not be familiar. We suggest that a facilitator begin (or continue) to use this vocabulary when setting up and processing the improvisations created by participants.

Here are some key terms:

- **Dramatic Arc:** refers to a scene or whole play as having a clear beginning, middle and ending, and identifies and tracks the dramatic tension that is being explored. An effective dramatic arc takes the players and viewers on a journey in which, at some point, someone or something is shifted or changed (see Appendix E, p. 215).
- **Setting:** the Where of any scene, should always be established in the opening moments. If a spectator is unclear around the setting of a scene, it becomes more difficult to engage with the content, so players need to decide upon (usually) one location and stick with it. Setting includes not just Where a scene happens, but also When; selecting a specific time period will definitely have an effect on the behaviour and actions of character.
- **Exits and Entrances:** a scene can start with an empty space. It can start with one person and another person entering at some point. It can start with two or more people already there. It can also end in all of these various ways. It is good practice to remind participants of these options through the improvising process, so the potential risk of scenes having a sameness about them can be avoided. Refining exits and entrances becomes part of shaping and polishing scenes that have been selected by the group for further development.
- **Blocking:** blocking is a theatre term that describes how players make use of the space. It should not be confused with how the word is used in improvisation (see Chapter 9.2, pp. 122–123). A lot of the visual interest in theatre involves creating interesting movement patterns on stage. Movement can tell the players a lot about their characters/roles, the mood being established and the conflict being explored. At the improvising stage, participants don't need to consider blocking in any detail, although considering how a character moves and what kinds of actions they engage in is part of effective improvising. In the later stages of making a presentation, the facilitator's "outside eye" can be of enormous importance both for sorting out "traffic jams" and watching to see how the movement clarifies the meanings being made for the audience.

12.3 Reviewing and reflecting on improvised scenes

The next stage of the process, following on from generating scenes through simultaneous improvisations, is to select, share and reflect on participant-chosen scenes in a more polished form. The dramatic structure that follows illustrates this process in practice; how-

Chapter Twelve
Crafting Scenes

ever there are a few additional things that a facilitator may want to keep in mind. Again, it is key to remind participants that this is not about "acting" or "performing," *per se*, but rather is about sharing each player's choices on what they feel has worked well. The focus for the group is to value what is being offered and to build constructive ideas that can move the scene forward. It is up to the facilitator to set this tone. If you have seen something being worked on and can suggest a focus for the group that is fine ("I wonder if it might be useful to pay careful attention to how the characters in this scene fail to understand each other at all?"). Alternately, you can ask each pair or group of presenters to determine what it is they'd like the watchers to attend to most. You might suggest that a scene be replayed, perhaps in a slightly different way (twice the speed, raising the emotional stakes, changing the Where, etc.). Accepting whatever suggestions are offered with an attitude of "Why not?" generates a sense of playfulness and creative freedom in the group. Maintaining a firm focus on the ideas and issues being presented, and steering away from more theatrical rehearsal types of comments, is key. This is not the stage in the process to comment on acting choices and other performative aspects of the work, as the goal is to keep the possibilities open. After all chosen scenes have been shared, it may be helpful to have a group discussion in which participants have the chance to weigh in on how they see the work going, the overall perspectives and points of view on the topic of crime that are emerging. The polishing and preparing stage comes in the next chapter, "Modes of sharing."

12.4 Drama structure: *Improvising Scenes from Research Materials*

In Chapter 9, we focused on spontaneous imagined material for improvisation, based on very brief catalysts or prompts. Here, we are interested in shifting the focus toward the process of translating written texts into dramatic form.

1. Preparing for the work

- **Grouping: Whole group in circle, followed by individual work**
- **Strategy: Writing scenarios based in research materials**
- **Administration: Research materials, dozens of copies of scenario slips (see Appendix H, p. 221), pen or pencils, a large old sheet to spread materials on in the centre of the circle**
- **Focus: To generate a large number of possible scenarios to improvise**

Facilitator: So here we are with all of this amazing material we have gathered. Sitting inside all this lies a world of possibilities that we're going to explore today. Unusually, we're going to begin by working individually because we need to generate a lot of ideas. If you think back over all the material we've gathered, there will be certain bits that you remember quite clearly. The process we're about to undergo asks you to consider all those pieces of material, even things you may have considered quite boring. The idea here is not about liking or not liking something, but rather to consider its possibilities.

To help you, there are some prompts on these slips of paper in this pile that we will use to plan scenarios based on our research. The "Who" is about the people in the scene. The "Where" and "When" is about the setting for the scene: where and when does it take place? The "What" is to address what you see the scene is about, in no more than a one-sentence summary. Then, finally, the "How" refers to any idea you may have as to how the scene could be played. As a murder mystery? As a song? As grand opera? As science fiction? For example:

Here we would suggest that the facilitator prepare an example by choosing a piece of material and offering a condensation:

FIGURE 2: Scenario slip example

SOURCE: Columbia News, 12/11/10, p. N5, "Teacher with a secret"

WHO: Teacher, 2 students

WHERE/WHEN: Office after school

WHAT: Kids ask for a drive home after teacher has helped with homework

WHY: What sign indicates that we should be worried about this?

HOW: As a scene or possibly a ballad or folk song?

Here's how it's going to work. Just pick up any five pieces of material and some scenario slips, along with a pen or pencil. Find a place to work on your own. First, begin looking through the material and when you find something that "clicks" for you, write your ideas onto a scenario slip, including where the idea came from (Source). Write the title, if available, or just two or three words, or a brief description if you're working with an image. This is important, as we'll need to be able to track back to the source later on. You may find that all five pieces of material generate ideas, or only some, or only one, or none. This will vary and that's okay. When you've finished going through this batch, put it back in the pile for others, and take five more sources and five more scenario slips. Let's try to keep this going, as our goal is to get as many scenario slips as possible from all of us. Any questions? Right, off you go.

This process may take some time, even though we are trying to work as quickly as we can. You want to encourage people to be thoughtful and try not to censor themselves at this point. All ideas are acceptable! Advise participants to write as legibly as they can, as we will be reading each other's slips later on. At the 20- or 25-minute mark, depending on the energy of the group, let participants know they should be finishing up what they're working on. If some have difficulties, you may prefer to have them work in small groups.

Right everyone, good work. Are all sources returned to the sheet in the centre? Now I'd like you to read through all the scenarios you have written, making sure they are readable. Just be aware of how many different ideas you allowed yourself to record. It's quite an amazing collection we'll have to work with now. Before we move on, does anybody have anything they want to say about that part of the process? Let's not talk about the material or your ideas, but rather the process.

2. Entering the work

- **Grouping: In pairs, or three if there is an odd number**
- **Strategy: Improvising from scenario slips**
- **Administration: Resource materials available, if needed; scenario slips, cardboard box, chart paper and markers**
- **Focus: To generate a large number of improvised scenes from scenario slips**

If there is a group of three, you can suggest to them that not every scenario they improvise needs to have all three of them in it. One of them can choose to sit and become the Outside Eye for the other two. They probably won't need to be reminded to take turns.

<u>Facilitator</u>: I'd like you to fold all of your scenario slips in half, then come into the circle and place your scenario slips in this box. Then, I'd like you to return to somewhere in the space with a partner. We have an uneven number, so we'll have one group of three. Now, we've all created scenarios from which we can begin to improvise. Here's how it's going to work: one of you, and you can take turns, will come here and take out a scenario slip. When you get back to your partner, you will read over the scenario and get ready to go. You'll need to decide who is who, if you need a block or a chair or any object we have available. You can consider who will speak first, or if one or both people enter the scene. If you have time, you might also come up with an opening line. Are you ready to begin? I'm going to give you one minute only to prepare before we all start improvising.

[*After a minute*] Right, stand by, begin your scenes.

[*After no more than two minutes*] Time's almost up … you have 30 seconds to find an ending for your scene.

Stop everyone, thank you. Talk to your partner about that. When you're ready, please return your slip to the box and take a new one. Let me shake the box up for a second or two before you take a new slip. If you get your old one, put it back and choose another one. Everybody ready? Here we go.

This process may repeat up to five times, based on your view of the group's energy level. Be sure that pairs reflect after each improvisation.

Facilitator: Well done everyone! That is hard work and you kept it up. Before we take a break, just talk to your partner about which of the four or five scenes you improvised together you feel has the most dramatic potential for our particular purposes. You might immediately agree on one, or you each might have a favourite, which is fine. You can give the one or two scenes you are choosing a tentative title each. We need to record these choices on some chart paper to keep a good record of what we've done. I'd like you to add your scenes to the chart paper before you take a quick break. See you back in ten minutes.

When working with groups outside a school environment, it is important to give people time to have a wash and brush up. A break may be the only time they have for having a chat and exchanging news. When the group comes together again, ask everyone to find a new partner. This whole process is repeated for a second round. The more improvised scenarios that can be generated, the more valuable the sorting process that comes next will be. If a group is really doing well, a third round with new partners is also possible. That said, a facilitator should closely monitor the energy level and commitment to this challenging work within the group.

3.a. Engaging in the work

- **Grouping: Individuals in their own spaces**
- **Strategy: Sorting and processing improvised scenarios**
- **Administration: Paper and pencil; questions (see below) on chart paper on wall**
- **Focus: To select one improvisation from each round**

Facilitator: Everybody come and take a piece of paper and a pencil and find your own space. Now, I'd like you to think back over the first round of improvised scenes and consider which one, if any, for you was working well in terms of the following three questions (on chart paper):

1. What was it about this scene that makes it memorable for you? Was it something said, or an action, or an interesting choice one of you made in the moment?
2. How does it connect to our topic (in this case, crime in our community)? What perspective does the scene take, or could take, that is of interest to you?
3. How do you see the potential for this scene? Could it include more people, could it be extended, could it include a monologue, could it become a movement piece, include a song, and so on?

Use these questions to help you make your selection of one of the scenes from the first round. Your answer will be a further guide for us later. If you don't feel that any one of them was working particularly well, that's fine, but it's likely that there is something memorable, even a moment, from what you created.

Good. Now turn your paper over and think back to the second rounds of improvising from the scenarios. Again, choose one scene that you feel merits further attention and follow the process as before.

Good. Now let's turn our papers back over to the first round and I'd like you all to get together with your partners from the first round.

3.b. Engaging in the work

- **Grouping: Pairs (from first round)**
- **Strategy: Re-improvising and sharing**
- **Administration: Paper and pencils on hand; scenario slips in centre**
- **Focus: To revisit and polish selected improvised scenarios**

<u>Facilitator</u>: Just share with your partner which of the improvisations you did together that you feel had potential. If you both agree on the same one, make sure you hear how each of you dealt with those questions, to enrich your understanding of that choice. If you have chosen different scenarios, you'll need to share your reasons for choosing each one. We probably only need a few minutes for this conversation.

You may agree together that you only want to work on one of your choices. On the other hand, you may feel that both choices are worth further exploration. Make that decision now.

Good. Now you have ten minutes to work on polishing your choice or choices of scenes. If you're going to do one scenario you'll have more time, and if you're agreeing to do both, you'll have about five minutes for each one. I'll let you know at the five-minute mark. Your focus is on advocating for your scene or scenes when you share them with the group. We're not concerned at this point on how polished these scenes are overall, but rather on the ideas in them that you are interested in sharing with us. That said, these short scenes do need to have good dramatic elements of a clear setting (your Where) and a clear beginning, middle and end. Find a freeze frame to start with and end with. In polished improvisation, the "polish" is about making things clear for those of us who are observing. Unlike the first improvising, which you did for yourselves, this time we're concerned with making things clear for all of us who are watching.

There are three things going on here. The first is dealing with time and how the facilitator sees the work needs to be moved along. Ten minutes may be seven minutes or twenty minutes, depending on the group. Remember that giving less time is always a good motivator! The second level of activity is in shifting your vocabulary to include more theatrical terms; how scenarios become scenes, etc. Thirdly, although we are moving into presentation, it is important to keep the emphasis off that element and on the process. It's not about show-ing, but rather is about sharing and making meaning together.

Which pair would like to begin with their first scene? We'll carry on clockwise around the room from there. Then, we can go back around again for any pairs who have a sec-ond scene to share. You can all stay in your spaces, and we'll just adjust ourselves to see. Observers, your task is to open yourself up to each of these experiences and after each one, when we're reflecting, we'll have the chance to talk about them, guided by these questions (on chart paper), and your own responses. Each scene will end with a freeze, because as audience and players, we need a moment to process what we've seen and heard. Right, first pair, are you ready to go? Everybody, can we all see? Great, let's begin.

Thank you, players. You can talk together about how that went, and everybody else turn to somebody close by and have a chat about that. [*About a minute.*] OK, who has some-thing they'd like to share?

If you need any prompts, return to the three questions posted on the wall. This kind of sharing needs to move along at a good pace to maintain the group's energy level. It's important to realize that when you are in "perfor-mance" mode, however careful you have been to downplay it, participants' attention will naturally be on their upcoming turn.

[*After a short reflective discussion of a couple of minutes*] Good. Now we need to make a record of this scene to help us remember it. So, let's give it a title. Perhaps the players have one in mind? If not, let's come up with one together. A good title will help to capture the focus of the scene. I'll write the titles out on chart paper and we'll post them in the space later. Right, who's next?

This sharing and reflecting process continues, then repeats with the second choices of the first round scenarios. At the end of this round:

Facilitator: I'm going to lay out all these sheets of chart paper with the titles of each scene on each one from this first round. Take a marker and visit as many of these scene titles as you want and you can add any thoughts you wish. These responses may be lines you remember, or think could be added, or perhaps a strong moment or gesture or emotion that should be kept in mind, or it may be some other connection you had with the scene that might extend or deepen it. Perhaps you have an idea of a way of performing this scene that might be useful? This is not about Valuing at this point, this is another chance to reflect. Of course you might want to talk together as you do this.

This is a 15-minute reflective activity and conversation should be encour-aged. Then the whole process repeats with participants moving to their second (and, if applicable, third) partners, polishing their chosen scenarios and sharing them in the whole group, as described above. Be mindful of how much time and energy this whole process will demand. You may need to spread this process out over a period of days or weeks, depending on how often and for what amount of time your group meets. As the group's facilitator, you are responsible for setting the tone. If you are not satisfied with the level of commitment or focus, either ask for a scene to be repeated by participants, for the purposes of clarity, or decide to stop the process for the moment. Taking a break to play a drama game, or to revisit research materials for more information/inspiration, may become part of the process.

4. Reflecting on the work

By the end of this process, your group should have anywhere between five and fifteen workable scenes to carry forward into the next stage of development. If you are working with a group that seems keen on writing, these scenes can certainly be written up in dialogue form, and (if appropriate to the group), this can be requested as a task to be carried out between sessions. These semi-scripted scenes, still open to improvisation and change, can be copied and distributed to the whole group. Some participant groups are very happy to have something tangible in their hands, while others are quite happy to keep things improvised and may never need a script of any kind. Again, it is your role as facilitator to feel out the group's needs and respond accordingly to them.

- **Grouping: Groups of four or five (in new configuration, not pairs from previous sections)**
- **Strategy: Scene development**
- **Administration: Paper and pens/pencils; chart paper and markers; music player; found objects as props; costume pieces if needed; chairs and blocks; research materials; laptop computer and LCD projector for slide shows/videos, etc.**
- **Focus: To further develop selected scenes in a group process; to be aware of how the scenes shape the meanings that underlie the work**

<u>Facilitator</u>: Look at all these sheets of paper and the wonderful ideas and thoughts and reflections you have added to enrich these scenes we have shared. This will help us immensely as we move forward. One of the things that makes the work so rich is that nobody owns anything; that is, we all own everything. So it always helps us to maintain that shared sense of ownership if we keep things shaken up a bit. Along these lines, I'm going to ask you to say goodbye for now to the partner you've been working with most recently and find yourself two or three other people to work with, preferably all or most of whom you have not improvised with before. So groups of three or four, please.

Your task as a group is to choose one scene, and collect the piece of paper that refers to it. And if somebody gets it before you, that's fine, just find another one. You'll have the chance to choose one you might miss out on this time, next time. Come and do that now please.

So now we're going to come together as a whole group for a few minutes to create a resource for ourselves of the sorts of things that are possible for us to try as we continue working on and shaping these scenes.

This is an opportunity for a facilitator to see what the group considers helpful or fun as possibilities. What can they draw on from previous workshop structures that might come into play here? Remind participants of some of the ways scenes could be explored further: hot-seating, tableaux, storytelling, sitting-down drama; changing timeframes, settings, adding or subtracting characters, adding music and/or sound, adding movement? By generating this list, participants should be able to recognize all the drama-based skills they have acquired that can now be applied to this part of the process.

Facilitator: Right, so you've seen this scene improvised and the list of ideas on your chart paper. You've also got lots of drama strategies at-hand to help you explore and discover more about the scene. What do you want to try first? Make sure everybody agrees. Then, who in the group will be responsible for facilitating what happens? For example, if you've chosen tableaux, then your volunteer facilitator could say, "Let's create three tableaux of this scene showing the beginning, middle and end of the scene. Then, I'd be really interested in seeing the final tableau set ten years after this scene takes place." Just before you begin, I want to remind you that after you've completed each strategy, be sure to take time to reflect together on what happened that was of interest, both in terms of the dramatic arc and in terms of the meanings we are hoping to offer to our audience. You might like to take some notes to act as reminders for the later work. Once you've tried one strategy, you'll very likely see in reflection where you'd like to go next. And someone new will take over as the volunteer facilitator for that strategy. Remember that all the work will have something to do with and say about crime in our community. Any questions?

This is an open-ended process and can take some time. Your role is to move from group to group, observing and offering support where needed. You are there to provide resources and to ask questions that deepen the work. Here are some questions and prompts that might be of use:

- How might you make your setting or time period a little clearer through your words and/or your actions?
- I wonder if you've thought about the kind of mood that's happening in this scene?

- What or who is it you want us to focus on or engage with in this scene?
- I wonder if you aren't trying to tell us too much here?
- What other ways are there for your main character to get what she wants?
- How could we point out the differences between these two people?
- What could you add or change to make the scene a little more surprising or a little less indistinct?
- Have you thought about putting a silence in this scene, maybe they've said everything they need to say, maybe neither of them can think of what to say, or maybe what needs to be said is too difficult and they can't find the words to say it?
- I wonder if it would help if one or both of you were doing something during this conversation? These could be separate tasks, or joint tasks, whatever you want to try.
- Sometimes a scene works better if the people in it don't talk directly about what's on their minds. What happens if the topic of the scene remains unspoken (subtext)?
- You might like to think about the dramatic power of turning the expected on its head. Reversals of expectation, especially around established power relationships, make great drama, but only if they come from places of truth.
- What would you like me to watch for as you improvise this scene?

These questions and prompts are offered as possibilities and you'll probably come up with many of your own. What you are seeing will tell you what to ask. The thing to be careful about is that you never tell anyone what should be done but rather, ask a question that will enable him or her to rethink and repair. Your questions should be designed to generate and encourage their process.

12.5 Questions for Reflection, Suggested Activity and Further Reading

Questions for Reflection

1. As our dramatic process moves more towards theatre, it is a good time to reflect upon and identify areas in which you feel quite comfortable, and areas in which you feel you still need more development. How could you use your strengths and how might you plan to develop the knowledge and skills that you feel are lacking? Where would you go and what might you do to gain this experience?
2. If your participants wish to move forward into some kind of presentation, in what areas would you need some assistance and whom might you call upon?

One of the things about applied drama/theatre is that no one is an expert in all areas of practice. Just as we suggest seeking outside expertise for the special needs of the group with which you may have little or no experience (for example, counsellors for at-risk youth groups or psychiatric nurses for mental health issues) and experts to assist in topic explorations, so facilitators may benefit greatly by collaborating with theatre artists of many types to help to raise the level of the dramatic work. That said, professionals need to be paid for their time, which means planning and budgeting for such assistance as part of your initial preparation.

Suggested Activity

Read a play that addresses the topic of crime (we list some suggestions below). Consider what aspects or elements of this play effectively address issues around crime. How might you make use of some of these creative ideas by adapting them for your participant group? This reading might also raise some useful questions to share with participants.

Further Reading: Plays on crime

Blank, J. & Jensen, E. (2004). *The exonerated.* New York: Dramatists Play Service. This play draws on interviews, letters, and court transcripts to tell the true stories of six American death row convicts who won their freedom due to wrongful conviction.

Kaufman, M. (2001). *The Laramie project.* New York: Dramatists Play Service. This verbatim play looks at a crime, the beating to death of a young gay man in Laramie, Wyoming. The New York theatre company Tectonic Theatre gathered interviews in the town following this event and created a play that had significant impact. These two plays are of interest and value for any applied drama facilitator to read, even if not working with the topic of crime.

Rose, R. (1955). *Twelve angry men.* Chicago: Dramatic Publishing. This popular play, an American classic, portrays the jury process held behind closed doors. It shows how the democratic process of determining guilt or innocence works. The film version is also recommended.

Further Reading

Ball, D. (1983). *Backwards and forwards: A technical manual for reading plays.* Carbondale, IL: Southern Illinois University Press. A highly regarded text on how to read and understand the structure of plays.

Spencer, S. (2002). *The playwright's guidebook: An insightful primer on the art of dramatic writing.* New York: Faber & Faber. A well-reviewed text on playwriting, useful for a facilitator who wishes to know more about the challenges of writing for theatre.

CHAPTER THIRTEEN
MODES OF SHARING

13.1 Thinking about the audience

In the traditional theatre the audience is valued primarily for the price they pay for their tickets. The "number of bums in seats" attitude still can prevail in many mainstream theatre companies, particularly profit-based ones that depend on ticket sales for survival. This is what performance theorist Richard Schechner (1988/2003) calls an "accidental audience" (p. 220); that is to say, the play is created and played to a general public audience. In applied theatre practice, audiences are otherwise; these audiences are invested in the subject matter of the theatre piece and/or the players involved in presenting it. Schechner calls this very different audience "integral," and their presence is considered by the players to be absolutely "necessary to accomplish the work of the show" (p. 220).

At this stage of the process, as participants move towards some kind of sharing, it is vital to think about what the group has worked on that it feels is of benefit. A key question to offer the group here is, "What is it about crime in our community (or other topic/issue) that we wish to communicate to an audience?" In moving from dramatic process toward a theatrical "product" of some kind, participants need to consider what it is they have created, what they want their work to say, and to whom. A group may choose to keep the work

To say any more about intuition, hunches, luck, trusting the process, vision would be next to futile. What I have learned in my years of making dances—and making narrative dances in particular—is that, like the pragmatist, you have to know what you are trying to accomplish; but like the idealist, you have to be open to many ways of getting there. In other words, I have to be both my own king and priest at the same time. Rule and serve at the same time. You have to look like you know what you are doing but you have to make sure that you don't. That is when the process becomes the most fun. And believe me, it takes years to perfect this. But that is where the inspiration lies, somewhere between knowing and not knowing.

– James Kudelka, *The Globe and Mail,*
May 7, 2012, A2

in-house, and this decision should be supported fully by a facilitator. However, if there is a wish to share the work with a wider audience, they may decide to only invite immediate family members. Perhaps they might consider also inviting close friends or colleagues. A group that expresses this wish will be most comfortable with quite a small audience, and will need to determine and agree how many people maximum will be present. If 25 chairs are available in the space, for example, the facilitator might suggest the chairs be put out in audience formation (of various kinds, see more on this below) for participants to get a better sense of how it will feel. On the other hand, the group may feel that what it has to say needs to be said to a particular part of the community (between 25 and 50). A youth group, for example, may want to share their work with members of the police department or local shopkeepers or social service agents (social workers, counsellors, street workers, and so on), whom they feel will benefit from hearing their stories. A more confident group might wish to invite a larger audience made up of a cross-section of the community (50 to 75 maximum). We recommend these audience size limitations as, unlike mainstream theatre, we are not just "putting on a show": engaging with audience members in a meaningful post-show conversation is an important part of the process. As the work develops, the size and target audience may change, and this is part of the process as well. However, the facilitator needs to be well-prepared to engage with audiences of all kinds. Maintaining the sense of a safe space is key at this point, and all group members need to be comfortable with the decisions being made around who will see their work.

13.2 Putting it all together

After deciding upon who the audience will be, and how large, then decisions can start to be made on how the disparate pieces that have been created can be put together. A group may choose simply to present a series of monologues and scenes that they have been working on without concern for overall structuring. This is a more informal work-in-progress approach that could involve the sharing of food and small group discussions with invited audience members around issues raised. As participants are an integral part of the post show conversations, they should be prepared to "host" members of the audience, either as a whole or in small groups. It helps to have a list of possible questions or prompts that they create beforehand and the facilitator's role is to float from group to group to keep discussions moving in this simple sharing model. In a model involving a larger, semi-public audience, the group will need to make more decisions and engage in a process of shaping the work. A group that makes this choice has to consider not only their own investment in the work, but also the potential engagement of an audience with it. Aesthetic qualities need to be considered, such as the presentation having a beginning, middle and "open-ended" finish, a clear focus, and elements like creative transitions, light, sound, props, set and costume. Often the wider audiences who will see this work will not have seen the issues being addressed done so through dramatic means. Paradoxically, some audience members may be regular theatregoers who bring with them expectations that this kind of community and process-based work may not meet. In each case, a facilitator should raise these points for the group to consider as they make collective choices around how and with whom they want to share their work.

Another consideration involves a group moving from the space in which they have been doing workshops and developing performance materials into a new space for the purposes of sharing their work. Whenever possible we recommend staying in the same space, as this can alleviate a lot of the understandable "stage fright" inexperienced participants may feel. That said, often a move into a venue of some kind (a theatre space, a community hall, a school gymnasium, and so on) may be deemed necessary to accommodate the audience that is to attend. As with all else, the facilitator should attend closely to how a group makes this move, and to alleviate as much as possible any concerns around this shift in location. It requires a lot of tact to help participants discover an effective theatrical framework for their dramatic process, without losing everything that has been gained in the process due to the pressures of presentation.

A sponsoring organization may also have a role to play at this stage, in terms of support around providing food and drink, publicity, posters, programs, or even the means to make use of a new venue. At all times, however, any involvement of the sponsors/funders should be fully and openly negotiated with the group.

13.3 Processing the process

A performing process has three parts: Pre-performance, Performance, and Post-performance (Schechner, 2002, p. 61). The pre- and post-performance components become areas for a facilitator to also consider with a group.

Some questions for pre-performance
- How does an audience enter the space?
- What will they see? What will they hear?
- What is the role of participants in the pre-performance? Will they serve food or drink? Will they act as docents greeting and explaining what is being displayed (chart papers of brainstorming, statistical charts, maps, images, research materials, scenario slips, etc.) to introduce audiences to the process? Will there be music (live or recorded)?
- How will the event be laid out in the facilitator's pre-performance remarks so that the audience is aware of what is going to happen? How will the audience be prepared to engage in a post-performance conversation of some kind?
- How will the space look? How will it be lit?

- How will audiences enter? What will they see?
- What is the facilitator's role in the pre-performance? How much should the facilitator say? How will s/he introduce both him/herself and the group? How will s/he facilitate the move from pre-performance to the beginning of the performance?
- Is the performance happening in the same space as the pre-performance, or does the audience move from one space into another? In either case, how will this transition work?

Some questions for post-performance
- What is going to happen after the performance? Will the audience have the opportunity to write comments and suggestions for the group? If so, how will this task be organized (blank space on the back of a program, or slips of paper, pencils and a comment box by the door, or an e-mail address)?
- Will the participants and audience remain together in a large group? Will participants and audience members break off into smaller discussion groups?
- If there are to be small discussion groups, who will lead the small group conversations? How will they prepare themselves? [*We recommend the group generate a list of prepared questions for this purpose*].
- Will there be food and drink involved at this stage?
- What is the role of the facilitator in each of these models? How can the facilitator allay concerns, or even fears, in participants around this engagement with their audience?
- What are the questions the group wishes to address?
- What are the needs of a sponsoring organization, if any, in this stage of the process? How can these needs be kept in balance with the needs of the group?
- How will the facilitator, if she is leading the post-show conversation, open up this post-performance process? How will she mediate any potential tensions that might occur (if, for example, audience members in power positions feel challenged by perspectives presented by the group)?
- What can be done to move the conversation from polite post-performance affirmations into something more meaningful?
- The questions presented in Figure 3, drawn from Prendergast's (2008) study *Teaching Spectatorship* are intended to help facilitators invite audiences into a deeper engagement with the presentation.

13.4 Drama strategies: *Ideas for Presentation*

We present a range of possibilities below for a facilitator and group to make decisions around as their work is shaped into a performance of some kind. These decisions are provisional to the extent that they remain changeable as the nature of

FIGURE 3: Post-performance questions for deeper engagement

- What did I recognize in the performance? What surprised me?
- How was the performance relevant to my life and experience?
- How did the performance stimulate my creativity and imagination?
- What puzzled me or confused me?
- What did I ignore or avoid?
- What was illustrated or represented by the performance?
- What were the social, political and cultural contexts of the performance?
- What perspectives were given by the performance?
- How valuable were these perspectives?
- What in the performance generated new thoughts?
- How suitable or significant was the form/content of the performance?
- How true and/or "right" was the performance?
- Where, and in what ways, does my interpretation agree or disagree with the interpretations of others?
- What can I compare and/or contrast the performance with?
- What new questions has this performance generated in me? How do they shift my being in the world? (Prendergast, 2008, p. 143)

the process dictates. At the same time, decisions do need to be made and a facilitator's role at this point is to encourage effective (and somewhat efficient) decision-making by the group. While a facilitator should never fully become the "Director" of the piece, as the group must maintain its power to shape and shift the work, s/he should recognize the need to make some kinds of directorial decisions on behalf of the group. This is a good time to repeat the mantra "Trust the Process" because however difficult this stage may feel, solutions emerge in the doing and most often everyone sees clearly when the "right" solution appears. The suggestions below are open to mixing, matching, modifying or remolding, as the group sees fit.

One way to help a group maintain focus on its overall objectives in this "putting it all together" process is to have the key question driving the process front and centre in the space. If possible, the facilitator can create a large banner of the group's theme with the overarching question—in this case, "What is it about crime in our community (or other topic/issue) that we wish to communicate to an audience?"—and display it prominently on a wall. The theme and this question become touchstones for the facilitator and group, to keep reminding them of the direction they wish to move in as the work is sorted, selected, ordered, framed and shaped in accord with the group's purpose for sharing with an audience.

1. *Assembling the audience*

It may be useful to consider the different kinds of theatre shapes that are available when we are working in a non-theatrical venue in order to select one that fits both the participants' comfort levels and best reflects the intentions of the presentation.

Proscenium: This traditional face-front audience-performer arrangement is recognizable and familiar to both participants and audiences. Inexperienced players may feel quite safe in this arrangement because of its familiarity and the distance it provides between spectator and stage. It is also easier for the audience to see and for the players to be seen. The limitations are that the distance can feel intimidating, so that players may believe the audience's expectations will be higher if the arrangement resembles too closely more traditional theatre forms. The fourth wall is present in this arrangement, which can create a divide that can be challenging to bridge. Stage movement can look quite flat in this staging option, limiting creative patterns of movement.

Thrust: In this arrangement, the stage space thrusts out into the audience, so that the audience sits around three sides, but the setting still can be framed with a background like a proscenium stage. This is the Elizabethan theatre style, as in Shakespeare's Globe Theatre, and reflective of a number of contemporary theatres. Advantages are an increased proximity between audience and players while maintaining the potential to use the upstage for visual effects such as screening statistics, quotes, images, etc. Thrust staging opens up additional entry and exit points, and entering from the audience becomes more possible. Limitations are that there are more demands made on players because of the closer engagement with the audience, including the challenge of more complex blocking and movement which will have to be more carefully planned and less improvisatory. There is also a heightened awareness of the audience with less of a fourth wall in place, which can interrupt the focus of relatively unskilled players. Also, thrust staging will involve players turning away from certain sections of the audience, which means their performance needs to be more three dimensional in order to be effective.

Alley: Alley seating places the audience on either side of the playing space, facing each other. It offers three distinct playing spaces, the middle and either end of the alley, which can be useful in terms of staging. The fourth wall is erased in this arrangement, and the players and audience are in close proximity. Audiences are more challenged to engage in alley arrangement, as they are visible to each other across the space. Players will be dealing with even greater levels of intimacy with the audience which will require higher levels of concentration due to possible distraction from audience members moving, reacting, or even simply being familiar to the player. Limitations are that exits and entrances are reduced again, as in proscenium staging, to either end of the alley. An option here is to place the players seated at both ends of the alley stage so they enter the playing space but never entirely exit.

Arena: This is theatre in the round, with many advantages. First, it will feel familiar to the group, as we have been working in this circle arrangement throughout the workshop structures presented herein. Indeed, the reader may recall the first structure we present is on the nature of the circle as a metaphor for dramatic process. Second, this arrangement allows for the greatest level of proximity and intimacy with an audience, often making audiences feel like they are inside the world of the drama alongside the players. Third, as the audience is so close, the technical challenges of vocal projection and face-front style of blocking and movement are negated. Finally, arena staging offers multiple entry and exit points for players. Limitations of arena are, as in alley staging: audiences can see and may be distracted by each other, or may feel intimidated by the intimacy. Also, players need to be more fluid in their blocking and movement than in other staging arrangements, as at any given time any one player's back will be turned away from a section of the audience. A facilitator should focus on the need for fluid movement if the group chooses arena staging.

Processional: There are two versions of this staging arrangement option. Both options provide an inherent sense of novelty, playfulness and energy with presenting dramatic work in this arrangement. Players are challenged with their improvisatory skills to respond to the unexpected, which is far more likely to occur in this arrangement than in the ones listed above.

a. The audience is taken on a "tour" by some kind of guide (possibly the facilitator) or guides—in or out of role—who move the audience from one area where they watch a scene within a larger space, to another area where a different dramatic event takes place. Depending upon the number of scenes, the players may have to move ahead in order to set up before the audience arrives. The advantages of this arrangement are that the staging feels very informal in that the audience gathers around the performance in a casual way, most often standing (obviating the need for seating). Close proximity and intimacy are present, and often projection and visibility are less of a problem. The space chosen for processional staging approaches can be used quite creatively, including the possibility of moving outside, or even to multiple sites within the community. Within one space, interesting use of space (closets, stairwells, bathrooms, etc.) can provide visual and contextual support for the work. Limitations are that outside spaces present the potential problem of poor weather, and long times spent on their feet can be wearying for an audience. Extraneous occurrences, such as traffic sounds, sirens, passersby, and so on, are also challenging, as there is little or no control over these events. Or,

b. The audience is divided into smaller groups and rotates (usually with a guide) from event to event, on an integrated schedule. The players remain in place and repeat their performance for each audience group. Advantages and limitations are similar to the first option, with one new challenge added in. In this staging choice, players repeat their work multiple times which can be very demanding, but they have the advantage of not having to move from space to space.

2. Sorting and selecting

It may be that participants are quite clear about and comfortable with their material so that the selecting and ordering is done almost organically and with ease. Participants can understandably feel very attached to certain works they have created, but the devising process always demands a giving over of individual desires to the needs of the group and the material being shaped as a whole. The topic, theme and overall focus of the presentation may have been decided earlier as part of the conversation to determine to whom the group wishes to present. Now the work of deciding which scenes and how to present them sets the group off on another journey of discovery in which all their group skills will be employed as they work democratically towards their presentation. However, as the sorting and selecting process is generally not an easy one, we offer the following suggestions:

- In groups of three or four, ask participants take a look at what has been created within the whole group and set up a presentational structure in list form that the group is prepared to defend. Each group can list this structure out on chart paper, and may include gaps or spaces where the group feels new material needs to be generated. Focus should be on including material that allows for equal involvement from everyone in the whole group and also includes a broad range of dramatic styles: monologues, scenes, movement sequences, tableaux, etc. The focus should be on what it is the whole group has agreed they wish to communicate most to their intended audience.

- As groups are discussing possibilities, the facilitator should circulate amongst groups encouraging participants to try sorting items into a possible Beginning section, Middle section and Ending section. Ideas for possible titles should be listed throughout the process, with one selected by the group before moving on. As well as this, participants should be invited to begin considering possibilities for a dramatic framework, a holding container of some kind (which will be the next step in the process, below). Notes on possible frameworks should be kept on a separate sheet of chart paper.
- When groups have completed these tasks, the whole group reconvenes to share what each group has proposed. Focus here is on presenting each overview with a view to how well it meets the goals of the whole group. Each group's contribution should be equally valued and the facilitator should offer positive insights whenever groups offer effective and creative ideas for shaping work into a performance.

Following this, small groups can meet again to debrief and the facilitator may invite groups to consider how they might adjust their structures to incorporate excellent ideas from others. This allows groups to keep their structures open to influence from the rest of the group, and allays the possibility of any group being overly attached to their own ideas at the expense of the whole group's process.

Back in the whole group, a general reflection is held around what it is the group is responding to most strongly. The facilitator then places three labels on the wall: Beginning, Middle and Ending. She also hands out markers, blank paper and has some kind of sticky tape available. This stage of the process allows for individuals to literally stand up for what it is they feel most vital to be included in the performance. This last part of sorting and selecting is adapted from Open Space, a self-organizing group process used around the world (see Prendergast, 2011). The facilitator then invites individual participants to write the name or title of an element they wish to see included in the presentation. As each person takes his or her turn writing and posting this element, he or she will also make a quick "claim" to the whole group expressing its perceived value as part of the overall presentation. The facilitator's role is to encourage participants to consider all the ideas presented, not just the ones developed in their own small groups, as ideas to support and advocate. It is useful to remind participants that even though someone might champion an element by placing it in one section of the presentation, its inclusion and placement will be provisional, as more sorting and ordering will be required.

At the end of this stage in the process, the wall should contain a number of selections, roughly ordered into three sections. Next, participants are invited to stand up and read over everything that has been posted, with a view to voting for their top three selections in each section—initialing against the selected elements stands as a vote.

Participants will need to agree on what kind of mark they wish to make. Checkmarks or X-es are anonymous, whereas initialing or signing names demands that each participant more publicly declares their choices. Numbers—1, 2, 3—should be avoided as their hierarchical nature may cause problems later on.

This sorting and selecting process may need to be repeated two or three times. After each round, the facilitator takes down those papers that have received few or no signatures/checkmarks. Letting go is part of the devising process, and reminding participants that this is a necessary, if difficult, part of the process is important at this point. All papers removed from the wall should be kept on-hand, however, as often pieces that have been let go may find their way back into the process later on. Finally, the group will arrive at an agreed-upon selection with a tentative sorting into sections.

This is a part of the process that needs to be managed carefully to ensure participants remain open to letting go of cherished ideas and pieces, and commit to whatever final selections have been made. Without commitment there is no sense of ownership, and without the shared ownership of material by everyone involved, the successful outcome of the process is endangered.

The next stage of the process involves finalizing the elements into an order that works best for the presentation, creating an effective dramatic framework that makes more coherent the disparate elements selected for presentation.

3. Ordering and framing

This section could also be titled "Framing and ordering" as these are parallel processes occurring and affecting each other at the same time.

Ordering: Ordering is not just about what-comes-next, although that is important. Ordering is also about considering the whole dramatic arc of the presentation, answering such questions as:

- What does the audience need to know?
- How do we introduce the audience to our topic and presentation on it?
- What are the essential points we must make?
- How varied are these points of view?
- How varied are the elements selected and how well arrayed (in terms of spacing out scenes, interspersing with movement, music, and/or monologues, and so on)?
- What are the shifts in tone and emotion throughout and how does ordering create both variety and coherence in this regard?
- What might be the climax or turning point of our presentation?
- What leads us into a satisfying sense of conclusion?
- What questions/solutions do we want the audience to take away?

- In a more focused way, ordering is also about deciding what connects the various elements we have selected. Some possibilities to consider:
  - What if the piece is more episodic, with elements that address the theme and key question, but are fairly independent of each other? Or,
  - How might there be a story carried throughout, with each element representing one aspect of a larger narrative? Or,
  - How might the piece include a protagonist-like character who threads through the whole presentation?
  - How might an antagonist figure (or figures) also be incorporated into this character-driven approach?
  - How might a chosen setting inform how elements are ordered and presented?

This ordering process can be done with the whole group working through the facilitator to rearrange selected pieces on the wall, so choices can be seen in a clear and visual way. One option is to lay out a taped line representing a dramatic arc on the wall and place selected elements on this line to help participants see how the presentation will be structured (see Appendix E, p. 215). Particular attention should be paid to the first piece that begins the presentation and the last piece that ends it. Considering a climactic piece that provides some kind of turning point is also valuable. Again, the ordering process is provisional and subject to change as the presentation continues to be put together.

Framing: The framework for the presentation is the container that holds all the elements of the presentation. It is a holding frame that collects together, in order to make sense of, all the disparate pieces being used. The framework says something about how things are connected or linked together, what unites them.

Whatever the group has chosen to open their presentation may greatly inform what kind of framework may be used. A scene in which someone is arrested for some kind of crime might allow the group to consider a holding cell in the local jail as a container out of which various characters tell their stories about how they got there. Alternately, if the presentation begins with a monologue delivered by someone affected by crime, then the framework might offer a movement and sound piece presenting a street front that shows various ways that crime affects members of a community. The transition possibility here (discussed in the next section) might be that every return to the street front, between parts of the presentation, may show differing kinds of crime occurring. A very popular and effective framework choice is a music and movement sequence. The energy helps drive a presentation forward and also engages audience attention. Another simple yet effective option for framing is to show how the players set up the stage for their presentation. Arranging boxes or chairs for the opening scene can be enough. Shifting these boxes or chairs then indicates clearly to an audience that we are moving into another scene, monologue or other aspect of the presentation. More abstract possibilities should also be encouraged: one of the richest frameworks from a group of students we have worked with took the audience on a tour through the protagonist's brain as he lay in a coma. Each "room" in the brain held a bureaucrat in charge of monitoring and recording a particular emotion, and memories were triggered by these various emotions that broke out of the framework into scenes and monologues. In another example of a linking device, a group who wanted to celebrate their community's history used the square dance as a metaphor for the military "British square" configuration of town planning, charting the growth of the community by adding street names as the dance was called.

Final moments in the presentation also require lots of thought and planning, as this is what the audience will be left with, and should be satisfying enough to serve as a good closing, but open enough to allow for continuing reflection and discussion. The presentation may close with some kind of revisiting of the opening, in a changed form to bookend the piece with the framework itself. Again, this can be as simple as the players taking chairs and boxes off stage, perhaps singing a song as they go. Or, it may mean returning to the street front to present a final vision from the group that represents what crime in their community means to them.

Taking a look at the pieces the group has let go of at this point can be very fruitful. Within a "deleted" piece there may lie a really lovely and imaginative idea for a framework that brings all the elements of the presentation together. One of the pleasures of this kind of work is that it is full of surprises

Putting it into action: Framework ideas need to be tried out, not just talked about. Small groups can take a framework possibility and put it on its feet to show the rest of the group. Again, as in all this sorting and ordering work, this is not a competition, but is rather a way for the group to share their work with a view to making decisions together.

4. Transitions and theatrical elements

Transitions: A transition is how a group moves from one piece to another. The traditional way to do this used to be a blackout, but it has fallen out of favour in contemporary theatre. This is just as well in the context of the community-based work that most often takes place in non-theatrical spaces with little or no stage lighting. However, scene changes can be as entertaining and significant as any other part of the show. The framework selected will have a direct effect on transitions as well. The more effective your framework, the more ideas it will offer for transitions and links between scenes. Music, movement and visuals (screened quotes, statistics or images) are often effective strategies for transitions. A narrator, lecturer, or tour-guide figure of some kind might lead the audience through the presentation, and will use direct address. A ritual of some kind can also be an effective framework. Some simple rituals to be considered:

- Chanting a repeated refrain
- Lighting and blowing out candles (check local fire codes first!)
- Processing into and out of the playing space to mark the beginning and end of the presentation
- Marking the perimeter of a circle before stepping into it to begin (with chalk, tape, significant props or other objects, etc.)
- Having the players stand in a line facing the audience with their own hands touching at waist level, elbows out, then slowly raising their hands in unison up and over their heads to indicate the raising of the curtain and reversing this gesture to signal the close

Whatever ritual elements the group wishes to use as part of the overall framework, these elements must be carried out with great precision, as ritual signifies oneness, the sense of what anthropologist Victor Turner calls "communitas" (Turner, 1969. p. 132).

Transitions, and the framework that supports them, work especially well with the conscious use of irony, contradiction and the reversal of expectations. For our model topic of crime, for example, historical criminals who comment ironically on the content of scenes and monologues, and who work hard to convince the audience of the value to be found in living a life of crime, might lead the framework and transitions. Never underestimate the power of humour in this regard!

Theatrical elements and devices: There are many kinds of theatrical elements and devices a group can make use of to strengthen their presentations. We offer a number of choices:

Sound/Silence

Silence can be used in a presentation to give an audience space to reflect. Allowing an audience to see something without necessarily hearing something also focuses their attention on the action being portrayed and its various interpretations. Sound effects, sound design, soundscapes (either made with found objects or with players' live or taped voices) are all theatrical devices that raise the level of a presentation. Including live music is something else that may be possible, if there are musicians within the group, or if the group wishes to collaborate with some community musicians.

Light/Dark

Light and dark elements in theatre can refer to having lighter and darker aspects of a play or performance (connecting to the genres of comedy and tragedy). A good presentation should attempt to include a balance of lighter and darker material. Light and dark can also refer to the visual elements of a performance, how light is used to create space and mood. In applied drama presentations, it is unlikely that stage lighting instruments will be available, so lighting may be as simple as turning off a few lights and keeping some lights on over the playing space. The use of an additional strong light source—for example, an overhead projector, a slide projector, a floodlight or powerful flashlight(s)—can be very effective especially when used with coloured gels to create an atmosphere. If participants remain on stage throughout, they can become effective lighting operators.

Stillness/Movement

As with silence, stillness can be palpably felt in performance. The stillness of the players' bodies before and after a scene, or the whole presentation itself, can be power-ful. The device of a monologue or scene that is still after a scene that has involved lots of movement provides good dramatic contrast. Movement always draws the eye, and skilled actors know how to selectively use stillness to focus an audience's roving atten-tion. Consider the use of statues and tableaux as devices to be pulled into a presentation. Movement, even subtle movement, can provide interesting dramatic tension when the movement suggests the opposite of what is being said. For example, someone talking on the phone in a casual way can be seen as quite tense through the nervous tapping of a pencil on a pad of paper. Again, the tapping might be picked up by those not in the scene to emphasize the emotional tone.

Props/Symbols

A decision needs to be made by the group whether to use props or to mime them. Mime requires some skill to be effective, needless to say, but props can become overused as well, becoming a kind of crutch for groups lacking confidence to lean on, as can cos-tumes and set pieces. In this, as in most things theatrical, simple is best. A prop that has the power to change itself—as a square of fabric that can become an apron, a shawl, a tablecloth, a baby or a sling—then moves toward becoming a symbol. A key prop in our imagined project on crime, for example, might be a length of heavy gauge chain that can symbolize a number of different things within the presentation.

Chorus/Repetition

The use of chorus, a group of people speaking together to represent a given commu-nity, has been an element of western and other theatre traditions over thousands of years. A chorus can be a framing device that weaves throughout a presentation, as a collective character that can comment and reflect on what is happening in the scenes and mono-logues presented. Speaking in chorus can be a good distancing effect, providing a critical perspective. Choral speaking can also involve breaking up a passage into solo or small groups, to create variety. Choral passages can be repeated, with varied pace, emotion, vocal quality, and so on. Repetition can be a forceful element incorporating movement, chanting, images and ritual. Repetition can be used throughout a presentation but should not slip over into predictability; effective repetition works best as variations on a theme.

Gesture/Images

Gesture is a movement intended to produce meaning. Great actors have great ability to use gesture to underpin their interpretation of a character and the text. Gestures can indicate mood, feeling, intention, relationship, and can also function as space for irony and contradiction. When a gesture contrasts strongly with words spoken—when, for example, a parent says "I love you" to a child then pats her politely on the head—the gesture can negate or question the sincerity of the words. Gesture can be used consciously, in choral and repeated ways by the whole group to indicate significant motifs.

Gesture is a kind of image, of course. Imagery onstage can be thought of as another form of text and can be used to create backdrops, to convey setting, information, mood, and so on. A facilitator can reflect with a group preparing for a presentation on what kinds of stage pictures the presentation offers, both in terms of how the players create interesting and engaging images within their scenes and monologues, and also how images are used as scenic elements via projections, posters, and/or paintings. The use of an image of a work of visual art, or a news photo, for example, can provide a compelling commentary on the content of a scene or monologue.

13.5 Questions for Reflection, Suggested Activity and Further Reading

Questions for Reflection

1. What are the benefits to the participants in taking this step, in "putting it all together" for some kind of public sharing?
2. In looking back at the drama contract negotiated between facilitator and participants, what might need to be revisited and renegotiated at this stage?
3. What are the expectations held by the funding or partnership group around a public presentation? Are these expectations congruent with those of the group and facilitator? Are they capable of being met?

Suggested Activity

How might you develop your skills as a director as you move towards presentation? You might be able to secure an assistant-directing role in a local professional or otherwise reputable theatre company. What are the differences you perceive between directing for text-based mainstream theatre and for applied drama presentations? What are the questions that emerge based on these differences and where or to whom might you go to find out some answers?

Further Reading

Ball, W. (1984). *A sense of direction: Some observations on the art of directing*. New York: Drama Books. A very readable text that has been around for a long time but still has value. A good start to reading more about the art of how directors work with actors to interpret a play.

Bray, E. (1991). *Playbuilding: A guide for group creation for plays with young people*. Paddington, NSW: Currency. A wonderfully exampled text that is very accessible and adaptable beyond working with young people. Bray takes the reader through the whole process of playbuilding in a thoughtful, detailed but not overwhelming way.

Neelands, J. & Dobson, W. (2008). *Advanced drama and theatre studies* (2nd ed.). London: Hodder & Stoughton. A marvellous practical and historical guide to making and appreciating theatre. Recommended chapters on devising and play analysis.

Oddey, A. (1996). *Devising theatre: A practical and theoretical handbook*. London: Routledge. This book provides a useful history of devised theatre and valuable advice to facilitators embarking on playbuilding.

Weigler, W. (2001). *Strategies for playbuilding: Helping groups translate issues into theatre*. Portsmouth, NH: Heinemann. Another excellent guide to devising plays written by an experienced community-based theatre director.

Chapter Fourteen
Reflecting, Exiting and Assessing

To wrap up and document an applied drama project requires reflecting upon how the project met the needs of the group, the funding agency/sponsor organization, the community beyond, and those of the facilitator. We recognize that facilitators will be working in and with very diverse settings and participant groups, and these inevitable differences raise challenges around creating a "one-size-fits-all" approach. All groups have different needs, interests and capabilities around reflecting upon and assessing their experiences; as well, funding or sponsoring agencies have preferred or imposed ways they wish the work to be documented and evaluated. A reflective assessment is incomplete without a consideration of the ways the community itself may have benefited from the outcomes of a group's experience. Finally, it is important that you, the facilitator, reflect on the learning depth and variety of experiences that have had an impact on you and on your practice.

In light of these challenges, we present here a range of strategies around finishing up and exiting an applied drama project through which readers may "graze" (as Donald Schön, 1983) suggests, so that approaching the end of a process, facilitators remain open to the possibilities of new processes emerging. In the strategies offered below, we remain rooted in a process-based approach that is collectively negotiated and within which participants and facilitators maintain ownership and a sense of control. You may work with groups that are not interested in processes of reflection and assessment, in which case you as facilitator may have to take on this responsibility. We offer some suggestions around how this facilitator-driven process can be undertaken in an ethical way.

We begin, in Section 14.1, by reflecting on an applied drama project that has carried out some kind of semi-public presentation. If, however, a group has not engaged in sharing beyond the parameters of the group itself, then Section 14.2 addresses ways for a group and facilitator to process their process. Exiting a community is one of the greatest challenges for a facilitator and often gets short shrift; in Section 14.3 we offer some process-based ways for a facilitator and group to acknowledge and honour the time they have spent together. Section 14.4 presents a range of assessment strategies available that move from more personal forms of reflection to more public ones.

14.1 Reflecting on presentation

Reflecting on the experience of a group's presentation needs to occur; a fuller and considered reflection should be viewed as an integral component of any dramatic process. This priority needs to be considered in any timetabling, so that a group does not disperse immediately following their presentation. If a funding body questions the need for follow-up meetings, it should be pointed out that this reflective phase offers opportunities to also begin the assessment process that is most often mandated by funders.

There is a lot to talk about at this stage. Asking a group how they would like to begin this process is one way to proceed. Another option is to offer participants the time to do some reflective writing on the presentation. This could be free writing or based on prompts. Here are some suggested questions, for either writing or talking:

- What did you learn about yourself from presenting our project?
- What have others helped you to know about yourself in this process?
- What are you grateful for that happened in this process?
- What challenges still remain for you?
- How did you feel before the presentation and how did those feelings change throughout and after the presentation?
- What were you thinking about when it was all over?
- What was it that surprised you in the presentation process? What made it so surprising?
- How did this performance fit in with other kinds of performances you have been involved with in your life?
- How did the multiple roles you have played in the drama affect the multiple roles you play in your own life?
- How do you see the value of performance in your own life as a result of this experience?

You can also invite the group to add questions they feel are not on this list, or to build a list of their own reflective questions. Whether participants write in response to any or all of these prompts, or simply wish to use them as discussion points, the process can move from paired discussion to small groups to the whole group. Here the facilitator's role is to encourage, support and keep the conversation flowing in productive directions. A facilitator should also reflect openly with the group, to model and make transparent her investment in the process. It is always good practice to let the discussion happen without too much comment. However, comments and reflections from the facilitator's perspective can bring key points together and note interesting gaps. For example, a group might reflect for some time on the audience response to their presentation. A facilitator will gather these thoughts together and then might say, "That's so interesting, because so much of my attention was on the reactions of the funding representatives that I think I missed some of what all of you experienced. But I can share a few of their comments that I think you'll appreciate hearing."

If the group's chosen mode of reflection is written then similar choices need to be presented and made. Where and when will the writing take place? Will it be individual writing only, or a more collective written response? How will the writing be shared? How will the writing be used, with participants' consent, as part of the formal assessment?

Another way to process the presentation is through drama:

Facilitator: Let's make a circle leaving a nice open space in the middle. Think about your personal reactions to the sharing we've done. What phrase or sentence is in your head? Let that thought carry you into the middle of the circle and inform your body as you take a shape that reflects that thought. So, one by one, moving one at a time, each of you move into the circle and add your image to what is there.

> What we produced was no earth-shaking blueprint for a just society, but a theatrical record of a particular journey of the imagination, which tried to engage with important real landmarks… [Presentation is] not the ultimate destination but simply [an] important way station. In the practice of community theatre it is the journey itself which is the destination.
>
> – John Salway, 2005, p. 128

[*When last person has joined in*] Just hold that position. On my signal, turn to a person near you, shake hands and exchange your thoughts. So for example, A might say to B, "I'm glad that's over!" and B says to A "It went so much better than I feared."

Good. Now each partner, remember the phrase spoken to you, make it your own, find a new partner to shake hands with and exchange comments. [*This process repeats until participants have met and exchanged with everyone else in the group.*]

I wonder what we discovered in that activity that might help our reflective process?

The next stage of reflection can be on the presentation itself:

- What did the group learn from the audience responses about how well everything was working?
- What elements seemed to be working most successfully, and what was it about them that made them work so well?
- What might we have done to enhance the effect of other elements?

- If we had the opportunity to revisit and extend this performance project, what might we wish to add or change?
- How might the work have been affected by the presence of people who had not been part of the process?
- How did the pre-performance stage of the presentation go?
- How might engagement with the audience prior to the presentation have had an effect on the post-show conversation(s)?
- In view of that, it might be worthwhile to ask what responses participants have heard from family, colleagues or friends who were there.
- What dramatic skills might we wish to work on if we were to repeat our presentation?
- What gets lost and what is gained when we share our work with an outside audience?

A lot of assessment and valuing statements are generated in these activities. How might a facilitator, with the group's permission, record their reflections? Although there will be valuable material in this stage, it may be that recording this will inhibit or otherwise constrain the group. If the group is hesitant, or the facilitator is aware that this is not appropriate for a particular group, then the best course of action is to let go of documentation in favour of maintaining the integrity of the group and its process.

The next phase involves reflecting on the entire project, over whatever period of time the group has been together. A facilitator needs to make clear that the focus for reflection is shifting when the group has exhausted what they wish to say about the presentation experience. Ideally, this next phase will occur in a second follow-up meeting, but if it has to be done in one session, the transition to the wider areas of assessment need to be clearly defined.

14.2 Reflecting on the process

A preparatory activity for beginning to reflect on an applied drama process is Jonothan Neelands and Tony Goode's (2000) drama strategy "Marking the Moment," "a reflective device to 'mark' a position or a moment in the drama where a feeling is aroused, or an understanding of the issue occurs" (p. 83). This may be accomplished by asking participants to reflect on memorable moments within the time span of the process, which could be either a strong feeling or an insight of some kind. Then, participants are asked to move to the actual location they were in, to the best of their recollection, and to take a frozen position that shows what they were doing in that moment. When the group has held these freezes for 20 to 30 seconds in silence, they can unfreeze, relax and share with someone close by what was on their mind in that moment. Another option here is to hand out paper and pens/pencils and ask participants to capture this memory in writing and/or drawing, and then sharing.

Another strategy that can follow from here, or can begin the process, is a version of brainstorming or mind-mapping. The facilitator prepares sheets of chart paper to represent each meeting the group has held. Each piece of chart paper should have in its centre the date this meeting was held, or Week One, Week Two, and so on, along with a short title indicating the focus of that workshop. These papers are placed randomly around the room and small groups (of three to five) form around each paper. The task is to write whatever memories arise around what happened in that session. These could be quotes of things said, or responses to the workshop, or drawn images of the work, or research material that was used. After two or three minutes, groups rotate and continue these processes until all chart papers have been visited. Then, participants go back and revisit their first chart paper and discuss what has been added. Each group goes on to revisit each paper to talk about it, and if they wish, to add additional comments, images, and so on.

Back in a whole group circle, participants can reflect on their conversations and the feelings and insights brought to the surface in this activity. If participants have written comments from Marking the Moment, time can be taken to add to these comments in light of this level of reflection. These mind-maps then become resources for the next stages of reflection and also as documentation for project reporting purposes.

Focusing on how the group functioned throughout the process *as a group* is a logical next step:

- What were the strengths of the group that developed over time?
- What were key moments when participants felt the group cohere, or when they felt more of a sense of trust and belonging within the group?
- How did the space(s) we worked in, and the environment around us, have an affect on our process?
- What did we discover working in a collaborative dramatic group process that could be applied to our lives and the society we live in?
- What do we understand about drama and dramatic process as a result of this experience? How has this changed from your initial understandings?
- In other words, how does working in process resonate with, or counterbalance or even resist the more individual, competitive and outcome-oriented values of our everyday world?

Role is another of the key concepts and strategies experienced by the group:

- What roles did each person take on throughout the timeline of the workshops?
- How has our understanding of role and its function in society shifted over the course of the process?

- What does role play open up as a way of exploring and building empathy for others, and of investigating expected versus unexpected social behaviours in a dramatic framework?
- What might be the differences of playing a role which depends on what you bring to it imaginatively and playing a role that is created by the group, as seen in *Being 14* and *Sitting-Down Drama*?
- What are the challenges and rewards of working in role?
- What has the opportunity for role play given us in relation to our everyday lives?

Improvisation is the third mode of dramatic process that drives this work:

- How did improvisational skills and abilities get developed over time?
- What discoveries did participants make around understanding themselves and others when improvising, putting role into action?
- What is a very memorable improvised experience and what made it so memorable?
- What might be the difference in playing yourself (nonfiction) in an improvisation as opposed to playing someone else (fiction)?
- What strategies did participants discover in practice to support and sustain their improvisations?
- What challenges still remain to be worked on?
- How important are the abilities to communicate and be playful in improvisational work?
- How do these capacities transfer into our daily lives?
- In a highly scripted world, how does improvisation invite a different way of being in the world?
- How do drama and theatre help us to see and interpret better what's happening between people and in the world at large?
- How do drama and theatre help us to interrogate personal, local and global events that affect us and others?

Many of these questions are quite philosophical and intended to provide space for discussions that can go more deeply into the impact of the work on participants. As ever, the facilitator should closely monitor the interest and comfort levels within the group when offering these reflective opportunities. That said, good reflective processes focus less on the What of what we did and the How of what we did and are more focused on the Why, the overall purpose and value of dramatic process for this particular group of people.

14.3 Exiting a community

Leaving an applied drama project has at least two levels, to varying degrees: leaving the participant group and the larger community.

Leaving the participant group

By this time, a healthy participant group should have the skills to plan their own closing experience. We suggest that a facilitator, immediately following on from carrying out the reflective phase of a project, ask the group what their wishes are for the group's final gathering. Of course, the group may carry on without the presence of the facilitator, or perhaps with a new facilitator, so the "exiting" process may be around the dissolution of the whole group, or the departure of the facilitator from the group, or both. No matter what the circumstances, here are some questions to pose and suggestions for possible ways to organize:

- What is it that the group wants to say to each other by carrying out a final event of some kind?
- What are some specific cultural activities connected to the group and its larger community that can inform how a group wishes to carry out its final meeting?
- Are there some drama activities the group wishes to revisit as part of this closing event? If so, what are they and how will they be ordered and organized?
- How might the idea of ritual help you to think about this event? Some examples may include gathering in the drama circle and offering words of reflection one person a time, perhaps passing a talking stick or candle. Corridor of Voices can be a powerful closing ritual (see Chapter 5), whether it is the facilitator who walks down the corridor, or each participant in turn.
- The sharing of food and drink is a very common part of an exit event, and including live or recorded music adds to the celebratory occasion.
- Participants may wish to have an "open mic" event as part of this kind of closing, sharing short performances of any kind.
- An effective final circle closing involves standing in silent recognition and acknowledgment of each person in the group, taking time to make eye contact with everyone, then turning and walking away from the circle feeling the support of the group carrying each person forward into the future.
- Creating a project scrapbook of some kind—either in hard copy format with cutting and pasting into a book and/or a digital version including photos, videos, and so on, to be placed online—can be a good closing activity, and can also serve double-duty (with full participant agreement) as a component of funding-based evaluation.

Leaving the community

Often a facilitator is a visitor to the participant community. Leaving the community is therefore just as important as leaving the group. A personal reflective question a facilitator might ask is: What did the group and I learn that we need to share, that we feel the community would benefit from knowing, beyond the performance (if there was one) or the documentation by the group? The notion of reciprocity is paramount here; the mutual sharing of resources and benefits as a kind of gift exchange. While there are far too many possibilities available here for us to name in any thorough way, here are a few suggestions:

- Offering to connect with anyone who wishes to work in this setting in the future, by leaving your contact information with the sponsoring agency.
- Volunteering to speak about the applied drama project to other community groups, at political, cultural or social gatherings, in schools, and so on. Representative members of the group should be involved with these opportunities whenever possible. Ideally, these should be framed as follow-up activities drawing from the discoveries made by the group that provide space for the group's voice to be heard.
- Asking the group to create some kind of welcome/introduction for future visitors and/or new group members. This could be in written, visual or video form. What would they like new facilitators/group members to know about their community before they arrive?
- Assuring the group that, even at a distance, you will be able to support any future activities they wish to carry out, by writing letters of reference for individuals or even the whole group (should they wish to apply for a grant to continue their process, for example).
- What personal-professional process can you engage in to ensure the departure is positive for you as facilitator? What have you learned from this experience? How have you documented your time in this project for your own archives? What might you take away as powerful memories? How well were you able to help participants negotiate their way through the diversity issues (of age, gender, ability, ethnicity, class, faith, etc.) that arose within the group? What painful, difficult, challenging moments do you need to probe in order to strengthen your practice? What are your strengths as a facilitator and what areas of your practice do you see as requiring development?

14.4 Reporting strategies

Our focus in this section turns to the needs and demands of a funding/sponsoring organization. Most often this will require the writing and submission of some kind of report that is a justification and/or validation of what has taken place in terms of the original proposal. The first of many levels of challenge here is that the very process you have been engaged in is a creative one, therefore dependent upon the participants to generate the content and participate in the exploration of where the content leads them. The parameters laid out in a funding proposal may often be a mismatch with the actual unfolding of the project. Or, it may be the case that you were carrying out the project as a member of an academic institution and so its evaluation will need to be tailored in terms of acceptable academic prose or reporting approaches, as a class credit or component of a research study. All of these are real challenges to be faced when assessing an applied drama project.

In many cases, a sponsoring agency will have prepared templates for assessment purposes. In our view, it is important to take as much time and effort preparing an assessment report as was taken soliciting the funding to carry it out. Professionalism in terms of clear and polished writing, thorough description and thoughtful analysis are all important. This high level of professionalism serves your own future career prospects very well, but it also honours your participants and the process you went through together. A slapdash last-minute assessment report reflects badly on both you as facilitator and how you regard your relationship to the group with whom you were engaged.

Another area of assessment, as a general guideline, is to keep an eye on how the process might have shifted somewhat (quite naturally) from the original proposal. If, for example, the funding was attached to some kind of public performance (which is most common) and your group chose not to share their work outside of the group, you must document when that shift occurred and how you made the funding agency aware of it. Accountability is the catch-word here! Folders and/or print-outs of e-mails or notes of phone conversations or meetings are valuable documentation to maintain throughout a project for these purposes.

Numbers are very important to funders, so documentation of attendance and levels of participation will probably be required. It is a reality in this field that shifting levels of attendance and participation are normal and not necessarily a reflection on the quality of the work being done. Guiding your funders through the participation process in an honest and sensitive way is key.

As you have never thrown anything away, you will have a lot of documentation available from the project itself by the time you reach the reporting stage. With your participants' full permission, you can make effective use of their brainstorming charts, mind-maps, research material, scenario slips, dramatic and reflective writing, presentation poster/programme, publicity materials and video documentation. While there might not be space available within a template report form for selections from this process-driven documentation, we advise you to create an appendix that selectively presents this material, again in ways that focuses attention onto your participants and their accomplishments.

The aesthetic effect of the report is extremely important as it reflects on your professionalism and the work of your group. Sharing this report with the group, and asking them to "approve" it by signing or by some other means, is ideal. A group of high-risk youth, for example, might agree to have their photo taken holding the report and offering their thumbs-up or thumbs-down response to what they have read, or you have read to them. This is a playful way to include participants in the assessment response beyond the group-driven valuing covered in earlier sections of this chapter. Yet, it still does the ethical task of ensuring that you do not revert to becoming the "all-knowing expert" who is solely responsible for translating the group's experiences into a form that may be very alien, or alienating, for participants.

14.5 Summary

Horace, the first century BCE philosopher, wrote that the art form of theatre should be both entertaining and beneficial to an audience (Ars poetica, n.d.). In a developed world that can be viewed as highly, even extremely, "dramatized" (Williams, 1975)—in which reality television shows and fictional dramas begin to look more and more alike, and 30-second advertisements present polished and perhaps even deeply moving dramatic scenes for the purposes of selling something—engaging in group dramatic process can feel and operate in distinctively different ways. As education and media critic Neil Postman writes in the accompanying text box, educators should consider what they do in schools as offering a counterbalance to the prevailing culture. In this handbook we are operating from a similar philosophical point of view: that the work of applied drama offers a vital alternative to automized thinking, habitual behaviours and (self-)imposed limits.

Engaging with a community in dramatic process that is open-ended, flexible and context-driven invites new ways to consider a world that is too often closed, inflexible and outcome-driven. We live in a rapidly changing global environment that can feel turbulent and chaotic, but drama offers processual ways to accept and function effectively within states of fluidity and ambiguity. Whatever the reason for a community to assemble and work in these ways, the value lies as much in the facilitated coming together with a common purpose as in any outside instrumental concerns.

[Education is a] counterbalance [to] the information biases of culture. Such biases, if left unchecked, are tyrannies, closing off our awareness of different metaphors of the world and of different opportunities for understanding and expression.

– Neil Postman, 1979, p. 46

Role and improvisation are the means by which we engage in dramatic process safely yet creatively to explore issues and ideas with which we wish to engage. Through this process, we learn that we can indeed exert some control over our lives as we discover the power of action and of our own words. Applied drama facilitation provides participants a space within which a way of being in the world can be both modelled and experienced: a way of being that is more interested in processes than products, more interested in identity as shifting and mutable rather than fixed, more interested in life as improvised and subject to change as opposed to scripted and unalterable. Recent brain research is beginning to show a robust relationship between the ways in which applied drama works best and how people work together and learn most effectively (Damasio, 2010; Kahneman, 2011; Siegel, 2007). From that research and our own practice we can take hope that applied drama processes will continue to expand and reach out, modifying and mediating training programs, community-based projects and institutional agendas of care and rehabilitation. Valuing human relationships, celebrating diverse cultures, and envisioning a more sustainable and just world are the central actions of applied drama practice.

> The great privilege of the theatre is the conversation that occurs while people are making something together.
>
> – Martha Burns and Paul Gross, 2009, p. 28

Afterword

Books require conclusions, which we would rather resist. Instead, we summarise the principles of applied drama facilitation presented throughout this handbook. These are offered to you, the skilled facilitator, the facilitator-in-training, or the interested reader, as a possible mandate or mantra for practice:

In applied drama,
- the encounter/engagement is processual and is
- based on participants' ideas and concerns;
- it functions through cooperation and collaboration
- under fictional circumstances
- by means of role and improvisation.
- It is driven by questions
- and tasks that are offered in conditional language as invitations.
- The position of facilitator is as a member of the group who holds the expertise of form;
- whereas the group has expertise in ways that will be different, especially with regard to content.
- Reflection is a key strategy woven throughout the process
- in order to examine the series of tiny "products" that, as part of a process,
- allow us to see where we are and where we wish to go through shared thought and decision-making.

Yet, like the world, the work remains generally unfinished (albeit not unpolished) and ever open to new possibilities.

Applied drama/theatre models based on Nancy King's 1978 continuum of observation

MODELS

PRIVATE	SEMI-PRIVATE	SEMI-PUBLIC	PUBLIC
Individual process	Paired or group process	Informal observation of process by invitation	Formal presentation open
Individual role play	Paired or group role play	(to funders, similar groups, family and friends)	to all (moving to performance)
Individual improvisation	Paired or group improvisation		

OBSERVATION CONTINUUM (King, 1978)

←------------------------------→

Private: work is unobserved; reflection is intrapersonal

Semi-Private: work is observed by others who are doing the same work; reflection is intra- and interpersonal

Semi-Public: work is shared with others who have concerns or a direct interest in the issues being presented; reflection is interactive with the audience

Public: the work is performed for an "accidental" audience; reflection is generally individual or with informal groups

Selected peer reviewed publications on applied drama, 1996–2012

AUTHOR(S)	DATE	INTENTION
Ackroyd, J.	2007	To train diabetes counsellors through drama
Arciuli, J., Carroll, J. & Cameron, D.	2008	To assist in the training of professionals working in the area of crisis management
Baim, C., Brookes, S. & Mountford, A.	2002	To offer drama and mask-based strategies for working with offenders in prisons and other people at risk
Baldwin, A.	2009	To enhance social and emotional wellbeing, support individual and communal resilience and self-efficacy, and encourage positive interpersonal interactions in indigenous communities
Cahill, H.	2010	To equip women and girls to talk openly about sex within a culture in which this is not the norm
Cameron, D. & Carroll, J.	2009	To suggest how some of the conventions developed in applied theatre may be of use to the designers of serious games (computer or video games used for educational purposes)
Cawthon, S.W. & Dawson, K.	2009	To make sustainable improvements in the learning culture of a classroom, school and school district
Chinyowa, K. C.	2011	To offer more participatory approaches to monitoring and evaluation practices in applied drama/theatre, particularly in African contexts
Chinyowa, K. C.	2009	To explore emergent paradigms of applied drama/theatre practice in Africa
Conroy, C.	2009	To present a themed issue on drama and theatre with people with disabilities (multiple authors follow)
Daboo, J.	2007	To explore issues surrounding self-harm with a group of Asian women in Britain
Fenech, A.	2010	To increase engagement in occupational therapy for patients with brain injuries or neurological diseases
Fonio, F. & Genicot, G.	2011	To employ drama education strategies in a second language program for postsecondary students

Franks, A.	2010	To discuss the use of drama in language and literacy education
Gallagher, K. & Neelands, J.	2011	To present a themed issue on applied drama/theatre in urban settings (multiple authors follow)
Goddard, J.	2012	To develop working relationships for young people with learning disabilities through drama
Grant, D. & Crossan, J.M.	2012	To consider how a failed element of a prison-based applied drama project ironically demonstrated success amongst the six participants in terms of their improved sense of self-worth
Grant, D., Elliott, J. & Morison, S.	2012	To show the effects of an arts project (including drama) with seniors with dementia
Haseman, B. & Winston, J.	2010	To present a themed issue on aesthetics in applied drama/theatre (multiple authors follow)
Heddon, D. & Mackey, S.	2012	To present a themed issue on the use of drama/theatre in environmental education (multiple authors follow)
Hunter, M. A.	2008	To collaborate in the production of a safe creative space in the context of a performance-based Peace Project
Hwang, H.	2009	To address questions around intercultural considerations of applied drama and the Eastern theory and practice of the art of cultivation
Joronen, K., Konu, A., Rankin, S. H. & Åstedt-Kurki, P.	2011	To present a quantitative study showing the positive effects of a drama-based anti-bullying program in Finland with students in Grades 4–5 (ages 9 to 10)
Joronen, K., Rankin, S. H. & Åstedt-Kurki, P.	2008	To increase knowledge and positive attitudes related to health behaviour among school children (a review of the literature on this topic)
Kersey, O.	2008	To use role play in a fourth grade class to prepare for a visit to an historical site and to potentially transform dominant historical narratives
Kettula-Kouttas, K.	2009	To introduce drama as a tool in higher education, in courses in professional ethics, marketing and forest economics
Libman, K.	1996	To use process drama in pre-service teacher education
Low, K.	2010	To use theatre and performance forms to place the individual and his/her emotional and physical wellbeing at the forefront of an approach that aims to tackle the AIDS pandemic in South Africa

Mages, W.	2004	To work with urban youth to develop conflict resolution capabilities, critical thinking skills and proficiency in discussion through improvisation
McLaren, J.	2010	To present and analyse the work of Clowns Without Borders, a dramatic arts-based intervention in communities dealing with HIV/AIDS in South Africa
Neelands, J.	2009	To claim that the ensemble approach of teaching drama provides young people with a model of democratic and pro-social living in schools
Nelson, B. Colby, R. & McIlrath, M.	2001	To use mantle of the expert with underachieving minority middle school students
Nicholson, H.	2005a	To theorize the roots and survey the range of practice of applied drama and applied theatre
O'Connor, P.	2000	To provide a language for intellectually disabled students to explore their own experiences and needs
O'Connor, P.	2007	To use process drama with mental health service providers to shift workplace attitudes that were discriminatory or stigmatizing
O'Connor, P., Holland, C. & O'Connor, B.	2007	To use process drama activities such as role play, hot-seating and writing in role to explore issues raised by a theatre-in-education production on family violence, child abuse and neglect
Piazzoli, E.	2010	To illustrate of process drama to enhance intercultural awareness for learners of Italian as an additional language
Pilkington, A.	2010	To use drama and oral history strategies with social science students to create and disseminate a video on diversity and equity issues in police training
Poulsen, J.	2009	To examine classroom leadership concepts in a pre-service teacher education program through drama
Pratt Cooney, M. & Sawilowsky, S.	2005	To support the use of process drama as an additional pedagogical tool for acting teachers
Rasmussen, B.	2010	To examine the relationship between drama, aesthetics and constructivist education
Roberts, G, Somers, J., Dawe, J., Passy, R., Mays, C., Carr, G., Shiers, D. & Smith, J.	2007	To support early intervention by increasing knowledge and understanding of early psychosis in a mental health education program incorporating interactive drama

Sánchez-Camus, R.	2009	To address youth issues and HIV/AIDS in a collaborative and participatory arts project in Ghana
Schonmann, S.	2005	To claim the need for balance between the instrumental function and the artistic-aesthetic function of drama and theatre work in education
Sinclair, C. & Grindrod, A.	2007	To develop a grassroots campaign for health promotion
Snyder-Young, D.	2011	To reflect on the struggles and tensions felt as co-facilitator of a Theatre of the Oppressed project in an urban charter school, especially around the temptation to influence the work
Stinson, M. & Winston, J.	2011	To present a themed issue on the use of drama in second language learning (multiple authors follow)
Tam, P.	2010	To use Carnival theory to reflect on drama pedagogy recently introduced into the Hong Kong curriculum
Van Vuuren, P. J.	2004	To draw on Joseph Campbell's (1949/2008) "Hero's Journey" and Morgan & Saxton's (1987) "taxonomy of personal engagement" to develop self-discovery and personal growth through applied drama
Wang, W.	2010	To consider the use of Boal's Theatre of the Oppressed techniques in a Taiwanese setting as a way to devise a community performance
Winston, J.	1998	To use an English folk tale to explore drug-related issues
Winston, J.	2007	To consider the role of applied drama in citizenship and human rights education in a themed issue (multiple authors follow)
Winston, J., Lo, C. & Wang, X.	2010	To look at two applied drama projects in China and Taiwan through the lenses of transnational, space and border crossing theories

BIOGRAPHY SHEET

NAME:_____

ADDRESS: _____   PLACE
                                                                        PICTURE
_____   HERE

_____ POSTAL CODE_____

PHONE: _____

OTHER CONTACT INFORMATION?

_____

_____

[Thank you for the following information. Please use the other side of the page if you need more space.]

WHAT REASONS LED YOU TO BE A PART OF THIS PROJECT?

WHAT SPECIAL SKILLS DO YOU HAVE? (DO YOU PLAY AN INSTRUMENT, DO CPR, SING …?)

IS THERE ANY PHYSICAL OR OTHER KIND OF PROBLEM OF WHICH I SHOULD BE AWARE THAT MIGHT INHIBIT YOUR WORK IN THIS PROJECT?

IS THERE ANYTHING THAT YOU WOULD LIKE ME TO KNOW?

Sitting-Down Drama

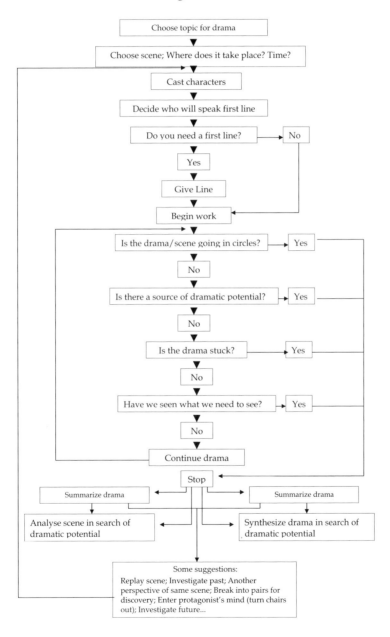

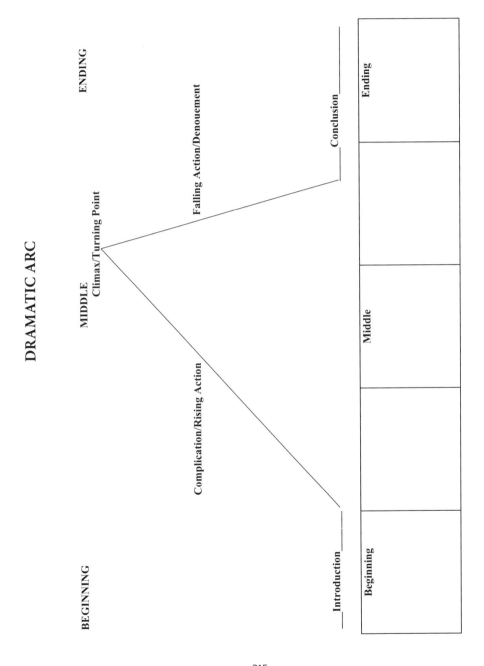

DRAMATIC ARC

INTERVIEW CONSENT FORM

[Adapted from the University of Tasmania, School of English, Journalism and European Languages]

Name of project_____

Name of interviewer_____

Facilitator or Funding Organization contact information_____

_____

1. I agree to be interviewed for the purposes of the project named above.
2. The purpose and nature of the interview has been explained to me by the interviewer and I have seen a description of the project on a separate page.
3. I agree that the interview may be electronically recorded.
4. Any questions that I asked about the purpose and nature of the interview have been answered to my satisfaction.
5. In the event of a public performance I agree that my words be included.
6. My name will not be used or cited or my identity otherwise disclosed without my permission.

Name of interviewee_____

Signature of interviewee_____

Date_____

****

6. I have explained the project and the implications of being interviewed to the interviewee and I believe that the consent is informed and that s/he understands the implications of participation.

Name of interviewer_____

Signature of interviewer_____

Date_____

Notes:

The Man Who Finds That His Son Has Become a Thief

Coming into the store at first angry
At the accusation, believing in
The word of his boy who has told him:
I didn't steal anything, honest.

Then becoming calmer, seeing that anger
Will not help in the business, listening painfully
As the other's evidence unfolds, so painfully slow.

Then seeing gradually that evidence
Almost as if tighten slowly around the neck
Of his son, at first vaguely circumstantial, then gathering damage,
Until there is present the unmistakable odour of guilt
Which seeps now into the mind and lays its poison.

Suddenly feeling sick and alone and afraid,
As if an unseen hand had slapped him in the face
For no reason whatsoever: wanting to get out
Into the street, the night, the darkness, anywhere to hide
The pain that must show in the face to these strangers, the fear.

It must be like this.
It could hardly be otherwise.

by Raymond Souster from *Collected Poems*,
© Oberon Press (1984). Reprinted with permission.

SCENARIO SLIPS

SOURCE:

WHO:

WHERE/WHEN:

WHAT:

WHY:

HOW:

SOURCE:

WHO:

WHERE/WHEN:

WHAT:

WHY:

HOW:

SOURCE:

WHO:

WHERE/WHEN:

WHAT:

WHY:

HOW:

Bibliography

Note: Texts, articles and media sources listed under Further Reading in each chapter are not repeated here.

A teaspoon of light: full performance [Video file]. (2012). Retrieved June 18, 2012 from http://www.youtube.com/watch?v=XWGpJaShQaU.

Ackroyd, J. (2004). *Role reconsidered: A re-evaluation of the relationship between the teacher-in-role and acting.* Stoke on Trent, UK: Trentham.

Ackroyd, J. (2007). Applied theatre: An exclusionary discourse? *Applied Theatre Researcher, 8*, Article 1. Retrieved December 6, 2012 from http://www.griffith.edu.au/education/griffith-institute-educational-research/research-expertise/applied-theatre-researcheridea-journal/issues

Arciuli, J., Carroll, J., & Cameron, D. (2008). The use of applied drama in crisis management: An empirical psychological study. *Australian Journal of Emergency Management, 23*(3), 3–8.

Ars poetica. (n.d.). In *Emory College of Arts and Sciences online.* Retrieved June 7, 2012 from http://www.english.emory.edu/DRAMA/ArsPoetica.html.

Baim, C., Brookes, S., & Mountford, A. (Eds.). (2002). *The Geese Theatre handbook: Drama with offenders and people at risk.* Winchester, UK: Waterside Press.

Baldwin, A. (2009). Applied theatre: Performing the future. *Australasian Psychiatry, 17*(S1), S133–136.

Barish, J. (1981). *The antitheatrical prejudice.* Berkeley, CA: University of California Press.

Barker, C. (1977/2010). *Theatre games: A new approach to drama training.* London, UK: Methuen.

Barron, F. (1988). Putting creativity to work. In R. Sternberg (Ed.), *The nature of creativity* (pp. 76–98). Cambridge: Cambridge University Press.

Beckerman, B. (1979). *Dynamics of drama: Theory and method of analysis.* New York: Drama Book Specialists.

Bell, E. (2008). *Theories of performance*. Thousand Oaks, CA: Sage.

Ben Chaim, D. (1984). *Distance in the theatre: The aesthetics of audience response*. Ann Arbor, MI: UMI Research Press.

Birdwhistell, R. L. (1970). *Kinesics and context: Essays on body motion communication*. Pittsburgh, PA: University of Pennsylvania Press.

Blumenfeld-Jones, D. (2004). Bodily-kinesthetic intelligence and the democratic ideal. In J. L. Kincheloe (Ed.), *Multiple intelligences revisited* (pp. 119–130). New York, NY: Peter Lang.

Boal, A. (1992/2002). *Games for actors and non-actors* (2nd ed.) (A. Jackson, Trans.). New York, NY: Routledge.

Bolton, G. (1984). *Drama as education: An argument for placing drama at the centre of the curriculum*. Harlow, UK: Longman.

Bolton, G. (October 1989). Poesis and mimesis [Keynote address]. Presented at *Council of Drama in Education* conference, St. Catherine's, Ontario.

Bolton, G. (1997). Dorothy Heathcote reflects with Gavin Bolton. In D. Davis (Ed.), *Interactive research in drama in education* (pp. 7–40). Stoke on Trent, UK: Trentham.

Bolton, G. (1998). *Acting in classroom drama: A critical analysis*. Stoke on Trent, UK: Trentham.

Bolton, G., & Heathcote, D. (1999). *So you want to use role-play? A new approach in how to plan*. Stoke on Trent, UK: Trentham.

Booker, C. (2004). *The seven basic plots: Why we tell stories*. London, UK: Continuum.

Booth, D., & Lundy, C. (1985). *Improvisation*. Don Mills, ON: Academic Press.

Booth, E. (1999). *The everyday work of art: Awakening the extraordinary in your daily life*. Napierville, IL: Sourcebooks.

Booth, M. (1991). *Theatre in the Victorian Age*. Cambridge, UK: Cambridge University Press.

Bowell, P., & Heap B. (2001). *Planning process drama*. London, UK: David Fulton.

Bowman, W., & Powell, K. (2007). The body in a state of music. In L. Bresler (Ed.), *International handbook of research in arts education: Part 2* (pp. 1087–1106). Dordrecht, NL: Springer.

Brecht, B. (2010). *The Caucasian chalk circle*. (A. Beaton, Trans.). London: Methuen.

Bresler, L. (Ed.). (2004). *Knowing bodies: Moving minds: Towards embodied teaching and learning*. Dordrecht, the Netherlands: Kluwer Academic Publishers.

Burns, M., & Gross, P. (2009). Photographic portrait. In V. Tony Hauser, *Stage presence/ Présence sur scène: Portraits by V. Tony Hauser* (p. 28). Toronto, ON: Studio Gallery Press.

Cahill, H. (2010). Re-thinking the fiction-reality boundary: Investigating the use of drama in HIV prevention projects in Vietnam. *Research in Drama Education: The Journal of Applied Theatre and Performance, 15*(2), 155–174.

Caine, R. N., Caine, G., McClintic, C., & Klimek, K. J. (2008). *12 brain/mind learning principles in action: Developing executive functions of the human brain*. Thousand Oaks, CA: Corwin.

Cameron, D., & Carroll, J. (2009). Lessons from applied drama: Conventions to help serious games developers. In O. Petrovic & A. Brand (Eds.), *Serious games on the move* (pp. 27–41). New York, NY: Springer-Verlag/Wien.

Campbell, J. (1949/2008). *Hero with a thousand faces* (3rd ed.). Novato, CA: New Worl Library.

Carlson, M. (2001). *The haunted stage: Theatre as memory machine*. Ann Arbor, MI: University of Michigan Press.

Carroll, J., & Cameron, D. (2003). To the Spice Islands: Interactive process drama. Retrieved April 26, 2010 from hypertext.rmit.edu.au/dac/papers/Carroll.pdf.

Carroll, J., & Cameron, D. (2005). Playing the game, role distance and digital performance. *Applied Theatre Researcher, 6*, [Article 11]. Retrieved October 8, 2010 from.http://www.griffith.edu.au/education/griffith-institute-educational-research/research-expertise/applied-theatre-researcheridea-journal/issues

Cavarero, A. (2000). *Relating narratives: Storytelling and selfhood*. London, UK & New York, NY: Routledge.

Cawthon, S. W., & Dawson, K. (2009). Drama for schools: Impact of a drama-based professional development program on teacher self-efficacy and authentic instruction. *Youth Theatre Journal, 23*(2), 144–161.

Chinyowa, K. C. (2009). Emerging paradigms for applied drama and theatre practice in African contexts. *Research in Drama Education: Journal of Applied Theatre and Performance, 14*(3), 329–346.

Chinyowa, K. C. (2011). Revisiting monitoring and evaluation strategies for applied drama and theatre practice in African contexts. *Research in Drama Education: Journal of Applied Theatre and Performance, 16*(3), 337–356.

Clark, B. (1971). *Group theatre*. London, UK: Pitman.

Cockburn, B. (2005, June 21). Sounds like Canada with host Sheila Rogers [Radio broadcast]. Toronto, ON: Canadian Broadcasting Corporation.

Conroy, C. (Ed.) (2009). On disability: Creative tensions in applied theatre [Themed issue]. *Research in Drama Education: Journal of Applied Theatre and Performance, 14*(1).

Conroy, C. (2010). *Theatre & body*. Basingstoke, UK: Palgrave Macmillan.

Courtney, R. (1980). *The dramatic curriculum*. London, ON: University of Western Ontario.

Croyden, M. (2003). *Conversations with Peter Brook 1970–2000*. New York, NY: Faber and Faber Inc.

Daboo, J. (2007). Unveiled: Interrogating the use of applied drama in multiple and specific sites. *Research in Drama Education: Journal of Applied Theatre and Performance, 12*(1), 55–64.

Damasio, A. (2010). *Self comes to mind: Constructing the conscious brain*. New York, NY: Pantheon.

Davidson, J. (2004). Embodied knowledge: Possibilities and constraints in arts education and curriculum. In L. Bresler (Ed.), *Knowing bodies: Moving minds: Towards embodied teaching and learning* (pp. 197–212). Dordrecht, the Netherlands: Kluwer Academic Publishers.

Davis, J. H. (2005). Redefining Ratso Rizzo: Learning from the arts about process and reflection. *Phi Delta Kappan, 87*(1), 11–17.

Deasy, R. (2001). Keynote: Tucson Symposium on the Arts. Tucson, AZ: February. [Based on the research that resulted in *Champions of Change: The Impact of the Arts on Learning*. 1998. NEA Partnerships in Arts Education and the Kennedy Centre. Washington, DC].

Deavere Smith, A. (1997). *Fires in the mirror: Crown Heights, Brooklyn and other identities*. New York, NY: Dramatists Play Service.

Deavere Smith, A. (2003). *Twilight Los Angeles, 1992*. New York, NY: Dramatists Play Service.

Dewey, J. (1938). *Experience and education*. Indianapolis, IN: Kappa Delta Pi Press.

Dewey, J. (1934/2005). *Art as experience*. New York, NY: Penguin.

Doll, W. (2008). Looking back to the future: A recursive retrospective. *Journal of the Canadian Association for Curriculum Studies, 6*(1), 3–20.

Eriksson, S. (2011). Distancing at close range: Making strange devices in Dorothy Heathcote's process drama Teaching Political Awareness through Drama. *Research in Drama Education: Journal of Applied Theatre and Performance, 16*(1), 101–123.

Fenech, A. (2010). Inspiring transformations through participation in drama for individuals with neuropalliative conditions. *Journal of Applied Arts and Health, 1*(1), 63–80.

Finlay-Johnson, H. (1911). *The dramatic method of teaching*. London, UK: Nisbet.

Fish, S. (1980). *Is there a text in this class? The authority of interpretive communities*. Cambridge, MA: Harvard University Press.

Fonio, F. & Genicot, G. (2011). The compatibility of drama language teaching and CEFR objectives – observations on a rationale for an artistic approach to foreign language teaching at an academic level. *Scenario, V*(2), 71–84.

Franks, A. (2010). Drama in teaching and learning language and literacy. In D. Wyse, R. Andrews & J. Hoffmann (Eds.), *The Routledge International Handbook of English, Language and Literacy Teaching* (pp. 242–253). London, UK: Routledge.

Freire, P. (1970/2000). *Pedagogy of the oppressed: 30th anniversary edition* (M. B. Ramos, Trans.). New York, NY: Continuum.

Freire, P. (1992/2004). *Pedagogy of hope: Reliving the pedagogy of the oppressed* (R.R. Barr, Trans.). New York, NY: Continuum.

Fulford, R. (1999). *The triumph of narrative: Storytelling the age of mass culture*. Toronto, ON: House of Anansi.

Gallagher, K., & Neelands, J. (Eds.). (2011). Drama and theatre in urban contexts [Themed issue]. *Research in Drama Education: Journal of Applied Theatre and Performance, 16*(2).

Giles, H. & Le Poire, B. A. (2006). The ubiquity and social meaningfulness of nonverbal communication. In V. Manusov & M. L. Patterson (Eds.), *The Sage handbook of nonverbal communication* (pp. xv–xxvi). Thousand Oaks, CA: Sage.

Goddard, J. (2012). Enacting change: Disability and the arts in Northern Ireland. *Journal of Arts and Communities, 3*(1), 49–56.

Goodwin, J. (2004). The productive postshow: Facilitating, understanding and optimizing personal narratives in audience talk following a personal narrative performance. *Theatre Topics, 14*(1), 317–338.

Govan, E., Nicholson, H., & Normington, K. (2007). *Making a performance: Devising histories and contemporary practices.* Abingdon, OX: Routledge.

Grant, D., & Crossan, J. M. (2012). Freedom to fail: The unintended consequences of a prison drama. *Performance Research, 17*(1), 97–100.

Grant, D., Elliott, J., & Morison, S. (2012). Holding eternity in an hour: A practical exploration of the arts in the health care of older people with dementia. *Journal of Applied Arts and Health, 2*(3), 237–255.

Gray, R., & Sinding, C. (2002). *Standing ovation: Performing social science research about cancer.* Walnut Creek, CA: AltaMira.

Greene, M. (1995). *Releasing the imagination: Essays on education, the arts and social change.* San Francisco, CA: Jossey-Bass.

Groundwater-Smith, S., Ewing, R., & Le Cornu, R. (1998/2006). *Teaching: Challenges & Dilemmas.* Melbourne, AU: Thomson.

Grumet, M. (1998). *Bitter milk: Women and teaching.* Amherst, MS: University of Massachusetts Press.

Grunwald, M. (Ed.). (2008). *Human haptic perception: Basics and applications.* Basel: Verlag.

Haidt, J. (2012). *The righteous mind: Why good people are divided by politics and religion.* New York, NY: Pantheon.

Hall, E. T. (1969). *The hidden dimension: An anthropologist examines Man's use of space in public and in private.* Garden City, NY: Anchor.

Halprin, A. (1995). *Moving toward life: Five decades of transformational dance* (Rachel Kaplan, Ed.). Hanover, NH: Wesleyan.

Hanisch, C. (2006). Introduction to her original paper "The personal is political" (1969). Retrieved February 22, 2012, from http://www.carolhanisch.org/CHwritings/PIP.html.

Hannaford, C. (1995/2005). *Smart moves: Why learning is not all in your head* (2nd ed.). Salt Lake City, UT: Great River Books.

Haseman, B. & Winston, J. (Eds.). (2010). The aesthetics of applied theatre and drama education [Themed issue]. *Research in Drama Education: Journal of Applied Theatre and Performance, 15*(4).

Heathcote, D. (1991). Improvisation. In L. Johnson & C. O'Neill (Eds.), *Dorothy Heathcote: Collected writing on education and drama* (pp. 44–48). London, UK: Hutchinson.

Heddon, D., & Mackey, S. (Eds.). (2012). Environmentalism [Themed issue]. *Research in Drama Education: Journal of Applied Theatre and Performance, 17*(2).

Hindin, M. J. (2007). Role theory. In G. Ritzer (Ed.), *The Blackwell Encyclopedia of Sociology* (pp. 3959–3962). Oxford: Blackwell.

Hodgson, J. & Richards, E. (1966/1974). *Improvisation.* London, UK: Methuen.

Homer. (2006). *The odyssey.* (R. Fagles, Trans.). London: Penguin.

Hunter, M. A. (2008). Cultivating the art of safe space. *Research in Drama Education: Journal of Applied Theatre and Performance, 13*(1), 5–21.

Hwang, H. (2009). Between artistic instrumentalism in applied drama and the notion of cultivation in Eastern theory and practice of art. In J. Shu & P. Chan (Eds.), *Planting trees of drama with global vision in local knowledge: IDEA 2007 dialogues* (pp. 91–98). Hong Kong: IDEA Publications.

John-Steiner, V. (2000). *Creative collaboration.* New York, NY: Oxford University Press.

Johnson, L., & O'Neill, C. (Eds.). (1991). *Dorothy Heathcote: Collected writings on education and drama.* Evanston, IL: Northwestern University Press.

Johnstone, K. (1987). *Impro: Improvisation and the theatre.* New York, NY: Routledge.

Johnstone, K. (1999). *Impro for storytellers.* New York, NY: Routledge/Theatre Arts Books.

Joronen, K., Konu, A., Rankin, S. H., & Åstedt-Kurki, P. (2011). An evaluation of a drama program to enhance social relationships and anti-bullying at elementary school: A controlled study. *Health Promotion International, 27*(1), 5–14.

Joronen, K., Rankin, S. H., & Åstedt-Kurki, P. (2008). School-based drama interventions in health promotion for children and adolescents: Systematic review. *Journal of Advanced Nursing, 63*(2), 116–131.

Kahneman, D. (2011). *Thinking, fast and slow.* Toronto: Doubleday.

Kandil, Y. (2012). *Effective methods of TfD Practice: Understanding the conditions that provide autonomy and empowerment for marginalized communities.* Unpublished dissertation study, University of Victoria.

Kao, S., & O'Neill, C. (1998). *Words into worlds: Learning a second language through process drama.* Stamford, CT: Ablex.

Kersey, O. (2008). Amendments to a national narrative: Children performing history in the Sutter's Fort Environmental Living Program. *Youth Theatre Journal, 22*(1), 108–126.

Kettula-Kouttas, K. (2009). Enhancing understanding: Drama as a tool in higher education. In J. Shu & P. Chan (Eds.), *Planting trees of drama with global vision in local knowledge: IDEA 2007 dialogues* (pp. 336–353). Hong Kong: IDEA Publications.

King, N. (1981). *A movement approach to acting.* Englewood Cliffs, NJ: Prentice-Hall.

Knowles, R. (2010). *Theatre & interculturalism.* Basingstoke, UK: Palgrave Macmillan.

Kudelka, J. (2012, May 7). Choreographing the undanceable. *The Globe and Mail.* Retrieved June 18, 2012 from http://www.theglobeandmail.com/arts/theatre-and-performance/choreographing-the-undanceable/article4107163/.

Levitin, D. J. (2008). *The world in six songs.* Toronto: Penguin.

Libman, K. (1996). Right from the start: An initial drama session for pre-service teachers. *Drama Matters, 1*(1), 67–72.

Lockford, L., & Pelias, R. (2004). Bodily poeticizing in theatrical improvisation: A typology of performative knowledge. *Theatre Topics, 14*(2), 431–443.

Low, K. (2010). Creating a space for the individual: Different theatre and performance-based approaches to sexual health communication in South Africa. *Journal of Applied Arts & Health, 1*(1), 111–126.

Mages, W. (2004). Urban Improv: A portrait of an educational drama organization. *Youth Theatre Journal, 18*(1), 30–44.

Mamet, D. (2000). *Three uses of the knife: On the nature and purpose of drama.* New York: Vintage.

Mar, R., Oatley, K., Hirsh, J., dela Paz, J., & Peterson, J. (2006). Bookworms versus nerds: Exposure to fiction versus non-fiction, divergent associations with social ability, and the simulation of fictional social worlds. *ScienceDirect: Journal of Research in Personality, 40,* 694–712. Retrieved from http://www.elsevier.com/locate/jrp.

McCloskey, D., & Gandevi, S. (1993). Aspects of proprioception. In S. C. Gandevia, D. J. Burke & M. Anthony (Eds.), *Science and practice in clinical neurology* (pp. 3–19). Cambridge, MS: Cambridge University Press.

McConachie, B. (2008). *Engaging audiences: A cognitive approach to spectating in the theatre.* New York, NY: Palgrave Macmillan.

McLaren, J. (2010). Storytelling, drama and play in psychosocial interventions for communities affected by HIV/AIDS in Southern Africa—developing pathways to locally sustainable care. *South African Theatre Journal, 24*(1), 67–81.

McNeill, D. (Ed.) (2005). Gesture: A psycholinguistic approach. In the Psycholinguistic Section, *The encyclopedia of language and linguistics* (2nd ed.). London, UK: Elsevier Press. Retrieved September 25, 2011, from http://mcneilllab.uchicago.edu/pdfs/gesture.a_psycholinguistic_approach.cambridge.encyclop.pdf.

Miller, C., & Saxton, J. (2004). *Into the story: Language in action through drama.* Portsmouth, NH: Heinemann.

Mimesis. (1986). In P. Hanks (Ed.), *Collins dictionary of the English language* (2nd ed., p. 979). London, UK: Collins.

Morgan, N., & Saxton, J. (1987). *Teaching drama: A mind of many wonders.* London, UK: Hutchinson.

Morgan, N., & Saxton, J. (1995/2006). *Asking better questions* (2nd ed.). Markham, ON: Pembroke.

Morgan, N., & Saxton, J. (2000). Influences around the word. *Drama Matters: The Journal of the Ohio Drama Education Exchange, 4*, 7–20.

National Association of Drama Therapy (n.d.). What is drama therapy? Retrieved October 15, 2010 from http://www.nadta.org/faqs.html.

Neelands, J. (1984). *Making sense of drama: A guide to classroom practice.* Portsmouth, NH: Heinemann.

Neelands, J. (2009). Acting together: Ensemble as a democratic process in art and life. *Research in Drama Education: Journal of Applied Theatre and Performance, 14*(2), 173–189.

Neelands, J., & Goode, T. (2000). *Structuring drama work: A handbook of available forms in theatre and drama.* Cambridge, UK: Cambridge University Press.

Nelson, B., Colby, R., & McIlrath, M. (2001). "Having their say": The effects of using role with an urban middle school class. *Youth Theatre Journal, 15*(1), 59–69.

Nicholson, H. (2005a). *Applied drama: The gift of theatre.* Basingstoke, UK: Palgrave Macmillan.

Nicholson, H. (2005b). On ethics. *Research in Drama Education: Journal of Applied Theatre and Performance, 10*(2), 119–125.

Norman, J. (1999, Summer). Brain right drama. *Drama Magazine* [UK], 8–14.

Nussbaum, M. (2010). *Not for profit: Why democracy needs the humanities.* Princeton, NJ: Princeton University Press.

Oatley, K. (2009). Changing our minds. Retrieved June 3, 2012, from http://greatergood.berkeley.edu/.

O'Connor, P. (2000). Down the yellow brick road. *Applied Theatre Researcher, 1* [Article 4]. Retrieved June 11, 2012 from http://www.griffith.edu.au/education/griffith-institute-educational-research/research-expertise/applied-theatre-researcheridea-journal/issues

O'Connor, P. (2007). Reflection and refraction—the dimpled mirror of process drama: How process drama assists people to reflect on their attitudes and behaviors associated with mental illness. *Youth Theatre Journal, 21*, 1–11.

O'Connor, P. (Ed.) (2010). *Creating democratic citizenship through drama education: The writings of Jonothan Neelands.* Stoke-on-Trent, UK: Trentham Books.

O'Connor, P., Holland, C., & O'Connor, B. (2007). The everyday becomes extraordinary: Conversations about family violence, through applied theatre. *Applied Theatre Researcher, 8* [Article 3]. Retrieved June 11, 2012 from http://www.griffith.edu.au/education/griffith-institute-educational-research/research-expertise/applied-theatre-researcheridea-journal/issues

Oddey, A. (1996). *Devising theatre: A practical and theoretical handbook.* London, UK: Routledge.

O'Neill, C. (1995). *Drama worlds: A framework for process drama.* Portsmouth, NH: Heinemann.

Osmond, C. (2007). Drama education and the body: "I am, therefore I think". In L. Bresler (Ed.), *International handbook of research in arts education: Part 2* (pp. 1109–1118). Dordrecht, NL: Springer.

O'Toole, J. (1992). *The process of drama: Negotiating art and meaning.* London, UK: Routledge.

O'Toole, J., & Lepp. M. (Eds.). (2000). *Drama for life: Stories of adult learning and empowerment.* Brisbane, AU: Playlab.

Partnership for 21st Century Skills. (n.d.). Framework for 21st century learning. Retrieved June 7, 2012 from http://www.p21.org/overview.

Patel, A. D. (2006). Musical rhythm, linguistic rhythm, and human evolution. *Music Perception: An Interdisciplinary Journal, 24*(1), 99–104.

Pavis, P. (1998). *Dictionary of the theatre: Terms, concepts and analysis* (C. Shantz, Trans.). Toronto: University of Toronto Press.

Pawar, S. (2012). A synopsis of process thought. Retrieved June 18, 2012 from http://www.ctr4process.org/about/process/Synopsis.shtml.

Piazzoli, E. (2010). Process drama and intercultural language learning: An experience of contemporary Italy. *Research in Drama Education: The Journal of Applied Theatre and Performance, 15*(3), 385–402.

Pilkington, A. (2010). How can film and drama be used on social science-based vocational programmes to engage participants? *Enhancing Learning in the Social Sciences, 3*(1), 1–21.

Pite, C. (2009). Photographic portrait. In V. Tony Hauser, *Stage presence/Présence sur scène: Portraits by V. Tony Hauser* (p. 128). Toronto, ON: Studio Gallery Press.

Poiesis. (1986). In P. Hanks (Ed.), *Collins dictionary of the English language* (2nd ed., p. 1183). London, UK: Collins.

Polanyi, M. (1967). *The tacit dimension.* New York, NY: Anchor Books.

Postman, N. (1979). *Teaching as a conserving activity.* New York, NY: Delacorte Press.

Poulsen, J. (2009). Teacher as performer: Using theatre/drama concepts and methodology to teach student teachers. In J. Shu & P. Chan (Eds.), *Planting trees of drama with global vision in local knowledge: IDEA 2007 dialogues* (pp. 440–449). Hong Kong: IDEA Publications.

Pratt Cooney, M., & Sawilowsky, S. (2005). Process drama and actor training. *Youth Theatre Journal, 19*(1), 55–70.

Prendergast, M. (2008). *Teaching spectatorship: Essays and poems on audience in performance.* Amherst, NY: Cambria Press.

Prendergast, M. (2011). Devoted and disgruntled: An Open Space Making a Scene conference [Review]. *Canadian Theatre Review, 148,* 100–103.

Prendergast, M., & Saxton, J. (2009). *Applied theatre: International case studies and challenges for practice.* Bristol, UK: Intellect.

Process philosophy. (October 2012). In *Stanford Encyclopedia of Philosophy online*. Retrieved November 15, 2012 from http://plato.stanford.edu/entries/process-philosophy/

Rasmussen, B. (2010). The "good enough" drama: Reinterpreting constructivist aesthetics and epistemology in drama education. *Research in Drama Education: The Journal of Applied Theatre and Performance, 15*(4), 529–546.

Reitman, J. (Director). (2009). *Up in the air* [Motion picture]. United States: Paramount Pictures.

Rideout, N. (2009). *Theatre & ethics*. Basingstoke, UK: Palgrave Macmillan.

Roberts, G., Somers, J., Dawe, J., Passy, R., Mays, C., Carr, G., Shiers, D., & Smith, J. (2007). On the edge: A drama-based mental health education programme on early psychosis for schools. *Early Intervention in Psychiatry, 1*, 168–176.

Salway, J. (2005). Bordering Utopia: Dissident community theatre in Sheffield. In P. Bellingham (Ed.), *Radical initiatives in interventionist & community drama* (pp. 109–129). Bristol, UK: Intellect.

Sánchez-Camus, R. (2009). The problem of application: Aesthetics in creativity and health. *Health Care Analysis, 17*(4), 345–355.

Saxton, J. (1990). Drama and aesthetics. *Association of British Columbia Drama Educators Journal, 10*(1), 1–9.

Schechner, R. (1981). Performers and spectators transported and transformed. *Kenyon Review, 3*(4), 83–113.

Schechner, R. (1988/2003). *Performance theory* (2nd ed.). New York, NY: Routledge.

Schechner, R. (1997). Believed-in theatre. *Performance Research, 2*(2), 76-91.

Schechner, R. (2002). *Performance studies: An introduction*. New York, NY: Routledge.

Schneider, J. J., Crumpler, T. P., & Rogers, T. (Eds.). (2006). *Process drama and multiple literacies: Addressing social, cultural and ethical issues*. Portsmouth, NH: Heinemann.

Schön, D. (1983). *The reflective practitioner: How professionals think in action*. New York, NY: Basic Books.

Schonmann, S. (2005). "Master" versus "servant": Contradictions in drama and theatre education. *Journal of Aesthetic Education, 39*(4), 31–39.

Schweitzer, P. (2006). *Reminiscence theatre: Making theatre from memories*. London, UK: Jessica Kingsley.

Sherrington, C. (1906/1966) *The integrative action of the nervous system*. New Haven, CT: Yale University Press.

Siegel, D. (2007). *The mindful brain: Reflection and attunement in the cultivation of well-being*. New York, NY: W.W. Norton & Company.

Sinclair, C., & Grindrod, A. (2007). Converging worlds: Fostering co-facilitation and relationships for health promotion through drama at the grassroots. *Applied Theatre Researcher, 8* [Article 5]. Retrieved June 11, 2012 from .http://www.griffith.edu.

au/education/griffith-institute-educational-research/research-expertise/applied-theatre-researcheridea-journal/issues

Slade, P. (1954). *Child drama.* London, UK: University of London.

Snyder-Young, D. (2011). Rehearsals for revolution? Theatre of the Oppressed, dominant discourses, and democratic tensions. *Research in Drama Education: The Journal of Applied Theatre and Performance, 16*(1), 29–45.

Spolin, V. (1963/1983). *Improvisation for the theatre* (2nd ed.). Evanston, IL: Northwestern University Press.

Spolin, V. (1963/1999). *Improvisation for the theatre* (3rd ed.). Evanston, IL: Northwestern University Press.

Stein, J. (Ed.). (1966). *The Random House dictionary of the English language* [unabridged]. New York, NY: Random House.

Sternberg, P. (1998). *Theatre for conflict resolution in the classroom and beyond.* Portsmouth, NH: Heinemann.

Stinson, M., & Winston, J. (Eds.). (2011). Drama and second language learning [Themed issue]. *Research in Drama Education: The Journal of Applied Theatre and Performance, 16*(4).

Stuart Fisher, A. (2005). Developing an ethics of practice in applied theatre: Badiou and fidelity to the truth of the event. *Research in Drama Education, 10*(2), 247–252.

Tam, P. (2010). The implications of Carnival theory for interpreting drama pedagogy. *Research in Drama Education: The Journal of Applied Theatre and Performance, 15*(2), 175–192.

Taylor, P. (2000). The drama classroom: Action, reflection, transformation. London, UK: Routledge.

Taylor, P. (2003). Musings on applied theatre: Toward a new theatron. *Drama Magazine: The Journal of National Drama UK, 10*(2), 37–43.

Terret, L. (2009). Who's got the power? Performance and self advocacy for people with learning disabilities. In T. Prentki & S. Preston (Eds.), *The applied theatre reader* (pp. 336–344). London, UK: Routledge.

Three Looms Waiting Part 1 [Video File]. (1971). [BBC Omnibus documentary on Dorothy Heathcote]. Retrieved June 18, 2012 from http://www.youtube.com/watch?v=f5jBNIEQrZs [Part 1 of 8].

Tobin, K. (2011). Introduction: Learning from a good mate. In J. Kincheloe, *Key works in critical pedagogy* (pp. xv–xxiv). Rotterdam, NL: Sense Publishers.

Turner, V. T. (1969). *The ritual process: Structure and anti-structure.* Ithaca, NY: Cornell University Press.

Turner, V. T. (1982). *From ritual to theatre: The human seriousness of play.* New York, NY: PAJ Publications.

Van Mentz, M. (1983/1989). *The effective use of role-play: A handbook for teachers and trainers.* New York, NY: Nichols.

Van Vuuren, P. J. (2004). Meeting the mentor: The role of the teacher-director in engineering a hero's journey for participants in an educational drama workshop series. *Research in Drama Education, 9*(2), 211–227.

Verbal and nonverbal communication (n.d.). Course material, Buffalo State University. Retrieved November 22, 2012 from http://faculty.buffalostate.edu/smithrd/UAE%20 Communication/Unit2.pdf

Vygotsky, L. (1978). *Mind in society: The development of higher psychological processes.* Cambridge, MA: Harvard University Press.

Wagner, B. J. (1976). *Dorothy Heathcote: Drama as a learning medium.* Washington, DC: National Education Association.

Wang, W. (2010). Transgressive local act: Tackling domestic violence with forum and popular theatre in *Sisterhood Bound as Yuan Ze Flowers. Research in Drama Education: The Journal of Applied Theatre and Performance, 15*(3), 413–429.

Way, B. (1967). *Development through drama.* London, UK: Longman.

Weigler, W. (2001). *Strategies for playbuilding: Helping groups translate issues into theatre.* Portsmouth, NH: Heinemann.

White, M. (2010). Developing guidelines for good practice in participatory arts-in-health-care contexts. *Journal of Applied Arts and Health, 1*(2), 139–155.

Williams, R. (1975). *Drama in a dramatized society: An inaugural lecture.* Cambridge, UK: Cambridge University Press.

Williams, T. (1944). *The glass menagerie.* New York: Random House.

Winston, J. (1998). *Drama, narrative and moral education.* London, UK: Falmer.

Winston, J. (2007). Citizenship, human rights and applied drama: Editorial [Special issue]. *Research in Drama Education: The Journal of Applied Theatre and Performance, 12*(3), 269–274.

Winston, J., Lo, C., & Wang, X. (2010). "Being in the state of crossing": Drama education and transnational space. *The Journal of Drama and Theatre Education in Asia, 1*(1), 7–24.

Wolfson, L., & Willinsky, J. (1998). What service learning can learn from situated learning. *Michigan Journal of Community Service Learning, 5*, 22–31.

Zannatou-Papacosta, M. (2002). *Dorothy Heathcote's use of drama for education: In search of a system.* Unpublished doctoral dissertation, University of Central England, Birmingham, UK.

241